ISBN: 978129022471

Published by:
HardPress Publishing
8345 NW 66TH ST #2561
MIAMI FL 33166-2626

Email: info@hardpress.net
Web: http://www.hardpress.net

MEMORIES

F. Myrick

MEMORIES

OF LIFE AT OXFORD, AND EXPERIENCES IN ITALY, GREECE, TURKEY, GERMANY, SPAIN, AND ELSEWHERE

By FREDERICK MEYRICK, M.A.

PREBENDARY OF LINCOLN AND RECTOR OF BLICKLING

LONDON

JOHN MURRAY, ALBEMARLE STREET

1905

PREFACE

THE following memories, enabling the reader to make first acquaintance with some of the persons named, and a better acquaintance with others, may, I believe, throw some sidelights on the course of events in England, specially, but not exclusively, in the latter phases of the Tractarian Movement at Oxford; and also, though again not exclusively, on the origin, growth, and value of the Old Catholic Reform Movement on the Continent; and through these on the fortunes of the Church of England and of the Church Catholic during the past half-century.

This is my excuse for publishing the following pages, to which must be added the not ignoble desire that an old man has to render his experiences of use in one way or another to the coming generation.

The memories are of the persons whom I have known, rather than of the places that I have visited, for which reason I have not allowed myself any lengthened description of foreign sights; and as to persons, I have, with a few exceptions, refrained from admitting into my gallery any that are still living.

F. MEYRICK.

BLICKLING,
    April, 1905.

CONTENTS

CONTENTS

CHAPTER VIII

CHAPTER IX

CHAPTER X

CHAPTER XI

CHAPTER XII

CHAPTER XIII

CHAPTER XIV

CONTENTS

CHAPTER XXI

CHAPTER XXII

APPENDIX

MEMORIES

CHAPTER I

Home and Oxford undergraduate days—Fellows and scholars
of Trinity College, Oxford—J. H. Newman.

My father and my grandfather were both of them
Doctors of Divinity, and both of them Vicars of
Ramsbury, a benefice that was in the gift of the Lord
Chancellor.   My grandfather came from South Wales,
being one of the Caermarthenshire Meyricks, who
were descended from Sir Francis Meyrick, second son
of Rowland Meyrick, the first Protestant Bishop of
Bangor in the sixteenth century, who himself belonged
to the house of Bodorgan in the Isle of Anglesea.
The Meyricks of Bodorgan trace their descent, I
believe, from one of the Welsh kinglets.   The family
motto is: 'Have God, have everything : God and
enough'—of course in Welsh.   Ramsbury was at
one time a Bishop's see, and the Latin title of the
Bishop, *Episcopus Corvinensis*, shows that the name
of the village was originally Ravensbury, which has
been corrupted into Ramsbury.   The church is a fine
building, in the Perpendicular style of architecture.
Attached to it was a private chapel, belonging to the
Littlecote family, which was kept locked, and went
under the name of Darrell's Aisle.   It was looked
upon by us with some awe, because the tomb that it
contained was supposed to be that of 'Wild Darrell.'
The more than tragic tale of Wild Darrell may be

I

found in the notes of Sir Walter Scott's *Rokeby*. It lived still in the village of Ramsbury (from which Littlecote is only two miles distant) with extravagant additions, such as are usual in stories handed down by oral tradition. I believe that the true account of the manner in which the Popham family came into possession of Littlecote on Darrell's death was this: Darrell had committed a savage murder, and his life was saved by the ability of Sir John Popham, whom he employed as his advocate. To show his gratitude, Darrell left him Littlecote in his will; but before he died, Popham had become Judge, and therefore it came to be believed that the trial had taken place before him as Judge, and that he had passed sentence on Darrell, declaring him innocent, being bribed to do so by the promise of succeeding to the Littlecote inheritance, whereas the trial was held in 1590, and Popham was appointed Lord Chief Justice in 1592. In my younger days a manuscript ballad was passed from hand to hand in Ramsbury, written with more than usual poetic power, of which I only now recollect one verse; it is based upon the false story of the Judge having been bribed:

' Not all the blood of all the Pophams
Can wash the Darrell stain away ;
Nor all the wealth of all the Darrells
Stead Popham on the Judgment Day.'

A stile just outside Ramsbury is known as Darrell's Stile, because legend reported that as Darrell was coming back from hunting he broke his neck in leaping it, his horse being frightened by the vision of a woman holding in her arms a child enveloped in flames. My eldest sister, Anne Meyrick, married John Popham, third son of General Leybourne Popham of Littlecote.

A story is told of one of my grandfather's predecessors which shows how greatly times have changed. Some Dissenters called Ranters, coming into the village for the first time, began to preach and to sing hymns under a wych-elm that grew in an irregular square at the end of the chief street of the village. The parishioners, indignant at the invasion, asked permission of the incumbent to take out the fire-engine—as they said, for exercise. Leave being granted, they dragged it up to the square and poured water on the preachers. Shaking, not the dust, but the mud from their feet, they took their departure, followed by the fire-engine, to the confines of the parish.

My grandfather, being a good scholar, became tutor to the young Duke of Somerset and his brother, which led to his taking pupils, first at Hungerford, and afterwards at Ramsbury, of which parish he was appointed incumbent by Lord Chancellor Thurlow. He is described as the pattern of a dignified clergyman of the day, in curled wig (dressed every day by the barber), buckles at his knees and on his shoes, and shovel-hat. A description of the life at Ramsbury is given by Moultrie in his poem ' The Dream of Life.'

My grandfather had four sons, two of whom entered the army, and two were ordained, according to the old-fashioned idea that a gentleman's sons must serve either the Crown or the Church. Of the two soldiers, one went through the Peninsular War, and the other saw active service in India. Both of them died in India.

The eldest son, Edward Graves Meyrick, who was my father, was fond of greyhounds. One day when he was taking some food to the kennel of a favourite hound, which was tied up on account of illness, the dog flew at him and bit him severely in the arm. Believing that the dog might be mad, he went straightway to the kitchen, and, without calling any-one's assistance, he heated a table-knife in the fire and cut out and seared the wound. My father kept grey-

hounds for some years, and won a number of prizes at
the Ashdown coursing meetings, which are now in my
possession.

The youngest son, Arthur, was interested in
mechanics, and long before the days of railroads and
steam-engines he made a bet with Lord Ducie that
a vehicle moved by steam would go from London to
Bath before a certain day. Before that day came we
received news that a steam-carriage had left London
and was going to Bath by the old Bath turnpike-road.
We made an expedition to a spot from whence we
might see it pass along the road. But we were disappointed, for before it had arrived at that point the
populace had risen and broken it to pieces, on the
ground that the new invention would take away work
from all those who were employed as coachmen or
stablemen, and would prevent the breeding of horses.

Arthur Meyrick made another prediction. He was
fond of hunting, and he used to say some seventy
years ago that before very long we should go out
riding, if not hunting, 'each on our own tea-kettle'—
an anticipation of the present motor-car and motor-
bicycle, of the future existence of which there was
in his day no prospect.

My brother, James Meyrick, had been scholar of
Queen's College, Oxford, on the Michel foundation
(now amalgamated with the old foundation), and he
took his degree of B.A. in 1839. After his ordination he became curate of Newport in the Isle of
Wight, and of Chilton in Berkshire, then Vicar of
Avebury and of Westbury in Wiltshire. At Westbury
his health broke down from overwork; an attack of
pleurisy turned to pneumonia, and he was obliged to
go abroad in search of health. He spent two winters
at Malaga in Spain with his sister, and a volume consisting mainly of his and her letters was subsequently
published, entitled *The Practical Working of the*

Church of Spain (1851), which served as a counterpoise to some extravagant imaginations as to the perfection of the Roman Catholic Church entertained at the time in England by men whose minds had been disturbed by Newman's secession. The motto taken for the volume was some words of Pugin, himself a Roman Catholic : 'Pleasant meadows, happy peasants, all holy monks, all holy priests, holy everybody. Such charity and such unity when every man was a Catholic—I once believed in this Utopia myself, but when tested by stern facts it all melts away like a dream.' A third winter he spent on the Nile with Lord Henry Scott, afterwards created Lord Montagu. During his absence his parish was left in charge of the Rev. Thomas Bowles and the Rev. A. H. Mackonochie, the last of whom became afterwards incumbent of St. Alban's, Holborn. Finding that he did not recover his health sufficiently to fulfil the duties of a parish clergyman as he estimated them, my brother resigned the cure of Westbury into the hands of the Bishop of Salisbury, and spent the remaining years of his life as an invalid at Bournemouth.

My cousin Thomas Meyrick was scholar of Corpus Christi College, Oxford, and took a first class in Classics in the year 1838, his name appearing in the same list with those of Dean Lake of Durham, Bishop Rigaud of Antigua, and Bishop Trower of Gibraltar. After taking his degree he resided in Oxford, and became a popular private tutor. He was an enthusiastic admirer and follower of Newman. In 1844, during my first year of residence as an undergraduate, I received a note from the Rev. R. G. Macmullen of Corpus Christi College, saying that my cousin was very ill. Going to see him, I found him in a state of great mental excitement, and hardly master of himself. He said that he wished to join the Church of Rome but was bound by a promise to Newman not

to do so. I went to Littlemore, where Newman was
then living, to consult him, and he gave me a letter
for my cousin, in which he said that he could not
authorize his secession, but he relieved him from the
obligation of any promise made to him. Recovering
to a certain degree, my cousin went to his home to
ask his father's permission to become a Romanist.
His father, an old Tory Protestant parson, said that
to save him from losing his mind (which appeared
likely from his excitement) he would give the leave,
though if it had been to save his life, he would not.
Soon afterwards he was received into the Roman
Church, and went to live for a time at the Roman
Catholic College at Prior Park, near Bath, where I
paid him a visit. Later on he joined the Jesuits,
and became extravagantly attached to the worship
of St. Mary. But ever since the excitement that
he underwent at the time of his secession he had
been liable to temporary fits of deep depression,
followed sometimes by unusually high spirits. The
Jesuits, wearied with his distressed and variable bearing, sent him to an asylum. The asylum was very
ill-managed in respect to the moral control exercised
over the patients, and it was governed by great violence. On one occasion my cousin tried to escape,
and, being caught, was brought back and placed in a
padded room with a strong man, who knocked him
down and then provoked him to fight, knocking him
down every time that he stood up, till 'the devil of
insubordination' was supposed to be subdued in him.
On a later occasion he succeeded in escaping; and
having hidden himself under the willows that fringe
the Thames at Putney during the day, he set off as
soon as it was dark and walked all the way to Wiltshire, and begged his brother to take him in and protect him. Indignant and angry with the Jesuits, he
broke off from them, and wrote a pamphlet (printed,

but not published) called *My Imprisonings ; or, Why I
left the Jesuits.* Time passed, and an imagination suggested itself to him that he had committed a sin in
leaving the Jesuits after having once been enrolled
among them and taken oaths of obedience. He again
joined them, but once more the depression and excitement seized him, and he was sent by the Jesuits to
an asylum in Ireland, from which he was delivered
by the Inspector of Asylums. After this he made a
solemn vow never to rejoin the Jesuits, and he went
to live in a lodging-house at Bournemouth, refusing
either to leave the Roman Church or to see a Roman
priest, or to go near the Roman or the English Church.
Thus many years passed. At length he had a partial
recovery, and again officiated as a Roman priest ; but
the recovery was not complete, and, indignant at not
receiving all his ' faculties,' he went to Rome in 1899
for redress, at the age of eighty-two, and was there
consigned to the care of some charitable nuns, who
looked after him until his death in 1903. Few know
the wrench that it was to those who left the Church of
England for Rome before Newman's secession in 1845
had made it easier to do so. Thomas Meyrick never
recovered from it.

In 1842, when I was fifteen years old, I exchanged
my Eton jacket for a coat, and went to Oxford to try
for a scholarship at Corpus. To my great surprise, at
the end of the examination I was given to understand
that I should have been elected, but that the Fellows
of the college thought that it would be better for me
not to come into residence at the University at so
early an age. They would be happy to see me next
year if I would come up again as a candidate. They
were very kind to me. One of them, the Rev. Charles
Balston, gave me a Boethius *De Consolatione,* which
I value for itself and its associations. Another of
the Fellows was Edward Greswell, a man of great

reputation as a scholar and theologian, author of a very popular *Harmonia Evangelica*, a Harmony of the Four Gospels in Greek. He was looked on with awe by undergraduates because he lived in a room filled with books, containing but one table, one tall reading-desk, two upright chairs, and no other furniture. (A few years later I found Professor Hengstenberg living in just such a room at Berlin ; for scholars of the old stamp were quite content with such surroundings.) It was said that, when anyone came to visit Greswell, he courteously pointed to one of the chairs, and said : 'You are welcome, sir. What can I do for you ?' Then his visitor would put before him some difficulty of scholarship or theology, which he would solve with the utmost patience ; and having made the point clear, he would then say : 'And is there anything else that I can do for you, sir ?' And on an answer being given in the negative, he would say, 'Then, good-morning, sir,' and turn at once to the tomes on his reading-desk. Mr. Greswell was interested in a candidate for the scholarship, young as I was, and having read the Latin essay, written in a round, boyish hand, passed it on the other Fellows with the words : 'What do you think of that for a lad of fifteen ?' This, being reported to me, so amazed me that it impressed that old boyish essay indelibly on my memory, and I can recall it now, though it is sixty years since.*

Another Fellow at Corpus at the time was the

---

* The subject was 'Brutus ante Cæsaris occisionem.' I had read Shakespeare's *Julius Cæsar*, and wrote : 'Brutus, literas quas per fenestram trajectas invenerat, legens : "Surge, interfice ! Cives orant, Roma jubet, Patria imperat." Mene igitur, mene orant cives ut surgam, ut interficiam ? Cives, Romani cives, voti compotes eritis ! Quemnam autem interficiam ? An amicum, quem e pueritia adamavi ? An socium, quem e fluvio pene inanimem eripui ?' (a vague memory of Cassius, not Brutus). 'An heroem, qui gloriam Romanam in exteras regiones extendit ? Imo tyrannum, imo sceleratum, qui libertates nostras sub pedibus conculcavit, invitus sed certus interficiam !' There was more of the same sort, I suppose.

Rev. R. G. Macmullen. When he wished to take his degree of B.D. (Bachelor of Divinity), as required by the statutes of his college, he had to read two original essays to the Regius Professor of Divinity in the Theological Schools. At the time Dr. Hampden was Regius Professor, and Mr. Macmullen was a Tractarian. The Regius Professor refused to pass his essays as a qualification for the degree of B.D., and Macmullen refused to offer others. The difficulty was not got over for a considerable time, during which Macmullen was said to be 'disputing daily in the school of one Tyrannus.' Macmullen at this time declared that he could become a Mahometan as soon as a Romanist ; nevertheless, he was carried down by the vortex caused by Newman's sinking. In the struggle for supremacy which afterwards took place within the Roman Church between Manning and Newman, Macmullen warmly took Newman's side. ' Newman's conversion is the greatest calamity which has befallen the Catholic Church in our day,' said one of Manning's partisans. ' No,' retorted Macmullen ; ' the greatest calamity to the Church in our day was the death of a woman '—Mrs. Manning—for that enabled Manning to be ordained in the Roman Church. Manning having reproved Macmullen for what he had said, Macmullen replied, ' I pity the man who repeated it to your Grace,' but did not withdraw it.

The next year, 1843, being now sixteen, instead of waiting for the Corpus Scholarship Examination, I went up as a candidate at Trinity College. This time I had some hopes, and was therefore in a greater state of excitement. I was then living in the Isle of Wight, and as the railway had not yet been made, except for a short part of the journey, I had to sleep at South-ampton, and travel by a coach which started at 4 a.m. Three times during the night I woke and half dressed myself, in terror lest the coach should start without me. On Trinity Monday, 1843, I was elected scholar of Trinity College, together with Wharton Marriott (age nineteen), W. Gifford Palgrave (age eighteen), W. Foxley Norris (age eighteen) ; and three of us came into residence in the following January — Marriott, Norris, and myself—the fourth, Palgrave, coming up a term later.

In January, 1844, the President of Trinity College was Dr. Ingram, who had some reputation as an antiquarian. He was succeeded in 1850 by Dr. Wilson.

The Senior Tutor was the Rev. Thomas Short. Tommy Short, as he was universally called, had been at Rugby as a master before Arnold's headmastership, and he had been already Tutor of Trinity College for a longer period than my sixteen years of life. He was the type of the genial High Churchman of the old school. He was regular in his life, never failing to attend college chapel on week-days, and taking a lectureship at a church in Abingdon, connected with Trinity College, on Sundays. He did not spare himself as a Tutor, was always kindly to the undergraduates, with whom he was very popular, and he was a leading figure in University politics. At one time the three most influential men in Oxford were Short of Trinity, Calcott of Lincoln, and Michell of Magdalen Hall. They were strong Tories, hating Radicals and Dissenters in the abstract, but full of kindness towards them in the concrete, and never forgetting that they must act towards their opponents with the forbearance of gentlemen, however much they abhorred their principles. After one of the Parliamentary Reform Bills, Short said that Parliament was now past praying for, and vowed that he would not use the prayer for Parliament any longer in chapel, but on second thoughts declared it required prayers all the more. He had eccentricities, which rather endeared him than otherwise to the undergraduate mind, because they amused it. He lectured in Aristotle's Rhetoric, and after a time he passed by many years the age at which Aristotle says that man's powers are at their best. It became a great enjoyment to various generations of undergraduates to hear him say, when he came to that particular passage, ' In those hot climates, you know, people come to their acme much sooner than with us.' Austerity was not a quality which men of Short's school either professed or inculcated. They liked their two glasses of port after dinner—seldom more, never in excess—and their game at whist with sixpenny points. And in dealing with undergraduates' peccadilloes they were more willing to be lenient than severe. They did not inspire into young men enthusiasm or strong devotion, but they made them upright, natural gentlemen, and it may be questioned whether that is not as good a foundation on which a character may be built, as Arnold's system, which appealed too soon to the young man's head, or Pusey's, which stirred too early the young man's heart. Short outlived many Oxford generations of contemporaries, and died an old man in the college which had so long been his home.

His nearest contemporary at the time was the Rev. Joseph Smith, always known under the name of the Bursar. He was the type of the old Oxford Don. It was enough once to see him walk across the quadrangle, with his head high in the air, his solemn gait, his spotless neckcloth, his academical gown bellying out behind him, to know his character. His essential quality was pompousness. Every day he took a sober walk by himself of two miles and back ; every day he appeared at the high table in Hall with a white waistcoat just showing its upper roll above his black waistcoat ; thence he marched sedately to the common-room, and after his two glasses of wine withdrew to his own room. He never knew an undergraduate by sight, but he was very condescending when in his bursarial capacity he was brought into contact with any of 'the youngsters.' He was a constant joy to the undergraduates; some story about 'the Bursar' was always afloat. He was greatest when a 'common-room' was going to be held on a hapless delinquent. Small offences were dealt with by the Dean of the college; but if he judged that a very serious penalty ought to be inflicted, a 'common-room' consisting of all the Fellows was called by the President, and the offender was summoned before it. It was a ceremony to make a young man quake, when he was asked by the President for an explanation or defence. At this moment the Bursar generally intervened with the words: 'Now, sir, take care what you say; for, remember, your existence is hanging on a thread!'

Here and there an undergraduate would rage at the Bursar's calm superiority instead of being delighted with it. One of them was so irritated that he declared his resolution of throwing an explosive ball into Bursar Smith's study, where he generally sat after tea. Hearing of this purpose shortly before it was to be accomplished, three of us determined that we must frustrate it. One of us, therefore, Wharton Marriott, went to the Bursar's room and asked him to be good enough not to sit in his study on that evening. After a time, as Marriott did not return to tell us the results of his mission, I, too, went to the Bursar's rooms. On my knocking at his door, he threw it open, brandishing a stout walking-stick in his hand. On seeing me, he went back to the table at which he had been sitting, in his front-room, with a book before him and his stick by his side. 'I ask no questions,' he said, 'but is it gunpowder?' On my saying I feared so, he resumed his reading, with the words, majestically pronounced: 'Then I sit here to-night.' The ball was not thrown, and the Bursar next day showed his magnanimity by making no inquiry whatever as to the disturbance that he had suffered. After many years the Bursar married an Irish widow, and disappeared from Oxford. Hopes were freely expressed that she might not be as submissive as the average undergraduate had been.

The Tutor that came next in seniority to Short was the Rev. H. P. Guillemard, a genial and kind-hearted man. But he was not a good teacher, and became the object of some good-natured jests among the scholars. His favourite lecture book was Thucydides. In giving a lecture on it he used Arnold's edition, and had open before him Göller's edition to which to refer. On coming to a hard passage he would turn to the book on the table, and say: 'Göller takes this passage as follows.' Among the scholars there was a witty and sarcastic man, E. T. Turner, who would have it that the supposed 'Göller' was really an English transla-tion, referred to when a difficulty occurred. We all knew that it was not so, but the jest suited a class of merry youngsters, and from that time 'cribs' went among us under the name of 'Göllers.' At one moment Guillemard came quite to the front in University affairs. W. G. Ward, Fellow of Balliol, having written a book called the *Ideal of the Christian Church*, was very properly condemned for it by the Convocation of the University, and his gown was taken away. But the Hebdomadal Board, the heads of all the colleges, who had the initiative in University legislation, thought it a good opportunity of condemning, not only Ward, but also J. H. Newman. This was not con-sidered fair, as Newman's offences had been com-mitted at a previous time, and use seemed to be made of the anger caused by Ward to condemn Newman. At this time Guillemard was Senior Proctor, and R. W. Church, of Oriel, was Junior Proctor. Accord-ing to the constitution of the University, whenever the two Proctors agree together to veto any proposal put before Convocation by the Council, their veto stops all proceedings. On the present occasion Church had a strong affection for Newman, and without difficulty he persuaded Guillemard, who also had a high regard for him, to co-operate with himself in vetoing the proposed condemnation. Accordingly, when the Vice-Chancellor said, ' Placetne vobis, domini magistri ?' the two Proctors rose, and Guillemard, as Senior Proctor, pronounced the magic words, ' Nobis Procuratoribus non placet,' on which the question fell to the ground and the Convocation broke up.

Ward was at this time (as always) a singular being. Among other Roman practices, he had been a strong advocate of celibacy. On the occasion of his condemnation he was allowed to defend himself, and was given an interval in the midst of his speech in which he might refresh himself. It was noticed that during this interval he occupied himself in reading a long letter. Very soon afterwards it came out that he was engaged to be married, and it was generally said in the University, with a smile, that the letter was ' from Fanny.' He was not a man of business. When he was Bursar at Balliol, the story runs that he could not get his accounts right at the end of the year till friends bethought them of looking through his books, and then they found within the pages banknotes, which he had put there for security when they were paid to him in behalf of the college, and had perfectly forgotten.

The ablest among the Fellows of Trinity was Arthur West Haddan. His interest was more in theology than in classics. For a time he had been curate to Newman at St. Mary's, Oxford, but he would not budge an inch from the Anglican position when Newman began to look Romewards. He was a man of great erudition and extraordinary laboriousness, as was shown by his edition of Thorndike's works for the Anglo-Catholic Library, and by the *Councils and Ecclesiastical Documents of Great Britain and Ireland*, of which he was joint editor with Bishop Stubbs. But his style was not good. Seeing the various sides of a question, and anxious not to overstate his case, he tried by means of parentheses to express the whole of what he thought in one sentence, instead of attaching other sentences containing the necessary modifications and limitations. This caused him to be a heavy and obscure writer. He had the same defect in his teaching, so that he was not a good Tutor. At the time of the University election he acted as secretary of Mr. Gladstone's committee, and in this capacity Mr. Gladstone owed him much. After many years' service as Tutor, he accepted the college living of Barton-on-the-Heath. But he never had higher preferment offered to him. This was probably owing to an uncompromising sturdiness of character, which made him dwell rather on the points in which he differed from an interlocutor than those on which they were agreed. But he more than deserved a canonry or a deanery, and perhaps such a post might have prolonged a very valuable life, for, owing to a misfortune that had happened to his father, he suffered from *res angusta domi*.

Haddan was a frequent contributor to the *Guardian* newspaper, which had been established and was mainly conducted by his brother, Thomas Haddan, and Sir Frederic Rogers, afterwards Lord Blachford. The paper was not at first a success, and in 1846 the editors put out a dignified appeal to their supporters, saying that the writers of the paper had other work that they might do, and that unless a wider circulation was effected the periodical would cease to be published. I had been a subscriber from the beginning, and this circular reached me as I was on a

Long Vacation reading-party at St. David's. It was a successful appeal, and soon the *Guardian* was established on a secure basis, superseding the *English Churchman*, which at that time was the organ in which the early Tractarians expressed their views.

The Mathematical Tutor was S. W. Wayte, a man of the greatest industry. At the time that he was reading for his double first class (which he got), E. T. Turner spread a tale abroad that every night at ten o'clock Wayte took green tea to keep himself awake, and at one o'clock some opium to make himself go to sleep. Of course he did not, but there was sufficient verisimilitude in the story to make it become a college jest. At a later date he was Secretary of the Oxford University Commission, and on the death of Dr. Wilson he was elected President of the college. In this office he devoted himself to the good of the undergraduates and other members of the college. Professor Freeman, being asked on one occasion what Wayte was doing, replied : 'I don't know, but I should suppose he is sitting in his chair thinking how he can do some kind act to someone, or else doing it.' He resigned the presidentship when he found the infirmities of age growing upon him.

The scholars at the time of my election formed a set apart from the commoners, sitting together at dinner in the hall at a table of their own, and regarding themselves as united by the very real bond of being on the same foundation, and therefore belonging to the household created by our founder, Sir Thomas Pope. The young scholars were gladly adopted into the brotherhood by their elders.

The senior scholar was W. Basil Jones, a very graceful scholar (he won the Ireland Scholarship) and a man of profound thought. He fell into a second class because he and others of the Trinity College scholars disdained merely 'to read for the schools,' thinking that our work was rather to master our books and learn our philosophy without regard to the specialities of the University examination, an error which the schools resented and revenged upon us.   He became a Fellow of University College, Archdeacon of York in the episcopate of Archbishop Thomson, and Bishop of St. David's in succession to Bishop Thirlwall.

The scholar next in order was George Ferguson Bowen, a hearty, genial man, who worked hard and got his first class.   After this it was noticed that he was for some time much less joyous in manner and more thoughtful in appearance than usual.   He was medi-tating on his future course of life.   Presently he burst in on a party of us with a countenance full of satis-faction : 'I say, you fellows, I have cast out the demon of asceticism' (by which he meant that he had given up the idea of a clerical life), 'and am going in for $\beta\acute{\iota}o\varsigma$ $\pi o\lambda\iota\tau\iota\kappa\acute{o}\varsigma$' (a life of politics).   He therefore left Oxford, where he might easily have got a Fellowship.   Five years later I found him as secretary to Sir Henry Ward at Corfu, which at that time belonged to England, together with the rest of the Septinsular Republic.   Sir Henry Ward was ruling his little kingdom as a benevolent despot, and Bowen was helping him by what his friends called his 'geniality,' and his enemies (in the *Edinburgh Review*) termed his 'uncontrollable garrulity.'   While at Corfu Bowen married the daughter of a Greek gentleman and re-ceived the honour of a Greek knighthood.   At a later date he was appointed Governor of several important English dependencies, and ended his life in London. He had hoped that his old college might have elected him its President on a vacancy occurring, but that did not take place.

The third of the scholars was Henry James Coleridge, the son of Mr. Justice Coleridge, of Ottery St. Mary, and brother of John Coleridge, afterwards Lord Chief Justice. He was a man of great refinement of mind and a sensitiveness that was somewhat excessive. After taking his degree (he got a first class) he was ordained, and he fell in love with the daughter of an old friend of his family. But he had already shown some tendency towards Rome, and for that reason the father of the young lady refused his consent. What might have been the effect of the marriage we cannot tell, but as it was, he carried out the anticipations that had been made of him, and joined the Church of Rome, following in the footsteps of Mr. Newman. He became a Jesuit, and for some years edited the Roman Catholic periodical called *The Month*.

The next scholar was Edward Augustus Freeman, known afterwards as the historian of the Norman Conquest. He was a man of very singular manners as an undergraduate. He paid no regard at all to what people might think of him, and he was in the habit of repeating poetry to himself as he walked in the streets, and occasionally leaping into the air when the poem moved him to any enthusiasm. He was bitterly disappointed at falling into a second class, but in spite of that he began, immediately the examination was over, to read history steadily with a view to the future. He gave himself so many pages a day to read, one half of them being the same that he had read the day before, and the other half new matter. His knowledge of architecture was extensive and enthusiastic, but the great study of his life was history, and his lighter occupation was writing articles for the *Saturday Review*, in which he did not spare his rivals or opponents. He had entertained great hopes of the Chicheley Professorship of Modern History, to which Commander Burrows was elected. Failing that, he went into the country and lived near Wells in Somersetshire, till in 1884 he was recalled to Oxford by being nominated Regius Professor of Modern History. He was warmly attached to the cause of modern Greek liberty, and held the Turks in abhorrence, which led him to take part in a series of anti-Turk pamphlets edited by Sir Arthur Elton. He was one of the only five men, that I knew of, who from the beginning detested the Crimean War. The other four were Lord Lothian, Canon Liddon, Lord Robert Cecil, and myself. He was a strong Liberal in politics, and failed to get into Parliament as a supporter of Mr. Gladstone. On his return to Oxford, however, he found that academic Liberalism had outstripped him, and he would often say, ' Can't they let it be as it was in our day ?' He died in 1892, in Spain, where he had gone chiefly to investigate some points of architecture. He had asked me to accompany him on his journey.

E. T. Turner, of whose wit and power of sarcasm I have already spoken, continued after his marriage to reside in the University as Registrar. H. Wilkins, who was deaf, was elected Fellow of Merton, and died early. Each of them got a first class.

The remaining scholar was W. G. Tupper, the most unselfish and sympathetic of men. After he had taken his degree, he would not offer himself for a Fellowship, because his income, though very moderate, was above the limit fixed by the founder of the college. He took charge of the House of Charity in Soho, and lived there among the poor. He died at an early age. He was brother of Martin Farquhar Tupper.

One of the commoners, who had already taken his degree, continued to reside in college, and lived in the scholars' set—J. L. Patterson. Socially he was the pleasantest of companions, with an infinite number of ' good stories ' always at hand, and ready in conversation ; but, as such men often are, he was superficial, and played on the surface of deep questions, which he was fond of touching upon. Carried away by the Newman stream, he joined the Church of Rome, and was made Bishop of Emmaus *in partibus*. In the rivalry between Manning and Newman he did not take any prominent or decided line. He was always pleasant to his fellow-religionists and to his old comrades. He died in 1902.

Balliol is only divided from Trinity by a wall, and two of the Balliol scholars, while belonging to a society of their own in Balliol, were often found among us in Trinity — James Riddell and Edwin Palmer. It is hard to speak too highly of either of these men.

James Riddell was the first Greek scholar of his day —far superior to Mr. Jowett, who was appointed in 1885 Regius Professor of Greek. On paying a visit to a friend, if he did not find him at home, he would scribble the object of his coming, on any stray piece of paper that he found, in exquisite Greek iambics. The following are specimens. The first is an invitation to me for a walk in the afternoon, and a 'wine' in the evening; the second asks me to meet him 'under the griffins'—that is, under the gateway leading into Trinity College (which was decorated with the figures of two griffins)—for a morning bathe. In both there is a pun on my name (Meyrick, μειράκιον or μειρακύλλιον—a young man) and his own name (Riddell—riddle, αἴνιγμα):

'Ιω φίλιστον ὄμμα Μειρακυλλίου,
'Ημῖν μὲν ἦν ξύνθημα καὶ πάλαι παγέν,
'Ως εἰ τοδ' ἧμαρ ζῶν ἄνομβρον εὖ σχέθοι,
῍Ωραν ὁδὸν στελοῦσιν ἀμφὶ δευτέραν.
'Αλλ' εἴ τί πού σοι ταῦτ' ἄραρε μήκετι,
Μὴ φροντίσῃς νῶν τοῦ πάλαι ξυνθήματος·
Καλῶς δ' ἐχόντων, ἀμμενῶ μολόντα σε
Τῶν Μασονείων δωμάτων ὕπαυλος ὤν.
Μὴ δ' οὖν ταχύνῃς θᾶσσον ἢ καθ' ἡδονήν.

Ἔν σοι γὰρ εἰμί· τοῦ χρόνου δ᾽ οὔ τοι φθονῶ.
Πάντως δ᾽ ὅπως παρ᾽ ἡμῖν ἑσπερᾶς ἔσει,
Φίλος φίλοισιν ξυμπότης, Βάκχου χάριν.
Εὖ δ᾽ οἶσθα γ᾽ ὅστις εἰμί· μῶν ἠνιξάμην;

The Μασονείων δωμάτων were Mason's lodgings, where he was then living. The second piece is shorter:

Ὅπως φανήσει, φαιδρὲ Μειρακύλλιον,
Γρίφοις ὑπ᾽ αὐτοῖς ἐν πύλαις ἑώθινος
Ὥραν φυλάσσων ἑβδομὴν μέσης ἀπὸ
Νυκτός· τό τ᾽ Αἴνιγμ᾽ ὅσπερ ἔγραψεν τάδε.

There are not many men who could scribble off such lines as those with a pencil on an old envelope in the time that another would be writing a message in English. He was not only a scholar; he was also the clearest-headed of thinkers. Our thoughts, I have heard him say, should not be tangled together like briars and brushwood, but should each separately spring into the air like a vigorous and independent tree. He stood in the foremost rank, not only intellectually, but also in physical exercises, which perhaps exacted too much of a student's frame. Whatever was the cause, he passed away in the early morning of his life, leaving behind him a very noble memory of one incapable of stooping to anything low or petty, or of conceiving any but high ideas clothed in fairest form.

His brother scholar, and afterwards brother-in-law, Edwin Palmer, was the first Latin scholar in the University, as Riddell was the first Greek scholar. Having won almost all the prizes and honours of the University that could be won, he became Professor of Latin, and subsequently Archdeacon of Oxford, having refused the deanery of Lincoln. He belonged to a remarkable family. His father was a specimen of the better race of clergy to be found in the English Church in the time of our fathers or grandfathers. He was contented with feeding a simple flock committed to him at Mixbury, and in giving the first impulse to his able sons in the course that they were to pursue. William Palmer, afterwards Fellow of Magdalen, who interested himself in an attempt to restore communion between the Oriental and the Anglican Churches; Roundell Palmer, afterwards Lord Selborne, Lord Chancellor of England; and Edwin Palmer, Professor and Archdeacon, were no common men. The Archdeacon was from his undergraduate days singularly complete. He could always be trusted for a sound judgment, and, if the case concerned himself, for acting on that judgment, while his sympathetic and affectionate nature made him a referee to many who were in perplexity or difficulty. At the same time, his boyish spirits never deserted him throughout his life.

Such was the society, consisting of men of high thinking and equally high conduct, into which Wharton Booth Marriott, William Foxley Norris, and myself, were admitted as younger brethren in January, 1844. A sketch of our undergraduate life for the next three years will be found contributed by me to the *Memorials of W. B. Marriott*, published in 1873.

Wharton Marriott was a man with great strength of character. He was strong in body, strong in mind, older than his contemporaries, and had gone through Eton. This made him take a leading position among us, and his healthy muscularity and genial wit and humour were very useful to repress any morbid tendencies towards asceticism which, under the circumstances of the University, might have sprung up among us. After taking his degree, he became Fellow of Exeter, and then a master at Eton. In 1871 he was elected Grinfield Lecturer at Oxford, and delivered a very valuable lecture on ' Terms of Gift and Offering in Scripture.' He was a great writer. Besides ephemeral articles and sermons, he composed a treatise on the Eucharist in reply to some statements and positions of the Rev. T. T. Carter. His *Vestiarium Christianum* is the best authority on the subject of ecclesiastical vestments at the present day. He died early, when he was only forty-eight. He was cousin to the Rev. C. Marriott, whose life Dean Burgon has written in his *Twelve Good Men*.

W. Foxley Norris and myself were assigned rooms in the same staircase in our first term, and from thence began a friendship which has continued unbroken down to the present year (1905). He was a man of sensitive, refined and affectionate disposition, very popular in the college, and unspoilt by his popularity. After taking his degree and being ordained, he filled several curacies, became Vicar of Buckingham, and was transferred thence by Bishop Mackarness to Witney (famous for its blankets), which he resigned in 1903. He is an honorary Canon of Christ Church Cathedral, and represented the clergy in Convocation for some years.

I have already stated that early in my undergraduate life I had to go to see J. H. Newman in behalf of my cousin. I had heard Newman's last sermon before the University when I was standing for a scholarship, and he had now retired to Littlemore, where he had established a quasi-monastery for himself and a few of his followers. I had been to it more than once with my cousin, who went to see Messrs. Dalgairns and St. John, who were resident there, and now I had to go on behalf of my cousin. I have two short notes which Newman wrote to me on the occasion. I was not brought into contact with him again until he published his *Apologia pro Vita mea* in answer to Charles Kingsley. This led to my writing two pamphlets—*But is not Kingsley right, after all?* and *On Dr. Newman's Rejection of Liguori*—in 1864. On the receipt of the first of these, Mr. Gladstone wrote on October 31, 1864 :

' DEAR MR. MEYRICK,
  ' Many thanks for your able and interesting pamphlet. Dr. Newman has had immeasurably the best of it in the rest of the controversy, but I think he will find it difficult to make a sufficient answer to you. Nor shall I be surprised if he proves to be of the same opinion.
                          ' Believe me,
                               ' Most faithfully yours,
                                    ' W. E. GLADSTONE.'

Eleven years after this, Mr. Gladstone having publicly praised Dr. Newman, I wrote a pamphlet— *Does Dr. Newman deserve Mr. Gladstone's Praises?* —on which I received the following letter from Mr. Gladstone, which is of extreme interest, as it contains his estimate of Dr. Newman's character :

                    ' 23, CARLTON HOUSE TERRACE,
                          ' *April* 26, 1875.
' DEAR MR. MEYRICK,
  ' I must not shrink from admitting that I follow with general assent the argument of the tract on my commendation of Dr. Newman, which you have so kindly sent me.
  ' I have, without doubt, spoken freely and largely of his merits, but indirectly and with reserve of his defects.
  ' To this I was moved by recollection of much kindness ; by my belief in his truthfulness of *intention ;* by my admiration of the disinterestedness which has marked his life, his content in an outward obscurity, his superiority to vulgar ambitions. I was sure, too, that he had, in dealing with me, repressed thoughts

and words of wrath ; and finally, as I was at this time in much correspondence with thorough-paced Vaticanists, I saw him shine morally in the contrast with them.   Besides a want of robustness of character, I have ventured to glance at an obliquity of intellect. The first he has shown by shrinking from the bold action to which his insight, and many of his avowals, should have led him, and also in his adopting for some time after his secession too much of the ordinary tone of the Romish controversialist.   The latter defect of his mind is too traceable in all his works, and the effect is, for practical purposes, you might as well argue with a Jesuit.   His mind seems to be nearly the opposite of Bishop Butler's, whom, nevertheless, he sincerely, but I should say ignorantly, worships, as the Athenians worshipped the unknown God.   He constantly reminds me of a very different man, Lord Westbury, in this great point, that he is befooled by the subtlety of his own intellect.   I always felt that Westbury, when he was wrong, lost the chance that we ordinary mortals possess of getting right, because we feel a greater difficulty in sustaining untrue propositions ; but in Westbury it was the same thing, in point of difficulty, to sustain a sound or unsound argument.   So it is with Dr. Newman.

' But I must not pursue further this very curious subject.
'Believe me,
'Most faithfully yours,
'W. E. GLADSTONE.

' Kingsley contrived to get defeated in his own case, while you, in a very short pamphlet, most conclusively established what he had really meant.'

I did not meet Dr. Newman again until he came to Oxford at the invitation of Dr. Percival (Bishop of Hereford), who was then President of Trinity College, in 1880, to dine at the High Table after having been elected an honorary Fellow of Trinity. He was then a bent old man, bedizened with pieces of red indicating that he was a Cardinal. I happened to have gone up to my old college on the same day, and I sat next but one to him at dinner, Henry Coleridge sitting between us. On hearing my name, he leant across, and said : ' I think I used to know Mr. Meyrick formerly ?' ' Yes,' I said, ' thirty-five years ago.' After dinner he went to the President's lodgings, and entered into un-polemical conversation with any of us that pleased to talk to him. At dinner his health was given by Professor Bryce, who congratulated him on having brought about a state of theological liberalism or indifferentism in Oxford, the one thing which from the beginning of his life to its end he abhorred. In the course of the day he paid a visit to his old and beloved friend, Dr. Pusey. ' Newman,' said Pusey, after the first greetings, ' the Oxford Liberals are playing you like a card against us who are trying to preserve the religious character of the University.' He was made much of during this visit. College Gardens were lighted in his honour, and he held receptions of admirers. But it was his old enemies, whom he had fought à outrance, and whose principles he hated now from the bottom of his heart, who flocked round him as their champion, and thanked him for what he had done in demolishing the power of the Church of England in Oxford.

It is an entire mistake to suppose that the religious movement in Oxford of the last century owes its origin to Newman, or required his help for its success. It would have taken place had Newman not existed, though the fire would not have blazed up so rapidly nor so fiercely if he had not been there to feed it.

But a steadily burning flame is in the end more useful and more effective than the furious and evanes-

cent upshooting of blazing tongues of fire ; and though
the Oxford revival would have been less picturesque
without Newman, it would have been more beneficial.
It would then have been under the direction of Keble,
Pusey, Palmer, Sewell, Rose, and others, who would
have kept it in its proper course. As soon as he had
joined it, Newman could not but be the controlling
power. He was one of those men who must be first,
and must stamp his own personality on others without
making concession in turn to them. From the first he
was the disquieting element in the body of associates ;
when Palmer tried to restrain his individuality by
giving a revising power to a committee, he broke away
from the shackles which would have been thus cast
around him. The result was that he made himself
master of the situation, and led his followers full upon
the rocks, on which they were broken to pieces, like
a wave when it dashes against a cliff. The Tractarian
Movement, as a concerted movement, failed, and turned
out a fiasco, because Newman led it. Keen as was his
intellect, Newman was never guided by his reason, but
always by his emotions ; and a man so constituted
cannot lead a host to victory, though he may stir up
in them the enthusiasm which, if directed aright,
insures success.

It is interesting to see the employment to which
Newman put his intellect. It was not the directing
force within him, but it was a faculty of extraordinary
power which he used, like a powerful slave to which
he gave his orders for reconciling to his own conscience any course that his will and affections had previously determined upon. It was so subtle that it
beguiled him, and easily persuaded him that anything
that he chose to do or to say was right. His mind
was naturally sceptical, like his brother's ; but his affections forced him to resolve by an act of will to be a
believer, and his intellect was then called on to justify

his resolution to himself and to the world. The more that this process went on—and it grew upon him with his years—belief lost the true character of belief, and became acceptance. Whether he gave an inward assent to a tenet or whether he did not, he would accept it if it came from a quarter to which he was inclined to pay deference. We know that in his heart he regarded the doctrine of the Pope's Infallibility the work of 'an insolent and aggressive faction'; nevertheless, as soon as it was declared, he accepted it, not with what we understand by belief, but with assent. So with the dogma of the Immaculate Conception : he accepted it when declared, and condescended to justify it by arguing in its favour from a known misreading in Irenæus, the true character of which he ignored until he was compelled to acknowledge it.

In argument he was not a scrupulous combatant, as was seen, in his controversy with Kingsley, by his framing the whole of his defence of Liguori's theory of truthfulness on the assumption that by the expression 'on just cause' Liguori meant 'in an extreme case,' and, after he had framed the defence, withdrawing the assumption in an appendix, without withdrawing the argument founded on it. His method of putting on an innocent face and passing off some fallacy as an undoubted axiom—e.g., that it is the world, the flesh, and the devil, not celibacy, which has caused and causes immoral life in a celibate clergy (as though no one had ever heard of the distinction between a cause and an occasion)—becomes provoking and monotonous when it has been noticed more than a certain number of times, and observed to be habitual.

Few men have been so conspicuous for bringing about that which they specially aimed at resisting as Dr. Newman. He organized the forces of Belief against Unbelief, and then, deserting his soldiers in the conflict, he fell back and hurled weapons on them from behind till they lost half their confidence. He was a dogmatist to his marrow, and yet his teaching and example drove man after man of his followers (to whom he gave only the choice of all or nothing) into scepticism. He loved the ecclesiastical character of Oxford, and he destroyed it. He loved the Church of England, and he assailed it with all his force and with envenomed weapons of offence. He loved the party which he led at the University, and he scattered it to the winds. His one object of abhorrence throughout his life was Liberalism, and he became the darling and the cat's-paw of Liberals, while he spread dismay and disorganization through the ranks of their opponents, whom he had betrayed. The old man must have winced as he sat, with bowed head, listening to the praises poured upon him by Professor Bryce on his last visit to Oxford. 'Such a scene,' said the Professor, 'could not have taken place till of late. Formerly religious bigotry would not allow any but a member of the Church to receive the honours of the University and the college, but we had changed all that. Now anyone intellectually eminent was welcomed, religious barriers were thrown down, and for that benefit Oxford was grateful to Dr. Newman.' This was the principle that Newman had been fighting against all his life, which he hated still with profoundest hatred, and, lo! he was represented as the champion who had caused it to triumph. And the representation was true. When Pusey said to him, 'Newman, the Oxford Liberals are playing you like a card against us,' by Liberals he did not mean Liberals in politics, but in theology—men whose object it was to drive all definite religion out of the University. Newman lived long enough to see the very men who would have stoned him as a bigot in his earlier career build his sepulchre, to the sound of drums and fifes in honour of one who had done so much to undermine and weaken the institution on which the continuance of religion as a powerful influence in England depends.

The record of Newman's life is a sad one. It is the record of one who, endowed with great powers, warm affections, strong will, high purpose, and a desire to do right, damaged profoundly the cause which he had most at heart, and promoted that which he most abhorred.

On Dr. Newman's death he became the object of a hero-worship which was most creditable to the generosity of Englishmen, but in many respects, as I thought, undeserved. Accordingly, I wrote an article in the *Churchman* deprecating this phase of the public mind, and showing how aptly the words of Vincentius Lirinensis respecting Origen and Tertullian applied in a lesser degree to Dr. Newman. Tertullian, who had been the champion and hero of the Church, deserted her, and became the ornament of the Montanist sect, which he enriched with the learning that he had brought from the Church ; while he assailed the Church with the bitterness he had borrowed from his new allies. Origen, according to Vincentius, was a man of many gifts, rare, singular, and strange, of great industry and patience, quick of wit, unrivalled in learning, so sweet of speech that honey seemed to drop from his mouth, so forcible in argument that he seemed to be able to make anything easy of acceptance, surrounded by friends and pupils who were ready to err with Origen rather than be right with anyone else. Both of these teachers, according to Vincentius, discrediting their earlier writings by later errors, became a great temptation to many. ' And surely,' continues Vincentius, ' a great temptation it is, when as he whom you think a prophet, a disciple of the prophets, whom you esteem a doctor and maintainer of the truth, whom you have highly reverenced, and most entirely loved, when he suddenly and privily bringeth in pernicious errors, which neither you can quickly spy, led away with prejudice of your old teacher, nor can easily bring your mind to condemn, hindered with love to your old master.' That was the frame of mind of many of Newman's friends and followers towards him.

At the beginning of my second term, W. G. Palgrave, who had been elected scholar with Marriott, Norris, and myself, came into residence. He differed from the rest of us in many ways. He was not only a man of great ability and great force of character, but also of inordinate ambition. At Oxford he tried to be foremost at once in the reading set and in the so-called 'fast' set, and consequently he failed in each case. After having done very well in the schools, he made up his mind that the sword, not the pen, was the instrument by which to force a path to favour in the present state of the world. He joined the army, but falling sick and being kindly received by some Jesuits, and finding himself altogether disappointed in his expectation of advancement, he gave up military life and became himself a Jesuit. Before much time had passed he hated the Jesuits and all their ways with the bitterest of hatred. Being appointed by Napoleon III. to obtain some information for him from Mecca, he feigned to be a Mahometan doctor of medicine, and made his journey to Mecca and back in safety. He wrote an account of his adventures, and in his book he gave a minute description of the Wahabees, whom he represented as the evil geniuses of Mahometanism. It did not require much reading between the lines to see that by Wahabees he meant Jesuits, and by Mahometanism the Roman Catholic Church. After his travels he came back to England, and went to Norwich, where I officiated at his marriage with his cousin. At this time he had been appointed as English Consul, or Consul-General, at Trebizond.

At the wedding breakfast he told his wife that she would have to wear the yashmak, or veil, in order to be like the Turkish ladies. I said to her that I did not often preach to a wife rebellion against her husband, and certainly I had never yet done so at the wedding breakfast, but that I had no hesitation in advising her to revolt if any such rule were laid upon her. They did not stay long at that post, and he died without having realized any of his ambitions except as a writer of travels.

It was during this term that Thomas B. Colenso came to Trinity from Cambridge, where he had resided one term, and joined the scholars' set. We were all at this time young men of slender means, and we none of us had any inclination towards extravagance. I suppose that, tuition included, our expenses did not exceed £150 a year. But Colenso was still more pinched, or, rather, he knew that his expenses necessarily, for the time, fell upon others. Consequently he gave it to be understood that he could not exercise hospitality. The rest of us respected him the more for his straightforwardness and courage, and felt much honoured when he came to our breakfasts or 'wines.' But he went too far. Once or twice a week he did without his regular dinner, to save expense, and this perhaps sowed the seeds of a rapid consumption, which carried him off soon after he had taken his degree. After his death, his brother, the Bishop of Natal, wrote to me to say that while his brother's mind was wandering he suddenly exclaimed : 'Ah, here's my friend Meyrick come to see me.' I calculated the time, and found that I was sleeping at the moment, and I tried to persuade myself that my spirit had gone to say farewell to him. The Bishop of Natal I only knew before he left England for South Africa, when he had adopted none of his rationalist or Higher Critical views. After his deposition, Bishop Gray sounded me as to the possibility of my accepting the post of Bishop of Maritzburg.

The two scholars next added to the existing body were Isaac Gregory Smith and George W. Cox.

I. G. Smith's scholarship was proved by his winning both the Hertford and the Ireland Scholarships, which are the tests of Latin and Greek scholarship. After his ordination he took charge of various parishes —Tedstone - Delamere, Great Malvern, and Great Shefford. He would make an ideal Dean of a cathedral, being at once a theologian and a poet, fond of metaphysical studies, and a man of earnest piety. But he is very retiring and self-repressive. He acted as examining chaplain to Bishop Basil Jones. He is a non-residentiary Canon of Worcester.

George W. Cox, who came up at the same time, succeeded to a baronetcy in his later life. During his Oxford career he was a strong High Churchman, more dogmatic than any of his associates. Suddenly (so far as his friends know) he changed his principles and opinions, and became as strongly rationalist as he had been Tractarian. On Bishop Colenso's death he was invited by Colenso's partisans to succeed him as Bishop of what had now become a sect. He accepted the invitation, but could find no Bishop to consecrate him, and he died incumbent of Scrayingham. He wrote many tales from classical history.

In 1846 Marriott, Norris, and myself, with G. E. Ranken, a scholar of University College, went on a long vacation reading-party to St. David's. Being assured of our own willingness to work, we took no tutor with us, which was a mistake so far as preparation for the schools went. We read from 7.30 a.m. to 2 p.m. (giving ourselves one hour's break at ten o'clock, when we attended the cathedral service), and from 7 to 10 p.m. The afternoon was given to exercise, chiefly bathing and rock-climbing. These last were not without the pleasurable excitement of some danger. On one occasion Marriott, walking in front of me, was swept from beneath a cliff by a wave, which was happily so massive as to carry him out to sea over some dangerous rocks. On another occasion I nearly fainted from exhaustion in swimming further than my physical powers permitted, and might have sunk had it not been for the encouragement given me by Henry Polehampton (an Oxford man, afterwards chaplain at Lucknow during the Mutiny), who had joined us on the day; and a few hours afterwards I caught him as he had missed his footing and was falling from a cliff to an abyss beneath him. Polehampton and several other Oxford men took the opportunity of our being at St. David's to visit it. Among them was Basil Jones, afterwards Bishop of St. David's. The old cathedral city, now sunk into a small village, had always appealed to him, and he had, with E. A. Freeman, written a valuable work on its history and antiquities. Hearing that I was going to St. David's, he addressed the following lines to me :

'FRIDERICO MEYRICK MENEVIAM ADITURO.

' And thou wilt wend to the West, my friend,
    To the happy sunset shore ;
And thou wilt greet the hallowed seat
    Where saints have sat of yore :
Where hour by hour the Minster tower
    Watcheth a dreary land,
Till the golden sun, his course y-run,
    Kindles the broken strand :
Where the waters sleep full dark and deep
    Beneath the waves' wild roll,
And give thee a token of peace unbroken
    That lies in the inner soul.

' Oh, sweet to me are the shades that be
    These thoughtful walls among,*
And the sullen swell of the nightly bell,
    And the quiet vesper-song :

---

* At Oxford.

And sweet to me in mine own countrie
    Broad flood and mountain gray,
With the silvery gleams of the flashing streams,
    And the woodlands green and gay :
But I'd give them all for the lights that fall
    On that dreary shore at even,—
For the song of the sea is its melody,
    And its beauty the sheen of heaven !'

June 12, 1846.

Perhaps it was Basil Jones's instigation, perhaps it was the very pitifulness of the scene that had been before our eyes for some weeks past, which made us write to the eminent architect, W. Butterfield, and ask him to come down and see if something could not be done towards the restoration of the cathedral. Mr. Butterfield came, and, immensely interested both in the old half-ruined building and in the zeal of a few penniless undergraduates who were set on restoring a cathedral, he lent us all his sympathy and help. When we had collected a little money, he gave us a design for the restoration of the screen—it was all that our purses would allow—and so began the restoration of St. David's Cathedral, which has since been so happily carried out, the progress of which Basil Jones was able to watch as Bishop of the diocese.

About this time there came up to Trinity a young freshman in whom Norris and I were interested— John E. Bowden. His father, author of the *Life of Gregory VII.*, had been a firm Anglican Churchman, but he died, and his widow got caught in the Newman stream, which landed her in Rome. She and Newman, who was her counsellor, wished John to have the advantage of an Oxford education, feeling secure of him in the end. After two years the *genius loci* seemed to be getting hold of him, and they thought it hardly safe for him to continue. So Newman looked at him through his spectacles, and said : ' Ah, John, your father would have been much grieved at your standing apart from your mother and the rest of the family.' What could the boy do? He had been taught to worship Newman, and to regard him as his father's old friend. It was only his father's memory that kept him straight, for he was guided more by his affections than by reasoning, and now that support was knocked away. But Newman had no right to say those words. His father had always been a faithful son of the Church of England, and his mother had no right to assume that he would have made a change of front because Newman did. John Bowden was ordained afterwards in the Roman Church, and was, I believe, a popular priest at the Brompton Oratory.

CHAPTER II

Fellowship at Trinity College, Oxford—Tutorship in Scotland—
Bishop Charles Wordsworth—John Keble.

AT the beginning of 1847, having taken my degree,
I was elected Fellow of Trinity College, being then
just past twenty years of age. About the same
time I received a proposal from Lady Lothian—Cecil,
Marchioness of Lothian—to take charge of her boys
during their holidays, which coincided with a part
of my vacations. Accordingly, I went to Eton and
picked up Lord Lothian, the eldest of the boys, and
travelled with him to Ingestre, the seat of Lady
Lothian's father, Earl Talbot, with whom she was
then staying. Lord Talbot was an old man, who died
about two years afterwards. He was surrounded by
a detachment of his tall sons and his one daughter.
The eldest of his sons was Lord Ingestre, who on his
father's death became Earl Talbot, and afterwards
succeeded to the earldom of Shrewsbury, having
proved to the satisfaction of the House of Lords that
he was nearest of kin to the late Earl. He had
been in the navy as a young man, and was, I believe,
sent home with the despatches giving an account of
the victory of Navarino. He retained something of
the bluff sailor character, whence the late Queen called
him her rough diamond. He married a Beresford,
and was the father of the four strikingly handsome
daughters : Lady Victoria, who died at Naples; Lady

Constance, who married her cousin, the eighth Marquis of Lothian; Lady Gertrude, Countess of Pembroke; and Lady Adelaide, Countess Brownlow. On my going to Ireland, he gave me an introduction to Lord George Beresford, Archbishop of Armagh, who died just before I was able to deliver it.

The next son was John Chetwynd Talbot, a very able lawyer, and a strong and firm Churchman. Living in Great George Street, Westminster, he seldom failed to attend the daily matins at Westminster Abbey, and he co-operated with Mr. Gladstone in the first phase of the latter's politics, while he was still member for Oxford. He looked very strong, but the strain of his incessant work broke him down. On one occasion, when there was a question whether some case should be continued or adjourned, he drew a sketch of a coffin, on which he wrote his own name, and handed it to the other counsel, telling him that that would be the result of continuing. His early death was a great loss to the moderate High Church party. He was the father of the present member for Oxford and of the Bishop of Rochester. He was guardian to his nephew, Lord Lothian, and his brothers and sister, and performed all the duties of the office with the greatest care and conscientiousness.

Another son of whom I saw a great deal at a later date was Gilbert Talbot. When I first knew him he was a strong Anglican, but his mind was upset by the Gorham case and Manning's representations of the meaning of that case, and he joined the Church of Rome, and, having been ordained, became a Monsignore.

Lady Lothian, the mother of my pupil, was one of the best women that I have known. But her husband was dead, and, like some other women (and men), she was carried away by the Newman stream, which bore

her to Rome.   After a time she took with her her two
daughters and her three youngest boys.   Let that be
enough to say of a most sorrowful, most lamentable
event.

My pupil Lord Lothian was a thorough Scotchman,
of a cool, calm judgment, which was never led astray
by enthusiasm, and guided rather by reason than by
the affections.   And it was a happy thing that he was
so.   On leaving Ingestre, I took him and his brother
to Scotland for a short trip, and in 1849 I went abroad
with him for a year's travelling in France, Italy, Sicily,
Malta, Corfu, Greece, Constantinople, Vienna, Salzburg, Venice, Milan, Switzerland, and the Rhine
country.   In October, 1850, he went into residence at
Christ Church, where I still continued his private tutor.
In the October term, 1853, he got a first class in
Classics, and in the April term, 1854, he got a first class
in the School of Law and Modern History which then
existed, and on January 30 he put on his B.A. gown.
The following year he went to India for a year, his
brother Schomberg, Lord Robert Cecil, and myself
seeing him off from Southampton on September 20.
Up to this time his health had been very good—so
good as perhaps to have tempted him to be careless
of the climate of India.   He came home in apparent
good health, and married his cousin, Lady Constance
Talbot, but soon signs of illness appeared.   One of
his legs would.drag at the end of a walk, and then his
hand began to shake, and at length a creeping palsy
so affected him that he was unable to move except in
a chair.   From this affection he never recovered, and
he died in the year 1870 at the age of thirty-six.   Had
he lived, he would have been, undoubtedly, a leading
English statesman.   He had a remarkable knowledge
of modern history, and seemed made for a Secretary
of State for Foreign Affairs.   Before he went to India
Lord Aberdeen had asked him to move the Address

in the House of Lords, but he cautiously abstained from committing himself to any party until he had had time to look round. I went to Scotland to officiate at his funeral at Jedburgh Abbey, and his widow erected a very beautiful monument to him (by G. F. Watts) in Blickling Church.

Having travelled to Newbattle Abbey, about a mile from Dalkeith and eight miles from Edinburgh, I there found my second pupil, Lord Schomberg Kerr. He was at this time a very engaging boy, with open face and affectionate manners, which he retained more or less throughout his life. It was said that each person that he spoke to went away with the impression that he liked him better than anyone else ; and yet there was not a shade of insincerity about him. He had just been withdrawn from Eton, and sent to Trinity College, Glenalmond, a school which Mr. Gladstone's energy had been instrumental in establishing in Scotland. It was at the present time in course of building, and Charles Wordsworth had given up the second mastership of Winchester to carry out a great experiment as its Warden. At present there were but fourteen boys; but it was to grow, as it did grow. The Sub-Warden was H. E. Moberly, of New College, a worthy fellow-workman with Charles Wordsworth. From Glenalmond Schomberg Kerr proceeded to New College, Oxford. But while he was in residence he was seized with an attack on his chest, which made his physician send him to Torquay, and prevented his finishing his Oxford career. In 1855 he went as an Attaché to Teheran, and on his return married the daughter of the Duke of Buccleuch. On his brother's death in 1870 he succeeded as the ninth Marquis of Lothian. He had two sons. The eldest, a bright young lad, popular with all who knew him, died before his father, being accidentally shot by a companion as he was riding in Australia.

The younger succeeded to the title on his father's death.

During our tour in Scotland in 1847 we went to see Trinity College, Glenalmond. Its Warden, Charles Wordsworth, was a man of a very high nature. A beautiful scholar,* a learned divine, with a halo round his name derived from his uncle the poet, he might have aspired to any office in the English Church. But he was absolutely unselfish and regardless of personal interests. The thought of building up the Scottish Church was placed before him, and his reputation as a scholar pointed him out as the man to commence and make successful the experiment of the school and college of Glenalmond, in which Mr. Gladstone and other Scottish Churchmen were deeply interested. He threw up his prospects in the South and accepted the post. From the wardenship of Glenalmond he passed to the bishopric of St. Andrews, an office not such as to satisfy an ambitious man, in which he gave more than he received. There he set himself the task of strengthening the Church of his adoption, and of persuading his Presbyterian fellow-countrymen to accept Episcopacy. Like his brother, the Bishop of Lincoln, he was an Anglican of the purest type—a pronounced opponent alike of Romanism and Puritanism, and entirely free from the mysticism and the mediævalism which of late years have invaded the Anglican Church and confounded the Anglican doctrine on the question of the Eucharist.

* What could be more exquisite than the following description of a tourist in Switzerland, scribbled by him in the travellers' book at the Grimsel?

χωρεῖν, καθεύδειν, ἐσθίειν, πίνειν, πάλιν
χωρεῖν, βαβαιὰξ ὡς καλὸν κεκραγέναι,
Κόντον τρίπηχυν χερσὶν οἰακοστροφεῖν,
Γαλλιστὶ βάζειν, τοὔνομ᾽ ἐν βίβλῳ γράφειν,
ὀμβροφόρον, ὡς τὰ πλεῖστα, βλασφημεῖν Δία·
τοιόσδ᾽ ὁ βίος ἐστι τῶν ὁδοιπόρων.

An invaluable work that Charles Wordsworth did was to resist the attempt made by Mr. Cheyne and Bishop Forbes to introduce into the Scottish Church the doctrine of the Objective Presence of Christ *in the elements*, and, in resisting that attempt, to show that that tenet was altogether alien to the Anglican Communion. The following letter which I received eighteen years ago, after I had published *Four Letters on the Neo-Eucharistical System*, shows how warmly the Bishop felt on the subject after the lapse of some thirty years :

'BISHOPSHALL, ST. ANDREWS,
' *March* 29, 1887.

' MY DEAR CANON MEYRICK,

' I have been reading with much interest your *Four Letters*. It is now very nearly thirty years ago that I had to go over the same ground—on occasion of our Eucharist controversy with Mr. Cheyne and Bishop Forbes : to encounter the same painful experiences from unscrupulous partisans ; and with the result of maintaining precisely the same conclusions as those which you have reached. In some respects, indeed, my experiences were still more painful; for I had to cope directly with Pusey (whom I scarcely knew personally) and with Keble, with whom I had been upon very friendly and intimate terms while at Winchester. Nevertheless, when all was over, Keble sent me as a present what I think was his last publication—*The Life of Bishop Wilson ;* and in that work— on the last page (972) of vol. ii.—curiously enough, you may see Bishop Wilson's repudiation of Keble's and Pusey's own doctrine of the Objective Presence ! At that time, apparently, in the Church of England " men slept " who ought to have been champions of the orthodox doctrine, and consequently you will now have very hard work to root up the tares which have since grown and spread so rankly and luxuriantly. I received scarcely any support or encouragement from any quarter, except from my dear brother (Bishop Christopher Wordsworth), who felt keenly on the matter and was most cordial, as you may see from p. 7 *et seq.* of *Letters to the Clergy*, which I am sending you.

'I don't know whether you have had occasion to take as complete a survey as I did (for I think I went over the entire field) of the Eucharistic teaching of Anglican divines ; so I am also sending you a copy of my "Notes to assist, etc.," which please to return at your leisure, for I have no other copy left (except one largely scored and added to), as you may like to trace the course of my investigations and compare it with your own. You will find the same exposure of mis-quotation and misapplication of Bishop Cosin's "Notes," of Maldonatus, Cassander, etc., and certain it is that my exhaustive inquiry led me to your con-clusion, viz., that the new doctrine had no standing whatever in the Church of England till the appearance of the work of Archdeacon Wilberforce, then on the highroad to the Church of Rome : the nearest ap-proaches to it are to be found in the suspicious period of the concluding years of the reign of Charles II., and during the short reign of his infatuated brother.

'Allow me to offer you my sincere thanks. You have done a great and valuable service—at, I am sure, no little cost to your own personal feelings—and never was such a service more needed.

                    'I am,
                        'Yours sincerely,
                            'CHARLES WORDSWORTH,
                                'Bishop of St. Andrews.

'I am very glad indeed to know that more than half the Bishops have recognised the value of the stand you have been making and the service you have done

—not a moment too soon ! I shall probably be gone, or at least quite enfeebled, before Liddon's *Life of Pusey* appears ; but I earnestly hope you will be alive and well and strong (if necessary) to carry on your testimony.'

Bishop Charles Wordsworth was as strongly opposed to the theory of a heavenly altar, to which the bread and wine are supposed to be transferred from earthly altars, and there converted into the glorified body and blood of Christ, and retransferred to earth, having become now a proper subject of worship (which is Bishop Gore's representation in his *Body of Christ*), and, indeed, to the theory of the existence of a continued sacrifice in heaven, as he was to the supposition that Christ's Objective Presence in the elements was brought about by consecration.

'The doctrine of the Saviour at the right hand of God, plainly taught in no less than a dozen passages of the New Testament, has been swallowed up by the notion of a continuous sacrifice carried on in heaven ; as though the great Sacrifice on the Cross had been grudgingly accepted or can be held to be less than perfect. The notion has arisen out of the prestige which it gives to the priesthood of the clergy ; but it has no foundation in the Word of God, and it obliterates the doctrine, which has abundant foundation in that Word.

'I confess I do not like the notion (now so popular) of our Lord's pleading His Sacrifice. It seems to clash with the doctrine of the Passion. The one Sacrifice on the Cross was full, perfect, and sufficient: the pleading of it seems to suggest either that the Sacrifice was insufficient or grudgingly accepted. That *we on earth* should plead it in prayers and Eucharist is right and natural. But the teaching that Christ in some way repeats or continues and pleads

His own Sacrifice upon the heavenly altar has no foundation in Holy Scripture.'*

On the subject of reunion with Presbyterians, after forty years' discussion with the heads of the Presbyterian Church, he was willing to accept the compromise that the existing generation of Presbyterian clergy should be left free to receive Episcopal ordination or not at their own option, provided that a threefold ministry was eventually accepted.

The last act of the Bishop was a grudging acceptance of Archbishop Benson's judgment in the Lincoln case —grudging because he thought it moved the centre of the Anglican position nearer to Rome—and a warning addressed to the Anglican Church against the theories of Old Testament criticism introduced from Germany by Canon Driver.   He died in 1893.

While still in Scotland with my two pupils I fell in with A. H. Clough, Fellow of Oriel, who was conducting a reading-party, in which, as he said, he aimed at 'plain living and high thinking.'   Unable to sympathize with the theological sentiments at the time common in Oxford, he slid off more and more into agnosticism.   It is sometimes said that agnosticism was originated after this date by Huxley, but it existed, name and thing, in the time of St. Paul, who says: 'For some have agnosticism of God (ἀγνωσίαν Θεοῦ); I say this to your shame' (1 Cor. xv. 34); and it must always exist.   Clough was more a poet than a theologian.   Some of his verses are more than pretty, and full of sad thought.   We were joined for a time in the Highlands by H. M. Birch, Lord Lothian's tutor at Eton.   Having been tutor to the Prince of Wales, and his initials being H. M., he was known as Her Majesty's Birch.

After a short stay at Newbattle we went to Lord Lothian's other Scottish home, Monteviot, in Rox-

* *Episcopate of Charles Wordsworth*, p. 137.

burghshire. At that time Monteviot was a singular house. From the front-door, which was of a very simple character, a long passage led straight to the drawing-room ; this passage was paved with flag-stones, and on each side ran a strip of gravel; the roof and sides of the passage were made of plain deal planks. It is reported that the late Queen said that she must go to Monteviot to see a house with a gravel path inside it. A commencement of a new and larger mansion had been made, which, I believe, is now occupied. But the old house was very comfortable and very pleasant. It was beautifully situated above the Teviot, and below a hill that rose behind it. The most striking personality at Monteviot was Robert Kerse, the keeper. He would have died for any of the family, and he never failed in courtesy ; but he had withal an independence of bearing not usual in the South. He regarded himself as having rights in respect to teaching his young lord fishing and shooting, which he firmly stood up for. A neighbour, Mr. Richardson, a friend of Sir Walter Scott, used occasionally to pay a visit, and, as he did not fish or shoot, Kerse looked upon him with displeasure. 'Ah !' he would say, 'if the mon Richardson is coming, there'll be no fishing the day.' He was inclined to look upon me at first as an enemy ; but when he found that I took part in the fishing, he came round, and at last we were such friends that he came to the Episcopal chapel to hear me preach and officiate. He was surprised at all 'the manœuvres' of sitting, standing, and kneeling, that he saw.

Later in the year I made acquaintance with my younger pupils : Ralph, now General Lord Ralph Kerr ; Walter, now Admiral Lord Walter Kerr ; and John, who was sent to school at Oscott, and died there.

In the same year A. P. Forbes was appointed

Bishop of Brechin. I had seen something of him in Oxford, and after his consecration saw him frequently in Scotland. He was a devout man, but not a good Bishop for the Scottish Church. He almost caused a schism in it by maintaining semi-Roman doctrine on the Eucharist, which Bishop Charles Wordsworth had to controvert, and he wrote an unsatisfactory book on the Thirty-nine Articles.

The incumbent of St. Mary's, Dalkeith—a little gem of a chapel built by the Duke of Buccleuch—was the Rev. J. Robertson. He, too, was a devout man, but he was weak and not well read. After a while he resigned his incumbency and became a Roman Catholic. Meantime he did much mischief to members of his congregation.

My brother being very ill, and unable to do his work as Vicar of Westbury in Wiltshire, I engaged Alexander Heriot Mackonochie as his curate as soon as the latter had been ordained. He was very earnest and self-devoted, but singularly stiff and narrow. It was said of him that he walked about the parish saying to himself, 'I am a priest'; and that if he had known that the fate of Christendom hung on his saying his prayers facing west, while he thought it 'catholic' to face east, he would have continued facing east without hesitation. His brother curate was the Rev. Thomas Bowles, and on my brother's resignation they both went to Wantage as curates under the Rev. W. Butler, afterwards Dean of Lincoln. When Mr. Hubbard was looking for the first incumbent of his new church, St. Alban's, Holborn, he asked me if I could recommend a suitable clergyman. I told him that I thought the Rev. T. Bowles, then curate at Wantage, was the right man. Mr. Hubbard wrote to Mr. Butler, saying that he understood that he had a curate named the Rev. T. Barnes (he had forgotten the exact name) who would be suitable for the post. Mr. Butler wrote back that he had no curate named Barnes, but that he strongly recommended his curate the Rev. A. H. Mackonochie. The consequence was, Mr. Hubbard entered into communication with Mr. Mackonochie, and finally appointed him. The way in which Mr. Mackonochie conducted the parish, which in many ways was not in accordance with the wishes of the founder, is well known, as well as his sad death in Scotland. Mr. Bowles became afterwards the Rector of Hendred, in the Diocese of Oxford, where he was worried by having a Roman Catholic squire, and he spent his last years at Abingdon, after he had become too infirm to hold his parish with advantage to the people.

About this time, while on a visit to the Rev. R. F. Wilson at Ampfield, I made acquaintance with the Rev. John Keble at Hursley, with whom I had frequent communications afterwards. He showed me over his church with some pride, as it had lately been restored. Most of it was new, but 'here,' he said, 'we have kept a part of the old church to hitch us on to earlier times.' Keble belonged to the old historical High Church section of the Church, and he looked with dread on the threatening aspect of the State, which had cut down the number of the Irish bishoprics, and was turning its attention to the English Church, which Lord Grey warned the Bishops 'they must set in order.' During the eighteenth century Churchmen had grown to put their trust in their State connection, and to confide rather in their rights as an establishment than as a branch of the Church of Christ. Keble saw the danger, and in a sermon preached before the University of Oxford in 1833, entitled 'National Apostasy,' he called on Churchmen to fall back on their inherent powers as their means of defence, and no longer to rest secure in the arms of a protector that

had become unfriendly. In the critical circumstances
of the day his call met with an extraordinarily vigorous
response. Men gathered together, resolved to recall
and stand by the principles and practices of the seven-
teenth-century divines, which were too much overlaid
and forgotten. The Church was a Church, not merely
an Establishment; it could stand on its' own feet if
the State turned against it, and it could prove from its
own principles that it had a right to be the Church of
the nation, whether a Parliamentary majority favoured
it or not; and there was yet time to save a national
apostasy. Hugh James Rose had been preaching the
same doctrine at Cambridge, and through these two
men a new spirit was infused into the English Church.
Keble's first follower was Isaac Williams, a poet and a
devotional writer, who had been his pupil in classics
and philosophy, and had learned to love the humility,
simplicity and cheerfulness which he found united
with masterly ability, depth, and power. Not at first,
but before long, J. H. Newman joined the growing
party, and at a still later time Dr. Pusey. These
adhesions, especially Newman's, changed its character
to a considerable extent. Newman grasped the direction of the movement, and turned it in the way in
which he, rather than Keble, would have it go. Keble,
not on the spot at Oxford, guileless as a child, and
having a warm affection for his colleagues and an
admiration of their ability, allowed himself to be
carried off his legs (it is his own expression) by them
for a time. Looking back in 1858, he said : 'I look now
upon my time with Newman and Pusey as a sort of
parenthesis in my life, and I have now returned again
to my old views, such as I had before. I see that I
was fairly carried off my legs by the sanguine views
they held and the effects that were showing themselves in all quarters.' 'Now that I have thrown off
Newman's yoke,' he said to Isaac Williams, 'these

things appear to me quite different' (*Williams' Auto-biography*, p. 118). Had the Tractarian Movement been in the hands of Keble, it would have had a very different result.

Mr. Keble continued at Hursley till his death, setting a conspicuous example—the English Church has shown others—of a wise, learned, and able man perfectly content to do the work which God had given him to do, however simple and obscure.

CHAPTER III

A year abroad—Pius IX.—Greece—Constantinople.

WHEN I went abroad with Lord Lothian in 1849, we crossed to Dieppe, and went on to Rouen. Among other places in Rouen, we visited the theological seminary, and were received by the Professor of Divinity, who courteously showed us over the building, and then sat down for a discussion with his unusual guests. His name was the Abbé Omer. He asked us if we came from Oxford, and on my replying in the affirmative, he said: 'Ah! the doctrines of Oxford are not far from those of the Catholic Church; you have all except one little point' (here he covered the whole of his fingers except just the tip) 'and that is the Papal Supremacy.' He argued (1) that the Pope held the supremacy from the Apostolic days, but that he did not exert it in the early ages; (2) that there must be an authority, and that Œcumenical Councils could not now be called; therefore it must be somewhere else; therefore it must be in the Pope; (3) that the promise 'I am with you' implied a perfect state of the Church, which therefore existed at present. So far as my French, helped out with Latin, allowed me, I replied (1) that his statement respecting the Pope's potential supremacy was an assumption, disproved by the voice of history and antiquity; (2) that there was great danger and presumption in using *a priori* argument and saying what *must* or *must not* be, for this

51   4—2

really means that *we think*, with our finite intelligence, that the Infinite Wisdom ought to, and therefore must, work in this way or that, which is prying into God's counsels; also that the authority of Œcumenical Councils was not abolished, though at present suspended, owing to the arbitrary conduct of the Pope in having severed himself, and that part of the Church which adhered to him, first from the Eastern Church, and then from us and other Western and Northern Churches; also that the erection of the Popedom into a monarchy was a poor device of man's wisdom to effect an end which God could fulfil in His own way, and which was effected until that human device was allowed to supersede the Divine plan; also that the Fathers made their appeal, not to any Bishop, but to the written Word of God, interpreted, when necessary, by the historical testimony of the past, shown in formal decisions of the Church; (3) that the promise 'I am with you' was fulfilled by our very existence, for without that presence Christianity must have perished with its first preachers, and that the promise did not guarantee that the sins of men should not mar the good purposes of God in the later, as they did in the earlier or Jewish, dispensation: for it was the privilege of the Church triumphant alone that the spirits of its members should go along with, and work in accordance with, the perfect will of God.

Passing to other subjects, the Abbé said that the French Church had suffered little by the Revolution of 1848. 'You had no revolution like the rest of Europe,' he continued. 'Are you not in fear of an outbreak in England?' 'No, thank God!' I said. 'Nor in Ireland?' 'Agitators have done harm there,' I answered. 'Ah, Smith O'Brien,' whose name was in the papers at the time. 'Yes, and before him O'Connell.' 'O'Connell!' he cried in a tone as if I had said 'St. Paul'; 'he won the emancipation of the

Catholics !'   Abroad he is generally looked upon as a saint, and no wonder, if they believe Padre Ventura's sermon about him ! As I rose up to go, I said smilingly, 'If you will give up your Romanism, we can then give up our Protestantism, and, see, we shall all be Catholics !' 'A beautiful hope !' he said. We parted with cordial good wishes.

At St. Cloud we saw Louis Napoleon. The year before he had been acting as a special constable in London, together with other householders, to put down a threatened Chartist riot, and was now President of the French Republic. While an exile in England, he made an offer of marriage to a young lady with whom I was acquainted. In refusing him she did not know that she was declining to be an Empress.

In Italy we had an interview with Pope Pius IX. At the beginning of his pontificate, Pius IX., finding the whole of Italy in effervescence, and resolved to form itself into one body politic instead of being divided into duchies, grand-duchies, Papal Dominions, and the Kingdom of the Two Sicilies, conceived a great idea. He would lead, not thwart, the popular impulse and will, and so constitute the Papacy the federal head of a United Italy, accepted as such, as he fondly hoped, by a general acclamation. Such a solution of the Italian question would gratify him for more reasons than one. He was an Italian, and, in spite of being an ecclesiastic, he could not help having some sympathy with the oppressed and divided Italian people. He would vindicate his position as a statesman, and deliver himself from the yoke of the Jesuits, who had long been governing at the Vatican. And, above all, he would give a new lease of power and prestige to the Pope as President of an Italian confederation as well as ruler in his own dominions. The Jesuits smiled grimly, and stood aside for him

to try his experiment. It failed utterly. He could
not control the forces that were set in motion with
his encouragement. The Reds were not going to
be satisfied with such an amount of liberty as the Pope
regarded as already excessive, and the Italian people
turned by a sure instinct to the House of Piedmont,
round which they should gather in order to form
themselves into a nation. He met with little sympathy. The Reds looked upon him as a traitor to
Italy because he would not go further with them ;
the Blacks (Neri) said in effect, 'We told you so ; see
what you have done for yourself and for the Church !'
He struggled on until the Reds assassinated his chief
minister, Rossi. Then he fled from his capital in
disguise, leaving Rome in the hands of the revolu-
tionists. A triumvirate with Aurelio Saffi at its head,
and with Garibaldi as its right hand, was proclaimed.
Then came the French intervention. We drove to the
Porta di San Pancrazio, and saw the ruined walls and
the marks of shells thrown by Marshal Oudinot's
army, still visible early in 1850. Shortly before the
entrance of the French, a fine scene was enacted in
the Forum, worthy of the spot and of its history.
Garibaldi summoned the people of Rome to an
assembly. Sitting on his horse, he told them that
the city was no longer defensible, and then, lifting up
his voice, he cried, ' Let all that love Italy follow me.'
With that he moved his horse towards one of the
gates not yet beset by the enemy, and, followed by a
body of devoted adherents, made his way to the North
of Italy, abiding his time and Cavour's. The Pope
did not dare at once to return. The city was subjected to a triumvirate of Cardinals, headed by Antonelli, and their authority was maintained by French
bayonets. The real ruler of Rome was General
Baraguay d'Hilliers. He was a courteous gentleman,
and did what he could to mitigate the hatred of the

Romans towards the French soldiers. We attended one of his receptions and one of his balls. At the latter, when his guests began to go away about twelve o'clock, in all good-humour he posted a sentinel at the door, who stolidly opposed his bayonet to those who would go out, with the words, 'On ne passe pas.' In this manner the ball was kept up till four o'clock. Antonelli and the other two Cardinals treated every one suspected of Liberalism—and that was the whole population, with the exception of the small party of Neri—with great severity, and Antonelli was known to be leading anything but an austere or moral life. Pope Pius meantime continued to live in the Kingdom of the Two Sicilies at Portici. It was here that we had an interview with him, being introduced by Prince Hohenlohe.

Pope Pius was sitting in a small room at a little table, dressed in his loose white robe (which is too much like a flannel dressing-grown), occupied as we came in with writing. According to Prince Hohenlohe's directions, we knelt on one knee at entering, and again on kissing his hand, for the Pope was still a Sovereign at that time. We then stood up and had a conversation with him for about a quarter of an hour. I had been introduced to him as a member of the University of Oxford, and he almost at once began to talk about it. Presently he said: 'Dr. Pusey is at Oxford.' I intimated that I was acquainted with him. 'He has done us a great deal of good,' he continued. 'The good that he has done is that he has taught people to believe that they cannot all come to the same truth while they indulge in unlicensed private judgment, but they must have some authority to guide them. And then,' he said, 'many will have recourse to the Apostolic See.' It was not a moment to enter into controversy with the Pope, so I bowed, without saying that there was authority apart from that of 'the Apostolic See.' After this he said that he knew Newman, St. John, and others with whom I was acquainted. Turning to my companion, he spoke about the Scottish dress, and especially the cairngorms which he was wearing, with which the Pope seemed much impressed. On a pause, he said that he would give us his benediction, for which we knelt accordingly, and he gave us his blessing with the promise of his prayers.

Pio Nono's appearance was prepossessing, from the great kindness of his expression; but he was already growing fat, and the lower part of his face was heavy. He was not a man of ability, and in trying to take the helm into his own hands in stormy times he made an utter failure. He had been elected as a Liberal Pope in opposition to Cardinal Lambruschini, whose appointment would have been the signal for a revolution, and he thought some concessions to popular feeling necessary. His Cardinals stood aloof as well as the Jesuits; the Roman nobles were nonentities, and he had only the populace to rest upon. As long as he let himself be carried away by them, he was their idol; the moment he stopped, he was the object of their abuse and obloquy. He trembled before the storm and fled. He had intended to take a Spanish ship for Majorca, but the King of the Two Sicilies received him on his knees and treated him with the respect shown to James II. by Louis XIV., begging him to remain in the Neapolitan dominions. From the time of his flight, Pius IX. gave up all his popular leanings, and threw himself back into the arms of the Jesuits, who had been waiting for him and wound their invisible cords around him more closely than ever. He had still a long pontificate before him, memorable for the declaration of the Immaculate Conception of St. Mary, and the decrees of the Vatican Council, constituting him infallible in matters of faith and morals, and the

Universal Bishop of the Church. He was to see the
entrance of the Italians into Rome on its abandonment by the French in 1870, and he died on February 7,
1878.

On the same day that we had our interview with
Pius IX. we visited the General of the Jesuits, to
whom we were introduced by Padre Costa, a Jesuit
Father attached to the Gesù in Naples. The General
was tall and thin, bent somewhat with age, but having
a keen and vigorous eye and brow and a kindly
expression. He remembered the reception of Thomas
Meyrick (p. 5) into the company, and had seen him
lately in Wales while on a visit to his English and
Irish subjects. He was, he said, an *ottimo giovane*.
The General was now residing in Naples, to be near
the Pope in his exile, and intended to stay there till
the Pope's return to Rome. The General of the
Jesuits is in Italy generally called the 'Black Pope.'
He rules the 'White Pope' (they are called 'Black'
and 'White' from their dresses), and through him the
Roman Catholic Church. From Ganganelli down-
wards, and before him, Popes have occasionally
attempted to assert their independence. Pius IX.
did so, to his own confusion. Leo XIII. struggled
feebly for liberty when he first became Pontiff. But
the Jesuits have made themselves a necessity as
supporters of the Vatican system, and Ganganelli's
example does not encourage Papal rebellion. The
declaration of the Immaculate Conception and of
the Papal Infallibility were both of them the work
of the Jesuits. They took the former dogma under
their patronage, not from believing it to be a truth,
but because by that means they were able to get
the better of the Dominicans, with whom they were
holding a controversy in the sixteenth century at
Rome. 'Let your reverence see,' wrote Cardinal
Lugo to a brother Jesuit in Madrid, 'that you and

yours take pains to reawaken the devotion of the Conception, which is very popular in Spain, in order that by this means we may turn off the attacks of the Dominicans, who are pressing us hard here. If we don't occupy them with some other matter, they will beat us in the controversy *De Auxiliis*.' Accordingly, the Jesuit Father Aquete was sent on a tour through Spain, preaching that 'the Virgin would rather be damned eternally and live with the devils than have been conceived in original sin.' Cardinal Lugo's plan of beating the Dominicans succeeded, and from that time the Jesuits, thrusting the Franciscans aside, took charge of the intrigue which ended in the decree of Pope Pius IX. in 1854.

Similarly in respect to Papal Infallibility. The dogma in its favour was issued, not because it was thought to be true—for all history and all experience contradicted it—but because the General of the Jesuits held it to be good policy to concentrate authority in the hands of the ' White Pope,' which would be really exercised by himself, the ' Black Pope.' In this intrigue, which ended in the Vatican Council's decrees, Cardinal Manning for once co-operated with the Jesuits, whom he heartily detested ; and not only he, but also the Protestant representative of Great Britain at Rome— Mr. Odo Russell—who had been living for twelve years in Rome in the society of Cardinals and Papal courtiers, and was anxious to strengthen the Papal throne against the seditious spirit with which he knew the city to be honeycombed. He thought that the only way of saving the Papal monarchy was by hedging it round with a prestige derived from superstition, and consequently, when Mr. Gladstone proposed that England should join in the Bavarian protest against the declaration of the dogma, Mr. Odo Russell, making himself the mouthpiece of Manning and the Vaticanist party, so represented the case to the Foreign Secretary, Lord Clarendon, that he opposed Mr. Gladstone's design, and defeated him in his own Cabinet. 'Dr. Döllinger,' writes Mr. Purcell, 'who was a *persona grata* to the King of Bavaria, suggested to King Louis II. that a coalition should be formed of the various States, whose Catholic subjects would be deprived, as he pretended, of their civil liberties by the setting up of the Pope's Infallibility, a dogma incompatible with their civil allegiance. Bavaria was to take the first step, and to propose to the English Government to issue in due form and order an invitation to France, Prussia, Austria, Bavaria, and Belgium, to make a common stand against the Vatican Council, and to present to the Sovereign Pontiff, through their respective representatives at the Holy See, a common declaration that the definition of Papal Infallibility was against public policy, and that the promulgation of any such dogma by the Council would be prohibited by international enactments. . . . On the occasion of the presentation by Prince Hohenlohe, the President of the Bavarian Ministry, of a formal proposal that the English Government should invite the Powers of Europe to intervene at the Vatican for the protection of the civil and religious liberty of their Catholic subjects, there was a prolonged and hot discussion in the Cabinet. In giving this information, Cardinal Manning said : "The Prime Minister, Mr. Gladstone, supported the Bavarian proposal on the grounds and by the arguments supplied to him by Acton ; but Lord Clarendon, better informed by Odo Russell, exposed one by one the fallacious statements and wilful distortions of fact. Finally, after a hot discussion, Mr. Gladstone was defeated in the Cabinet, the Bavarian proposal was rejected, and the Vatican Council was left in peace to do God's work. . . ." Had Dr. Döllinger's plan succeeded, and the Powers of Europe taken common action against the Pope and the Council, the moral influence of the Opposition would have become almost irresistible, and the united action of the majority of the Fathers of the Council have been broken, or so weakened as to have rendered them helpless to resist the final demand, insisted upon by the Opposition, of proroguing the Council. ". . . Had the Council been prorogued," continued Manning, "according to the designs of the Opposition, owing to events—the Franco-German War, the seizure of Rome, the persecution of Catholics in Germany by Bismarck— it would have been prorogued *sine die*. The Council, with the Pope a prisoner in the Vatican, could not have met again, and the Pope's Infallibility would have been undefined even to this day"' (*Life of Manning*, xvi, pp. 432-436). It is singular that the definition of the Pope's Infallibility should have been brought about by a coalition of the General of the Jesuits, an English convert, and a Protestant diplomatist.

The present General, Father Martin, a Spaniard, lives partly in Rome, partly at Fiesole, and once a year he goes to Paris to hold a conclave of the heads of the Order inferior to himself, to whom he gives his orders as to their political and social conduct, and with whom he examines their reports on the industrial, banking, and agricultural enterprises of the Society. It is said that, being absent from Rome in 1898 for eight days, he found on his return 4,000 letters waiting for him, and that after a stay at Fiesole of four months, during which only the more pressing communications were forwarded to him, 60,000 letters accumulated for him in Rome, requiring his personal supervision. He constitutes himself the unseen protector of the Vatican, and hates the Italian kingdom with an implacable hatred. The condemnation of Americanism by Leo. XIII. on February 21, 1899, is said to be due to an intrigue of Father Martin and an Italian journalist named Olinto Spadoni. Finding

Americanism—that is, a comparatively liberal theology —was spreading, Spadoni, who was the Roman correspondent of the *New York World*, called on the General, to concert measures for crushing it. The result of their consultation was that Father Martin undertook to see that Archbishop Ireland should be summoned to Rome, and that Leo XIII. should issue a Letter condemning Americanism, and Spadoni agreed to bring out a journal to combat the American views, which was to be circulated in thousands. But how was the expense thus incurred to be met ? 'There are good works,' said the General significantly, ' for which we know how to find compensation.' The General carried out his part, so far as Archbishop Ireland and the Pope's Letter were concerned ; but when Spadoni applied for his expenses, Father Martin refused his demand, and wrote to Cardinal Franchi to say that he had 'felicitated' Spadoni on his idea of publishing a Catholic journal, but had made no promise of pecuniary assistance. Spadoni, indignant at the deception, carried the case into the Italian courts of law, claiming his out-of-pocket expenses and 20,000 lire for his personal services. The court took cognizance of the case on November 18, 1903, and I am not aware that judgment has yet been given. This story, recounted by the *Nazione*, the *Sentinella Valdese*, and the *Chrétien Français*, indicates the power that the ' Black Pope' exercises over the 'White,' and it shows us the value of Papal Encyclicals as personal acts of infallible authority. The Papal treasury is said to be replenished out of the coffers of the Society, whose wealth is fabulous, and this is one of the causes of the subserviency of the 'White Pope,' but not the only one. Jesuitism has absorbed Romanism ; the faith of Ignatius Loyola and the moral theology satirized by Pascal are now the faith and moral theology of the whole Roman Catholic Church.

In Rome we saw a good deal of Mr. and Mrs. Harris and Mr. and Mrs. Monsell. Mrs. Harris and Mrs. Monsell were sisters, daughters of Lord Inchiquin, and sisters of Smith O'Brien, who at the time was instigating the 'cabbage-garden rising' in Ireland. It was said that, as the two sisters were leaving Naples, a steamer from England met their outgoing steamer, and that the captain, being asked as they passed for news from England, replied that there was none, except that 'that rascal Smith O'Brien had been hanged,' which, however, turned out to be untrue. Mr. Harris, the brother of Lord Malmesbury, was afterwards appointed Bishop of Gibraltar, and did much for the British congregations on the Continent, and by his courtesy and piety raised the estimation in which the English Church was held by the heads of the Greek Church. The Patriarch of Constantinople was much pleased at his second name, which was Amyand. 'Ah!' said the Patriarch, 'most suitable for a Bishop — 'Αμίαντος, the unstained.' In 1873 he came to Torquay, and lodged in the same house with me, both of us having broken down in health. On March 16, 1874, he died there.

The party had come to Italy in 1849 for Mr. Monsell's health, who was far gone in consumption, and died at Naples, to which city we accompanied them, together with Sir John Harington. Returning to England after her husband's death, Mrs. Monsell became Superior of the Clewer Sisterhood. I did not see her again until it was my lot to summon her to the death-bed of Bishop Harris in 1874, when she stayed for a week with us. It was interesting to note how she was the same woman before her work at Clewer began and now when her life was nearly being brought to a close. In the comparatively young wife of 1849 and the comparatively aged Mother Superior of 1874 there was apparent the same character, the same individuality. She was as deeply a religious woman in 1849 as in 1874, and she was as bright, merry, buoyant, cheerful, almost playful, in 1874 as in 1849. She was not lifted up, as some women have been, by a position of authority, nor was she stiffened into a female ecclesiastic. She did not walk about saying to herself that she was a Lady Abbess, or a Mother Elderess, or a Church dignitary of any kind. She was Mother Superior, but all the time she was Mrs. Monsell ; and her simple, unaffected behaviour as a kind-hearted lady, and her Irish humour, helped her to do her work as the head of a religious society, and saved her from many of the failures, mistakes, and faults which Miss Sellon and others in like position committed. Her honest and loyal obedience to her Bishop (Samuel Wilberforce), the memory which she cherished of her husband, who had died peacefully in the faith of the English Church, her experience of the religion on the Continent, and her own sound sense, kept her a faithful and loving member of the Church of England, and thus she escaped a rock on which it appeared at one time that Anglican sisterhoods were destined to founder, which is yet a serious danger to them.

From Italy we went to Sicily, at that time ruled by General Filangieri for the King of Naples ; thence to Malta, where I fell in for the last time with J. E. Bowden (p. 35), and went with him to the services for Holy Week, very beautifully rendered in St. John's Church, Valetta ; thence to Corfu, where we were hospitably received by the Lord High Commissioner, Sir Henry Ward : for at this time the Septinsular Republic formed by the seven islands Corfu, Paxo, Ithaca, Cephalonia, Santa Maura, Zante, Cerigo, was a dependency of Great Britain. From 1386 to 1797 the islands were under Venetian rule. Then for twelve years they were subject either to Russia or to France, and in 1809 they were conquered by the British, and by the Treaty of Paris in 1815 were recognised as being under British protection. A Constitution was given them by Sir Thomas Maitland, known in the Mediterranean as King Tom, consisting of a Lord High Commissioner, representing the English Sovereign; a Senate of five members, nominated by the Lord High Commissioner; and a Legislative Assembly of forty members. The Assembly, which only met every third year, and then sat for only three months, was in session at the time of my arrival, and they were in a very discontented and riotous frame of mind, the five members for Cephalonia pressing for immediate incorporation with Greece, a question which the Lord High Commissioner did not allow to be debated. On April 13 we were engaged to ride with His Excellency, but so threatening a disturbance took place in the Assembly that the President appealed to the Lord High Commissioner to support his authority. His Excellency ordered a sergeant and guard and thirty policemen to be in readiness, but the excitement cooled down, and they were not needed. Sir Henry thought it right to remain on the spot, that he might, if necessary, dissolve the Parliament. Meantime we went for our ride with two of his daughters and an Aide-de-camp, and after two or three hours, when peace was now assured, he joined us. When Lord Derby was Prime Minister, he commissioned Mr. Gladstone, whose position as a Peelite was at the time undefined, to proceed to Corfu and to hand over the Septinsular Republic to Greece, which Mr. Gladstone's love of Greece made him very willing to do. It was a generous act on the part of England, for Greece wanted territory and subjects, and the Corfiotes desired annexation; and it was also a piece of good policy, as the position of the islands did not make them of much value to us, and it was not satisfactory to be answerable for the acts of roving Greek islanders.

Lady Ward was sister to Mrs. Bowden, mother of J. E. Bowden (p. 35), and I had met two of the Misses Ward at the Observatory, Oxford, the house of Manuel Johnson, a friend of the Bowdens and a well-known character at Oxford. His Excellency's chaplain was Mr. Skinner, afterwards incumbent of St. Barnabas, London, a friend of Dr. Pusey; and G. F. Bowen (p. 17) was his secretary.

From Corfu we travelled to Patras and Corinth, passing on our way Missolonghi, where Mavrocordato, in the War of Independence, with 500 men beat off the Turks with 14,000 men in 1824, and in 1826 the garrison, when blockaded by Ibrahim Pasha and Raschid Pasha with 34,000 men, having eaten their last crust, cut their way through the enemy, while those left behind blew up themselves and the town by firing the powder-magazine. It was at Missolonghi that Byron died in 1824. Turning inland, we reached the Monastery of Megaspelion, where Bishop Germanus first unfurled the banner of Greek independence in 1821. Megaspelion is perched on the face of a precipitous cliff, a hundred feet from the top and many hundred feet from the bottom. The church is in a vast natural cavern, and the residences of the monks are built without order on a rock projecting from the mouth of the cavern, at the outer edge of which a blank wall has been built, with a few windows opening into the monks' quarters. The ascent is by a winding path. It served as a safe retreat to the Greeks in the War of Independence, and was vainly besieged by Ibrahim Pasha in 1826. There were 270 kaloyers (monks), who elected their Abbot annually, and occupied themselves chiefly in agriculture—very simple folk.

The night before we reached Megaspelion we slept at Vostizza, the ancient Ægium, once the chief town of the Achæan League, where we were kindly received by Kyr Soterios Poniatopulos, to whom we had an introduction. Unfortunately, he could not speak Italian or French, and our Oxford and Eton Greek would not serve as a means of communication until we had learnt a few rules of pronunciation and grammar. Our host, with many smiles and bows, made us sit down on a daïs, and took a chair facing us, dressed in a dark jacket bound with fur, purple waistcoat, white *fustianelle* or flounces, white leggings, slippers, and red cap with purple tassel. When we had gazed at each other for a little time, servants brought lighted pipes about 3 feet long, which we gravely smoked; then another servant brought a tray with a tumbler of preserve on it, two small tumblers of water, two filigree silver cups and spoons. What to do with them? My first attempt was to put some of the preserve into the cups. That not being right, I tried to mix it with the water. On this our host ran across to us, and without a word, but with much laughter from all of us, took a spoonful of the preserve and gave it to me to eat, and then put one of the tumblers of water in my hand to drink. In a short time coffee was brought in two little cups, and while we were drinking it a friend of our host, who could talk English, a grandson of Admiral Miaulis, of the War of Independence, arrived. The two Greek gentlemen told us that Greece was at that time divided between two parties, the Russian and the anti-Russian parties, the latter of which was subdivided into the English and French parties. The first of these parties worshipped Russia as the natural enemy of Turkey and protector of Eastern Christians. The second looked to England and France to set a Greek once more on the throne of Constantinople as the successor of the Byzantine Emperor when the Turks should be driven out of Europe, and it feared the rivalry of

St. Petersburg. This cause of antagonism between Greece and Russia still exists, and makes an animosity between the two nations.

On reaching Athens, we found the English fleet lying off the Piræus, blockading the Greek capital. It had been sent by Lord Palmerston to exact compensation for the loss of Mr. Finlay the historian's garden, which had been taken from him, and for injury done to Don Pacifico's house, and to demand an apology for Lieutenant Breen having been seized and imprisoned, through a misunderstanding, at Patras, together with some British sailors. Pacifico was a Jew whose house had been broken into by an Athenian mob because they had been forbidden to burn the effigy of a Jew on Good Friday according to custom. He was under the protection of England because he belonged to the Septinsular Republic. The English fleet made a gallant show in the Bay of Salamis, consisting of the *Queen*, the *Howe*, the *Caledonia*, the *Vengeance*, the *Powerful*, the *Bellerophon*, the *Ganges*, the *Scourge*, the *Spiteful*, the *Firebrand*, and the *Dragon*. In spite of the blockade, we lived at the Hôtel d'Angleterre in Athens, and passed freely backwards and forwards between the city and the fleet. On April 27, 1850, King Otho gave way, and it happened that we—unmistakable Englishmen by our dress—met him in the crowded street on the day of the surrender. Of course we took off our hats, and he courteously bowed to us. The commander of the *Scourge* was Lord Frederic Kerr, uncle of Lord Lothian, and we spent several days on his ship. At a later date I saw much of him at Newbattle Abbey in Scotland and at Blickling Hall, Norfolk, which was lent to him for several years by his nephew. He was a man wise and kind, and his quiet humour made him a delightful companion.

5—2

Some of those who had taken part in the War of Greek Independence were still living, and among them General Church, to whom we brought an introduction from his nephew, Dean Church. In the Greek War he played the part of Garibaldi's Englishman (Colonel Peard) in the Italian *risorgimento*, and made the name of Englishman honoured in Greece.

Two of the greatest benefactors that Greece has ever had were carrying on their beneficent work at this time—Dr. and Mrs. Hill. Archbishop Lycurgus of Syros has left a graphic account, written at the time of Mrs. Hill's death, of the way in which they undertook their mission. 'Fanny M. Hill (Φανὴ M. Χίλλ), learning in America the utter ruin and desolation of Greece, caused by the savagery and brutality of the barbarians, and feeling for her, said to her reverend and good husband : "Come, let us go to Greece, to inspire courage, instruct, and teach the Holy Gospel to those who, with unexampled bravery and nobleness, have shaken off the heavy yoke of slavery which has oppressed them for 400 years." The Rev. Dr. Hill agreed to the proposal of his dear wife. So they came to Athens, and established the girls' school which bears their name, where they carried on their work as teachers with zealous enthusiasm and unexampled self-denial, without interfering with the religious opinions of the young girls instructed by them, whence their school became famous and admired throughout Greece. The women that have been remarkable for piety, virtue, and Christian life were the pupils of Fanny Hill. The wives and mothers that have been remarkable for public spirit and simple life were her pupils. Eternal gratitude is due to this venerable lady that has been taken from us, who devoted the whole of her life to the moulding of our nation. Her memory shall remain deathless and ageless, and her name shall be engraven in golden letters, which shall never be obliterated, in the hearts of the Grecian people.'

It was in 1830 that Dr. and Mrs. Hill came and settled down among the ruins which marked where Athens had been and was to be, and seeing the imperious need that Greece had of the education which Turkish barbarism had denied her, they immediately opened a school for boys and girls. It was the only school to be found in Greece during the first years of the restored nation, and it was quite gratuitous. Dr. and Mrs. Hill arranged to take one girl from each of the ten divisions of Greece on the condition of her going back to her own district and there devoting herself to educational work. By this means education was spread throughout Greece. The wealthier classes came and begged that their children, too, might be received, when they saw the excellent education given to their poorer neighbours ; and this was done, superior schools being instituted for them. With the fees thus gained the Hills engaged English and American teachers to superintend the schools both of rich and poor, which soon began to multiply. On Otho's accession the State undertook the education of boys, placing that of girls unreservedly in the hands of Dr. and Mrs. Hill. In this important sphere Dr. Hill laboured for fifty-two years, and Mrs. Hill for fifty-four years — supported all along morally and financially by the American Episcopal Church—and during this time some three generations of Greek women passed through their hands drawn from almost every family in the kingdom. In 1881 the King publicly returned the nation's thanks to them, and in 1882, when Dr. Hill died, Professor Diomede Cyriacus, the most learned ecclesiastic in Athens, made a funeral oration over him, as the spokesman of Greek sympathy and sorrow. At the end of his oration he apostrophized him as follows : ' Yes, venerable man, thou art gone to the other life, to the Heavenly Father of us all, leaving to us a beloved memory. Not only those of thy household, to whom thou didst bear so deep an affection, will remember thee for ever with praise ; not only in America, to which thou hast been an honour, will thy name be never forgotten ; but Greece too, which to-day receives thy body into its bosom, thy second country, to which thou didst consecrate thy whole life and offer such noble services, will never forget thee. Her history will enrol thy name among the friends of Greece who have done most for her regeneration. Γαῖαν ἔχοις ἐλαφράν !' Dr. Hill was chaplain to the British Embassy in 1850, and when he died he had reached the age of ninety-one. His wife did not long survive him. Two months before her death she wrote to me expressing her 'sympathy in the gratification felt in the favourable results (now everywhere appearing) of the Anglo-Continental Society's efforts to promote a healthy reformation among the National Churches of Europe through the instrumentality of the English Church.'

At the Hôtel d'Angleterre we joined parties with Miss Nightingale and her uncle, Mr. Bracebridge, and with them went over the ruins of the Parthenon, the Erectheium, the Propylæa, the Temple of Victory, the Areopagus, and the other glories of the Acropolis, most of which were shattered by the explosion of the Turkish powder magazine 200 years ago, the pillars, of Pentelican marble, still lying where they then fell. *There* stood once the statue of the Parthenos, wrought by Phidias in gold and ivory, and not far off was that other statue of Athena Promachos in bronze, armed with spear, helmet, and shield, which looked down on St. Paul when he made his address on Mars' Hill. Miss Nightingale was much interested by finding flitting about the ruins a number of the 'owls' which were sacred to Athena. Miss Nightingale was not at this time the famous person that she afterwards became. The Crimean War was not yet, nor the Netley Hospital. Few people have done so much to raise their own sex and to promote the comfort of the sick and wounded soldier as Florence Nightingale.

After a fortnight at Athens we resolved on an expedition into Peloponnesus, and for this purpose we sold ourselves for so much a week to our guide, Andrea Prindisi, whom we had brought with us from Patras. He was then bound to take charge of us and conduct us to the places agreed on, which were Corinth, Mycenæ, Argos, Tiryns, Tripolizza, Tegea, Mantinea, Messene, Sparta, and back. At Corinth, to which we went by steamer, Andrea engaged saddle-horses for us and himself, and baggage-horses and men for our luggage. On the horses' backs we carried everything that we were to use, including sheets and blankets, and every evening Andrea sent on one of the men to hire and wash a cottage in which we might sleep. At Corinth there were remaining only seven columns of the old city, but there was the Acro-Corinthus, which no wars or revolutions could destroy, and from it there was a magnificent view to the west over Achaia, to the east Salamis, to the south Peloponnesus, and to the north Megara and the Corinthian Gulf. The treasures of Mycenæ had not yet been dug out, but we saw the Gate of Lions, the Treasury of Atreus, and the Tomb of Agamemnon (so called). Near Tiryns was fought a gallant battle in the War of Independence, when Ypsilanti and Colocotroni defeated Pasha Dramali. In the Plain of Mantinea we noted the site of the five battles fought there in old days, in one of which Epaminondas was killed. The evening before reaching Sparta we slept in the Monastery of Vurkano, on the slopes of Mount Ithomé.

It was an undisciplined and dirty place. At night I was lying on the floor of the guest-chamber, my companion occupying the daïs, when in the darkness I felt a centipede crawling across my face. I seized him and threw him to the other end of the room; but I had no matches, and imagination represented the room full of centipedes for the rest of the night. In Sparta there is little except the natural features of the country to mark the site of the stern old city—'Seges ubi Sparta.'

On our return to Athens we spent a week there, in which we visited the temples at Sunium and Egina, and then resold ourselves to Andrea Prindisi for an expedition in Northern Greece as far as Thermopylæ. Andrea took great care of us, and we escaped the bandits with whom our friends threatened us, but only by the skin of our teeth. From Thebes to Lebadea there are two roads—one by the pass of Zagara, the other by the side of Lake Copais. We were taking the Zagara road, and had passed the little village of Panaghia, when the villagers, headed by their pope, came running after us. 'We have something to tell you—Θέλομεν να ὁμιλήσωμεν τίποτε,' they cried. 'Δὲν ἔχομεν καιρόν—We have not time,' said Andrea, turning his back on them. 'Very well; good-day to you—Ὥρα καλή σᾶς!' replied the pope significantly. Thinking better of it, Andrea went back and made inquiries, when he learnt that two travellers, probably Englishmen, had been seized by robbers in the Pass of Zagara. What had become of them was not known, but some of the horses and muleteers had fled back 'naked'—i.e., without saddles and bridles or cloaks. 'What are we to do, Andrea?' 'Will you not go back to Thebes?' 'Certainly not.' 'Then, we must take the other road by Lake Copais.' This we accordingly did, and on arriving at Lebadea found that the travellers had been Danes, who had been robbed of everything ; and one of them had been injured by a bandit having struck him in the breast with the butt-end of his gun, which is not shaped like ours, but sharp at the upper and lower ends.

We had already passed Platæa, Leuctra, Thespiæ, as well as Thebes, and we now came to the Cave of Trophonius, Orchomenos, Chæroneia, Delphi, the Fountain of Castalia—all of them full of classical associations—and then, winding round the foot of Mount Parnassus, we crossed into Doris. As we were descending a steep road under the shadow of Parnassus, Andrea said to us, 'This is the most dangerous spot, signori. You must keep your watches and purses, because, the *palikari* expect Englishmen to have them, and if you were without them they might cut off your ears ; but if you have any trinkets that you specially value, give them to me.' We handed him some pencil-cases, when he gravely cut a hole in his wooden saddle and stowed them in it, saying, 'Now, signori, they will not find them there.' The muleteers ceased their cries, and we moved on in silence. Just in the *posto cattivissimo* I looked up and saw, on a bank above, a party of men dressed in *fustianelle*, and carrying long formidable guns. 'There are the robbers, Andrea,' I said. 'Oh, signor, where ? No, thanks to heaven ; they are the road-police ! I will give my men such a good dinner as soon as we reach the plain.'

We reached the Plain of Doris (the most luxuriant spot in Greece, such as Arcadia ought to be and is not) in safety, and learnt that the previous day the *palikari* had plundered a village just off our course. In the evening we reached Thermopylæ, and took up our quarters in a khan (an uninhabited, unfurnished build-ing for the reception of travellers), which last week had been held for two days by the brigands against the Greek soldiers. It was situated in a pestiferous marsh, the effects of which we afterwards felt, and we were victimized by mosquitoes.

The next day we eagerly sought the pass in which the noblest battle in the world's history was fought. *There* Leonidas and his 300 Spartans, with the Thespian volunteers, made their last stand, attacked on both sides by Xerxes' overwhelming forces, the rest of the Greek army having retired. *There* they fell, every man of them, except Aristodemus, who, being half blind, and not having hurried to join his devoted comrades, went ever afterwards by the name of 'the man that was afraid.' *There* once stood the monument, afterwards erected, with the glorious inscription :

> ' Tell the Spartans, passer-by,
> At their bidding here we lie.'*

But it was difficult to fix the exact spot, for the pass was formerly made by Mount Œta on one side, and the Malian Gulf on the other ; but now the sea has retired, and the pass is too wide to be held by such a handful of men as Leonidas' little band of patriots. It is something to have stood on the spot where 300 self-devoted men saved Western civilization from being overwhelmed by Asiatic despotism.

Passing along the shore of the Euripus southwards, we reached Chalcis of Eubœa, still connected with the mainland by a bridge originally built in the twenty-first year of the Peloponnesian War, and Aulis, the scene of Iphigenia's sacrifice, and thence we took a boat to Marathon. Thus, we landed much where the Persians had landed, and whence they fled after their defeat by Miltiades. From the Plain of Marathon, Andrea conducted us back to Athens, where we

---

* The translation by James Riddell, p. 20, of the original :

> Ὦ ξεῖν', ἀγγέλλειν Λακεδαιμονίοις ὅτι τῇδε
> κείμεθα, τοῖς κείνων ῥήμασι πειθόμενοι.

parted from him. He was a faithful and trustworthy guide, who took great care of his charges. We engaged him at Patras, as he was acquainted with Italian, which was our medium of conversation with him. He was a tall and strong man, although he retained the old-world practice of having himself bled periodically and whenever he felt ill.

On June 11 we went on board a steamer for Constantinople, and passed by Syra (now Syros), Scio (Chios), Smyrna, and Mitylene. At Smyrna the malarial fever, caught in the marshes of Thermopylæ, and perhaps conveyed by the mosquitoes, made itself felt, and by the time that we reached Constantinople I was quite ill with it. Fortunately, William and Edwin Palmer (p. 21) were expecting us there, and Edwin Palmer took charge of me till I recovered. By the time that I was convalescent, my companion, Lord Lothian, also had a slight attack of the fever.

William Palmer, the elder brother of Lord Selborne and of Edwin Palmer, had come to hold an interview with the Patriarch of Constantinople, and, if the interview were satisfactory, to be received into the Oriental Church. He had always had a great inclination towards that Church. In 1839 the Grand-Duke Alexander of Russia paid a visit to Oxford with the Duke of Wellington, and William Palmer, being then a Fellow of Magdalen College, presented a petition to him in favour of the union of the Russian and Anglican Churches, and asking for His Imperial Highness's protection and countenance if he should go to Russia to study the theology and ritual of the Russian Church. The next year, having obtained a letter of recommendation from Dr. Routh, the President of his college (which, however, Archbishop Howley declined to countersign), he carried out his plan, and travelled to St. Petersburg with introductions to the Ober Procuror (the Emperor's representative in the Russian Synod), who was at that time Count Pratasoff, and to some others that were ecclesiastics or interested in ecclesiastical things. With them, including Philaret, Metropolitan of Moscow, he held learned discussions on points of theology—such as the Divine Procession, Transubstantiation, the Mass, icons—on which there was difference of doctrine between the Russian, Latin, and Anglican Churches. In these discussions he demanded to be recognised and acknowledged as orthodox, on the score of his being a member of the Anglican Church. The authorities of the Russian Church disallowed his claim while offering to receive him, as a convert, into their Church. This was not what Palmer wanted, and after about a year's visit to Russia he returned to Oxford. Having spent the next ten years at Magdalen College, partly as Tutor, partly as student, he resolved to pay a visit to the head of the Oriental Church, the Patriarch of Constantinople, being ready now, if his claim of the equality of the Churches was rejected, to submit individually to the Greek Church.

On July 4 we took a caique (skiff) to the Fanar, the headquarters of the Eastern Church in Constantinople, and called at the patriarchal residence, for W. Palmer to have his desired interview. It happened, however, that at the moment a Synod was being held. We were therefore admitted, not into the Synod hall, but into an adjoining room, in which were the Proto-syncellus (the chief chaplain and minister of the Patriarch) and the deacons in attendance on the Bishops, who were sitting silently on the daïs which ran round the room, dressed in long black cassocks and smoking long pipes. Sweetmeats and pipes were offered to us, and W. Palmer held some conversation with the Proto-syncellus, who is the only person authorized to enter the Synod hall while a meeting is going on. The Synod consisted of the Patriarch of

Constantinople, three ex-Patriarchs, the Patriarch of Jerusalem, and some Bishops and Archbishops. The reason why there are generally three or four ex-Patriarchs is not creditable to the Eastern Church. A Patriarch is elected by the Fanariotes. After three or four years he offends the leading Fanariotes (who answer in a way to the Roman Cardinals and Congregations), or the Jesuits, or the French or English or Russian Ambassador, and he is warned that he had better resign. If he does not take the warning, a firman (order) is promptly obtained from the Sultan, exiling him from Turkey. The Patriarch of Jerusalem resided at this time at Constantinople, though contrary to the canons, on the plea that the capital is a better centre for business, and that his presence added weight to the Constantinople Synod. The subject for discussion at the Synod was the recognition of the Church of Greece proper, which was advocated by an Athenian Archimandrite and Professor named Misael, who succeeded in obtaining the desired recognition. In each of the newly-emancipated countries the Fanar is very jealous of the independent and national character given to the Churches, and desires to keep them under the immediate control of the Patriarch in a manner unacceptable to a self-governed nation. In each case the Fanar, after a struggle, has to yield.

Owing to the session of the Synod, Palmer was not able to see the authorities of the Fanar, nor, when he did have his interview, was it satisfactory to him. Had he been baptized with three immersions ? No ; it was not the Anglican custom. Had he, at least, had water three times poured upon him ? Probably not ; he could not be certain of it. Then he must be baptized again. But that would mean that he had not been a Christian down to the present moment, and he could not believe that ; and he knew that his father, by whom he had been baptized, was a very careful ministrant. That might be so; but it was a rule of the Church that a child should be thrice immersed, and he must now submit to regard his previous baptism as null, and be baptized aright. Thus, it appeared that Constantinople was stiffer in its unbending adherence to rules than St. Petersburg. Palmer bowed and withdrew. He could not acknowledge that he had now to begin the Christian life.

The Palmers travelled with us, when we left Constantinople, as far as the Dardanelles, whence they took a boat to Mount Athos, to visit the monasteries, or *lavras*, whither I was prevented from accompanying them by a return of my malarial fever. Subsequently W. Palmer went to Rome, in the hope that Passaglia might convince him of the truth of Romanism, for, as he said quaintly, he was in a bad plight. He was dissatisfied with the English Church, the Greek Church would not accept him except on a condition to which he could not assent, and he could not believe the Roman doctrines. Newman had built a bridge for himself, and had crossed by it; but 'as soon as I try to do the same, I find myself in the position of an elephant under whose feet the planks give way at the first step,' Passaglia's arguments having failed to convince him, in spite of his desire to be convinced, he was begged to go into a retreat, and after three days' fasting, praying, and preaching he was asked if he could not now embrace the Roman theory. No; he was intellectually unaffected. 'Well,' said Passaglia, 'my soul for yours. Join us, and you shall in time be satisfied.' 'When such a good man as Passaglia made such an offer,' said Palmer afterwards in his half-humorous way, 'it was not to be despised.' So he joined the Roman Church. 'And are you now satisfied of its truth?' I asked him some years later. 'No,' he replied. 'Intellectually I am exactly in the same position as before; but I am more comfortable in my present communion.' After his conversion, he lived for the most part in Rome, and occupied himself in writing *Egyptian Chronicles*, which interested him as an antiquarian pursuit. He died and was buried in Rome. Dr. Newman said of him in 1882 : 'Whatever might be the criticisms of those who saw him casually, no one who saw him much could be insensible to his many and winning virtues—to his simplicity, to his unselfishness, to his gentleness and patience, to his singular meekness, to his zeal for the truth and his honesty whether in seeking or in defending it, and to his calmness and cheerfulness in pain, perplexity, and disappointment.' There was, indeed, only one thing that William Palmer lacked, and that was the common-sense which looks at a thing all round and makes allowance for conflicting principles. Not having this, he became an ecclesiastical Don Quixote ; he was a man of noble soul, unselfish, honest, true, lovable, but lost to his friends, to his Church, to the name and fame that might have been his, by his inability to re-concile himself to the conditions of imperfect humanity and human institutions, untaught by the wisdom of Butler.

Among many objects of exceeding interest at Con-stantinople, Santa Sophia stands first. It was once the cathedral church of Constantinople, built by Justinian on the site of a church, erected by Constantine and dedicated to the Holy Wisdom, which had been burnt down, and it will be the cathedral church of Con-stantinople again when the Turks are driven from Europe. Of course it is of the Byzantine style of architecture, very beautiful, but at present much marred by disfigurements introduced by the Mahom-etans. The mosaics are concealed by whitewash, through which, however, may be perhaps traced heads of our Lord, of Constantine, and of Justinian. The walls are disfigured by large shields hung upon them, containing texts from the Koran in golden letters on a green ground, and the faces of the cherubim are erased, though their wings remain. The Turkish *kiblah*, which marks the direction of Mecca, is a little to the right of where the altar stood, and towards this point the Mahometans direct their prayers and arrange their kneeling-mats, which gives the impression at first of the church being awry. On the occasion of our second visit the Turks were beginning their mid-day prayers, during which we were allowed only in the gallery, whence we were able to watch them. The mattings were placed in the direction of the *kiblah*, and between them were spaces of about 6 feet. On the mattings the worshippers sat cross-legged in rows. Imaums led the prayers from a raised platform in a loud, ringing chant. From time to time the worshippers rose and touched the ground with their foreheads, and then reseated themselves exactly at the same moment with military regularity. When the prayers were over, some left the mosque, some gathered round different imaums, who expounded to them the Koran. As we were entering the mosque, and were about to draw slippers over our shoes, according to rule, a Turk came up to our guide, and said that we were sons of dogs and should be bastinadoed if we went in. And when we were walking in the nave after the prayers were over, a little boy walked resolutely up and spat on my umbrella with a face of righteous self-approbation tempered by alarm at his audacity.

The bazaars at Constantinople are not as interesting as in some other Eastern cities. The bazaar for arms and other valuables is separate from the rest, and kept under lock and key. While we were bargaining at a stall for a blade which my companion wished to buy, the Turk, who had been sitting cross-legged on it playing with his rosary of amber beads, suddenly leapt to his feet uttering the most incoherent exclamations, dashed down on our guide, whom he twisted about, feeling in his pockets and sleeves, then fell upon Lord Lothian and myself in like manner. He had lost his beads, and supposed that we had stolen them, on understanding which our indignant astonishment gave way to amusement, the sight of which more enraged the angry Turk. A great crowd of Mussulmans gathered round us, cursing all our ancestors, and our guide gave us to understand that we had better move on, as it was hardly safe to remain. We walked to another part of the bazaar, where our Turk presently followed us with the blade, and offered it for sale in a crest-fallen manner, having meantime found his beads.

Sir Stratford Canning—afterwards Lord Stratford de Redcliffe—was our Ambassador at Constantinople, ' bear-leader of the Turk,' as E. A. Freeman expressed it. He was at the time living at Therapia, the summer residence of the Ambassadors, which is much cooler than the city, as it lies northwards towards the Euxine Sea. In visiting him and Lady Canning, we sailed up the Bosporus, which is more like a noble river, blue and rapid, running down from the sea, than an arm of the sea itself. The current is accompanied by a north wind, so that it is much easier to descend than to ascend it. From Therapia we could look straight up to the Black Sea, over which a misty vapour was hanging. The hills on each side of the Bosporus are soft and pretty, but somewhat tame.

The Dardanelles are of the same character, but still tamer. Here we were the guests of the Consul, F. W. Calvert, and it had been our intention to take a boat to Mount Athos, but a return of my malarial fever made it necessary for me to take a steamer to Trieste, which carried us by Troy, Tenedos, Mitylene, Smyrna, Syros, Cythera (Cerigo), Pylos (Navarino), Zante, Corfu, Meleda, to Trieste, whence we went at once to the Caves of Adelsberg. These caves have a singular

6

charm. They extend two or three miles underground, for the most part like a vast gallery decorated by stalactites and stalagmites of fantastic shapes, and occasionally opening from the gallery into large halls on either side, similarly ornamented. A stream flows through them, in which the fish have lost their eyesight from disuse. It took us about three hours to explore the grotto, and the refreshing coolness of the underground air took away the remains of my malarial fever, which did not return again.

From Vienna, which we reached by railway from Trieste, we steamed up the Danube to Lintz, and thence on to Gmunden, Ischl, Salzburg, and Hallein. After Italy and Greece, this is the most beautiful part of Europe, but it has not the associations of Italy and Greece. At Hallein we visited a singular salt-mine. We made our entrance into it at the top of a high hill. After walking a little way, we reached a steep shoot, down which we slid, holding by a rope to steady ourselves; then another walk and slide, and another. About halfway down in the bowels of the hill there was a large artificial lake lighted by glimmering lamps round its edge, which we crossed in a ghostly boat; then more walks and slides, till we reached the bottom of the hill, where the exit of the mine was. The salt appeared to be first absorbed by water, which was then carried by pipes elsewhere and evaporated, leaving the salt behind it.

Having returned to Trieste, we proceeded viâ Venice, Padua, Verona, Milan, to Monza (where we saw the iron crown of Lombardy, and also General Radetzky, who, with Jellachich, saved the Austrian Empire in the year of revolutions, and was now keeping down North Italy under Austrian rule by military force), thence by Como, Lucerne, Cologne, Ostend to Dover.

CHAPTER IV

MY first occupation on reaching England was to vote in the election of the President of Trinity College, Oxford, Dr. Ingram having died while I was in Switzerland. There were two candidates: Thomas Legh Claughton, for whom the junior Fellows voted; and Dr. Wilson, who was the candidate of the senior Fellows. We were equally divided, when at the last moment the oldest member of our body unexpectedly appeared, and turned the scale in favour of Dr. Wilson.

T. L. Claughton, formerly scholar of Trinity, had married Lady Ward's daughter, and was at this time Rector of Kidderminster, in the working of which parish he had been so successful that many young men offered themselves as his curates without salary, that they might learn his system. He was Professor of Poetry at Oxford, and it fell to him to write the Installation Ode when Lord Derby became Chancellor of the University. He was appointed Bishop of Rochester, and, when the diocese was divided, he passed to St. Albans. He was a man of great geniality as well as piety, with a singular charm of manner, and it was characteristic of him that when, years afterwards, he confirmed my eldest son, he spoke kindly to him after the service, as the son of an old friend.

In October, 1850, Lord Lothian came into residence

at Christ Church, and, as I was still his tutor, I made acquaintance with most of his associates and friends. The first among these was Lord Robert Cecil (Lord Salisbury). He was rather senior to Lord Lothian, and having taken his B.A. degree, became a Fellow of All Souls. By his father's advice he had not gone up for a class, but he was recognised as the ablest of his contemporaries, and when lists of future Ministers were made by us, after the way of young men, he was always put in the first place as Prime Minister; Lord Lothian was to be the future Foreign Secretary (as he would have been but for his failure of health); Lord Carnarvon, Colonial Secretary; Lord Harrowby, Home Secretary; F. Lygon (Lord Beauchamp) was also to hold office; and Charles H. Alderson (son of Baron Alderson, afterwards one of the Ecclesiastical Commissioners, and now Sir Charles Alderson) was to be Lord Chancellor. It was an idle exercise of the imagination, but it showed how much was thought of the capacity of Lord Robert Cecil. He himself had an anticipation of the future. I was sitting with him on the terrace of Hatfield House, when we saw the late Lord Derby (Lord Stanley) coming towards us. 'Here,' said Cecil, looking through his half-closed eyes (a trick he had)—'here comes the future leader of the Conservative party.' 'Not,' I said, 'if Bright's saying about him is true' ('A very promising young man: he hates the Bishops and despises his father—very promising!'). 'Ah,' said Cecil, 'but he is his father's son.' Lord Stanley's rivalry, however, never turned out to be a serious cause of dread. Cecil having gone into the house, I took a walk with Lord Stanley, in the course of which he spoke very earnestly on Church rates, on which he had just published a pamphlet, and on the law of entail, which he thought should not allow anyone to settle his estates for more than one generation.

Lord Robert Cecil while at Oxford occasionally joined in the debates of the Union Society, taking the strong Tory side, and speaking sometimes with a young man's vehemence. I recollect his declaiming that Sir Robert Peel, for breaking up the Conservative party, should be left to lie in the grave of infamy which his tergiversation had dug. But that was not an example of his usual style.

There were two or three things that brought me and Cecil together for some years. One was that we were both interested in the welfare of the same persons; another, that he took a keen interest in a series of letters that passed between myself and Cardinal Manning on the moral theology of the Church of Rome (especially the theories of truthfulness and honesty), which arose out of a discussion in which he had taken part. The following are criticisms that he made on the correspondence:

'*September* 14, 1853.

'MY DEAR MEYRICK,—I am very much obliged to you for the loan of your letter, as the perusal has been very interesting to me. You have smashed Manning thoroughly, but, after all, it is breaking a fly upon the wheel. It is marvellous that a man of his talent and, I presume, sincerity should argue in such a fashion. The theory he tries to put into Liguori's mouth is almost as bad as the actual reality. Undoubtedly, the amount stolen is a gauge of the evil intent, if the thief has a perfect and thorough "advertence" of the difference of the injury inflicted by a theft of 5s. and a theft of 5s. 6d. But that is a distinction calculated only for an ideal race of thieves, who, before they steal, carefully collect the statistics of their victims' fortune and their booty's value, and then sit down and make an elaborate calculation of the

exact extent of the injury they are about to inflict.   It
is too ludicrous.'

' *May*, 1854.

' I think I can see what Manning means by his
shuffling about *gravitas materiæ* not by itself constituting the test of a crime's heinousness or mor-
talness — viz., that though theoretically it is a distinct element of guilt, and that therefore, by the
hypothesis, its presence or absence would make the
distinction between mortal and venial sin ; yet that, as
a fact, *advertentia* always varies precisely as *gravitas*—
the hue of mental contempt of God always corresponds
exactly to the degree of actual objective injury—and
that therefore *gravitas* never can vary from 5s. to
5s. 6d. without *advertentia* varying too, and therefore the hue of guilt can never be determined by facts
purely external to the mind of the culprit.   Of course
this involves a Utopian race of accurately calculating
thieves, who never deceive themselves or are deceived.
But the theory hangs together.'

' *June* 14, 1854.

' I agree, of course, that my view involves a charge
of inaccuracy of apprehension against him, or of inaccuracy of expression against those whom he is back-
ing ; but it seemed to me the only one that in charity
could be put together to save him from the accusation
of hopeless muddleness of mind.'

' *January* 24, 1855.

' I heard to-day a thing which I ought to tell you
as a set-off to all the attacks you have suffered *in re*
Liguori.   The Bishop of Oxford [Samuel Wilberforce]
told Miss Alderson that your articles [on " Truthfulness and Theft "] " had done more to delay the
Archdeacon's [Robert Isaac Wilberforce's] secession
almost than anything."   What is true of one must be
true of many.'

Another thing that brought Lord Robert Cecil and myself together at this time was the Oxford University Reform Bill. The Bill had been introduced mainly to alter the government of the University by abolishing the oligarchy of the Hebdomadal Board, which held the initiative in University legislation, and consisted solely of the heads of colleges and halls. In its later stages Mr. Heywood carried some clauses opening the University and colleges to Dissenters, and so altering, not only its constitution, but its character. On June 26, 1854, there met in my rooms at Trinity College Charles Marriott of Oriel, H. A. Woodgate of St. John's, and Lord Robert Cecil of All Souls, and we determined on a petition of the residents at Oxford against the admission of Dissenters. Four days later Marriott of Oriel, Mozley of Magdalen, Shadforth of University, Rawlinson of Exeter, and Pritchard of Balliol, met in my rooms, and we determined on a non-resident petition also. The following are extracts from letters of Lord Robert Cecil referring to the Bill:

'As to the Bill, I quite agree in your view of its blots. . . . You will already have got my list of times of second reading, etc. Whether Lord Derby will support the petition or not, it seems to me that it would clearly be a slight, and most impolitic, to present it through anyone but him. Except with his aid, you have no chance of carrying the petition. I understand that he expresses himself indifferent on the subject, so possibly the petition may have the effect of helping to decide him. . . . I have done as you bid me. I gave Lord Derby the paper this afternoon, and he promised to consider of it. . . . I saw Lord Derby last night, and he told me he had written to the Vice-Chancellor, suggesting your plan and pressing very strongly on him not to make any proposal that was likely to be rejected by Convocation, as it would materially injure the University's case in Parliament. I hope that it is not too late.'

On July 7, 1854, the Bill passed its second reading in the House of Lords.

On my appointment as Preacher at the Chapel Royal, Whitehall, I wrote to Lord Robert Cecil for information as to the congregation. He replied: 'I never was at Whitehall Chapel myself, but I understand that the congregation is aristocratic, official, and M.P.-ish, the last two elements preponderating. Sewell tried the experiment of preaching to them on the morality of politics, but he only succeeded in disgusting them. It don't pay. Most of the world won't stand the spiritual power invading the secular province, and in that repugnance I think they bear witness to a great truth. If you are really inclined to stir them up, keep up a vigorous fire on ambition and love of men's praise. It is a doctrine of which they hear little enough. We have not got thoroughly out of the old Jewish notion of parading the temporal rewards of doing one's duty.' I took for my subject 'The Outcast and Poor of London,' which in 1855 had not become a popular and favourite topic, as it has done since that time.

The cordial relations between Lord Robert Cecil and myself were not to last. His marriage and my marriage made a great difference, but the *coup de grâce* was given to them by my voting for Gladstone as member for the University of Oxford in 1865. The following letter is very different in tone from the letters that had preceded it, and was my last letter from Lord Robert Cecil:

'I was very sorry to hear of your decision. The conflict is not one of men, but of principles. If your adhesion should fail to bring Gladstone in, of course you may have no cause to regret your vote. But if you should be successful in giving the sanction of the University to the statesman who has avowed his intention of pulling down the Irish Church, I think the time is not far distant when you will regret your vote very much. The position of us Conservative Churchmen in Parliament is disheartening enough. We fight the battle of the Church for six years to the best of our ability, getting the strength of the Conservative party to be employed in her behalf ; at the end of that time we go to the great Church constituency to give us the sanction of its authority. We are disavowed, and the seal of the University approval is placed upon the acts of the statesman who has just declared war against one-half of the Established Church upon principles that will destroy the whole of it. Do you think that such a state of things is likely to warm the enthusiasm of the party which alone can protect the Established Church ?

'Ever yours truly,
'ROBERT G. CECIL.'

Of the contemporaries of Lord Lothian at Christ Church, I saw most of F. Lygon (Lord Beauchamp). Lygon was a man of very strong will, stronger than his judgment, who took a deep interest in Church matters. I was associated with him at the Union Society, in which I held successively the offices of secretary, treasurer, and president, and we were secretaries of the Oxford Architectural Society together. After taking his degree, he was elected a Fellow of All Souls, and as long as he resided we breakfasted together once a week. At a later period he took a great interest in the new Lectionary of 1871, and in everything that affected the welfare of the Church. He gave me Thomas Aquinas' *Summa Theologiæ*, which indicated his tastes. In 1890 I spent a few days with him at his beautiful place near Malvern—Madresfield Court.

Of elder men, my chief associates out of my own college were H. L. Mansel, afterwards Dean of St. Paul's, at this time Fellow of St. John's College; Charles Marriott, Fellow of Oriel; James B. Mozley, Fellow of Magdalen; and J. W. Burgon, Fellow of Oriel. Mansel was a short, bullet-headed man, who was not at first known beyond his college walls, except as an excellent private tutor in logic and ethics. Somewhat suddenly he came forward in the University, which found that it had in him a metaphysician and philosopher of first-rate ability. For years he had been studying German theology and philosophy, and now he showed himself their uncompromising opponent and antagonist, capable of meeting them in argument, and of enlivening his arguments by a wit which is not always the property of a philosopher.

His Bampton Lectures took the University by storm. They were entitled *The Limits of Religious Thought*, and dealt with very abstruse subjects in language which, though wonderfully clear, required some familiarity with philosophical terms to be fully apprehended. Nevertheless, they were attended by crowds of hearers, not only by Masters of Arts, or even undergraduates; but townsfolk and college scouts stood in the aisles to hear them. This was partly because of the reputation of the preacher, who was now Reader in Moral and Metaphysical Philosophy at Magdalen College, partly because it was felt by the more thoughtful members of the University that the subject which he had selected was vital to Christianity in its struggle with rationalism, and that it was in good hands. Rationalism, sometimes calling itself idealism, sometimes criticism, professes to decide, independently of all external revelation, what is the true nature of God, and the manner in which He must manifest Himself to the world; and it claims authoritatively to determine, by the unerring judgment of a faculty termed reason or moral sense, or some similar title, whether an alleged revelation, or any parts of it, are true or false. Mansel proves that no such faculty exists. We are unable to grasp and comprehend the nature of a Being who is at once Absolute, Infinite, and First Cause. These attributes cannot be reconciled by us ; they appear to our minds to involve contradictions : not that they are contradictory, but that we cannot reconcile them. Thus, the nature of God is beyond the limits of logical thought. But it is not beyond the limits of religious belief. The spheres of logical thought and of belief are not conterminous, for we can believe that which transcends thought, on the supposition that the difficulties which present themselves may be accounted for by the limitation of our faculties of apprehension and conception, not by an inherent impossibility of their being removed, seeing that they may be (and doubtless are) non-existent to higher intelligences. In this case our wisdom is to accept what is revealed, acquiescing in our present ignorance of many things ; and our reasoning powers should rather be exercised on the evidence of a revelation than on its subject and contents. Mansel's charge into the ranks of the rationalists was very effective, because in combating them he used their own weapon, philosophy ; and the orthodox party felt comforted at the first metaphysician in the University being on their side.

Mansel was by no means a bookworm, though his memory was stored with the results of much reading. He took an active part in the business of the University on the Conservative side, both in the Tutors' Association—which was formed for the consideration of the changes proposed by the Oxford Commission— and afterwards in the newly constituted Hebdomadal Council, or governing body of the University, to which he was at once elected. His quick wit made him very popular socially. He delighted in good and clever jests, which seemed to come bubbling from him spontaneously, and he could not refrain from puns, good or bad. He loved to throw a joke into the form of Latin or English verse. Some of these *jeux d'esprit* were hardly intelligible except to University men, but to them they were delicious—*e.g.*, the application of the then well-known lines of Aldrich (whose manual of logic was at that time universally studied), relating to logical moods called 'subaltern' and 'general,' to the alleged promotion of some young officers on no other grounds than their relationship to senior officers, regarding which the newspapers were storming. 'It is a case,' said Mansel, 'of

> 'Quinque subalterni, totidem generalibus orti,
> Nomen habent nullum, nec, si bene colligis, usum.'

That is, 'Five subaltern moods, springing from an equal number of general moods, have no name or use if you argue rightly.' But the words will equally well bear the translation: 'Five subalterns, sons of as many generals, have no name (reputation) and are of no use, if you come to a right conclusion.'

Again, when it was proposed in the Hebdomadal Council to allow a man to qualify for his doctor's degree by merely writing two essays, Mansel scribbled down and handed to us (as Proctor I was member of the Council at the time) the doggerel:

> 'The degree of D.D.
> 'Tis proposed to convey
> To an A double S
> By a double S.A. (essay).'

Mansel was appointed Professor of Ecclesiastical History by Lord Derby, and two years later Dean of St. Paul's by Disraeli. Unhappily, his health broke down, and a most valuable career came too quickly to an end when he was but fifty-one. He loved his University, and left behind him a declaration of 'his deep-rooted and increasing conviction that sound religious philosophy will flourish or fade within her walls according as she perseveres or neglects to study the works and cultivate the spirit of her great son and teacher, Bishop Butler.'

Oxford allowed a band of hostile examiners, headed by Mr. Mark Pattison, to strike Butler's works from the list of standard books appointed for the final examination in the University, whereby they determined that he should no longer be studied as of yore. Nor has Butler been restored to the place of honour which he held, and which he ought to hold, by the side of Aristotle, Plato, and Bacon. And Mansel's prediction has been verified.

Charles Marriott, Fellow of Oriel, came to the help of Dr. Pusey when the latter was deserted by Newman, and left more or less lonely. He acted as his lieutenant, and did an immense amount of work, which made no show and brought no name to himself, such as editing some volumes of the 'Library of the Fathers,' which was done with consummate care. In addition to his literary work, he took pains to break down the barriers between 'Dons' and undergraduates, which he thought to be a great evil to both. With this end, he asked such freshmen and undergraduates as he made acquaintance with to walk with him, and to breakfast, and to evening receptions in the common-room. But he was wanting in some of the qualifications for success in these attempts. He was singularly silent, and could not suggest topics of conversation to his young friends; while they were, for the most part, too awestruck to bring any forward themselves. I have walked with him for two hours, as an undergraduate, without a word passing between us, and this was the character of all his walks of the same kind. He would sometimes apologize on the ground that he was 'deficient in imagination,' but we used to think that his mind was running on the literary work in which he had been engaged in the morning. We liked to walk with him in spite of his muteness, knowing the great kindness of his heart.

His breakfasts (charmingly described in Burgon's *Twelve Good Men*) were still more singular. He would ask any whose names suggested themselves, and then he would invite any whom he chanced to meet, not counting heads. Consequently the table was laid for, say, twelve, and sixteen would arrive. The breakfast-table being full, Marriott would clear a space on his writing-table, tossing books and papers on the sofa, and having a new cloth laid and more breakfast ordered. When that difficulty was got over, there was the further difficulty of conversation, unless there was someone to lead it. I recollect the satisfaction that I felt on one occasion, when Marriott had swept in Bishop Charles Harris of Gibraltar, who I knew would talk. And yet we all liked to come, and we never laughed at him, for we knew that he was a first-class man in Classics—a thing which goes a long way with undergraduates—and we were assured that in any perplexity or trouble there would be no kinder counsellor. In his common-room parties, held for making acquaintances between younger and older men, he did not say much more than 'How do you do?' to each person, but this was valued. In 1850 C. Marriott succeeded C. P. Eden as Vicar of St. Mary's, the well-known University church, where Eden had succeeded Newman in 1843, and he soon won the love of his parishioners. In 1855 he had a stroke of paralysis after walking back from Radley, and in 1858 he died. He was cousin of my friend and contemporary, Wharton B. Marriottt.

James B. Mozley, Fellow of Magdalen College, often

confused with his brother, Tom Mozley, was one of the most thoughtful men in Oxford. Two of his brothers were married to two of Newman's sisters, and he therefore naturally came up to the University (where he matriculated at Oriel) in sympathy with Newman's views. When, however, Newman deserted the Church of England, Mozley did not hesitate as to the line that he should adopt : ' So now he has come to a point where I cannot follow him. But I cannot help that. No one, of course, can prophesy the course of his own mind, but I feel at present [1845] that I could no more leave the Church of England than I could fly. What the upshot of this is to be we have yet to see. We are in the struggle. One's spiritual home is a stormy and unsettled one ; but, still, it is one's home ; at least, it is mine ' (*Letters*, p. 168). His steadfast affection to the Church of England arose to a great extent from the love that he bore (like Keble) to Charles I., Andrewes, Laud, and the Caroline divines. Speaking of one of the first deserters to Rome, he said : 'He never cared much about the Church of England. All his very youthful days he was a Liberal, afterwards he altered in deference to Newman and Froude ; but he never had any feeling for the Church. He never cared about her best men nor her interesting periods. He never cared a jot for Charles I., or Laud, and all the rest of them. He has not, and never had, any historical, poetical, or romantic associations connected with her' (*ibid.*, p. 147). The article in the *Christian Remembrancer* on Newman's secession fell to Mozley to write, and its tone was firm and decisive: ' I expect it will annoy some people, but the fact is not to be avoided that a new relation is begun between Newman and the English Church, and someone must be the person to express that new relation. I have had the office, and a most disagreeable one it has been ; but I feel strongly that, staying in the English Church as I do, I stayed to support her, and not to give her up, or to stand loosely by her' (*ibid.*, p. 173).

Mozley was co-editor with Mr. Scott of Hoxton of the *Christian Remembrancer*, to which, at his request, I made several contributions. The *Christian Remembrancer* at this time was the organ of the Oxford party, but when Mozley found that he differed from most of his friends at the time of the Gorham judgment, with respect to the effect of Baptism, he resigned the editorship. In 1855 he wrote his great work on Predestination, the ablest and most philosophical book on that mysterious subject that has ever been written. The following year he accepted the college living of Old Shoreham, whence he was recalled by Mr. Gladstone to Oxford to fill the post of Regius Professor of Divinity in 1861. There he did good work in behalf of the Christian faith by sermons and lectures, whose reputation is still growing. He died in 1878.

J. W. Burgon, born at Smyrna, became, after taking his degree, a Fellow of Oriel College. He was a man of great piety, learning, courage, and unselfishness, and he combined in a most singular manner simplicity with shrewdness, gentleness with violence, impressiveness with grotesqueness, impulsiveness with resolution. He had a host of adversaries; those that did not know him personally hated him for the unsparing way in which he called a spade a spade; but friends and opponents alike, who knew him well, loved him. The work of his life was defensive—defensive of his University, of his Church, and of the Christian revelation. The University was at the time a Church institution, where the teachers were clergy, and the young men who were intended for the ministry were taught and trained together with the future squirearchy. In consequence of the misdirection of the Tractarian Movement, Oxford bore an ill-repute, and the adversaries of the Church took advantage of this existing ill-feeling to deprive it of its religious character. This was done finally by Lord Coleridge's Universities' Test Act. The assailing party did not see that their success would necessarily cause the institution of the diocesan theological colleges—which have since sprung up—in which the training and teaching would be of a far less liberal and manly type than that which used to be supplied by the Universities, while young men at the Universities would be exposed to serious risk when their lectures were given them by men who might be agnostics or rationalists or Romanists. Burgon fought his best for the retention of the religious and Church character of Oxford, but in vain. In the last Parliamentary Commission (1876) he was nominated by Lord Salisbury as a member, in order to represent one side of University opinion. Mr. Osborn Morgan and Mr. Lowe objected to him in the House of Commons, and Lord Salisbury unchivalrously begged Burgon to withdraw his name. 'I unconditionally set Lord Salisbury free to act in any way he pleases,' wrote Burgon. 'Far be it from me to embarrass my party, or to hesitate about jumping overboard in order ever so little to lighten the ship.' Mr. Osborne Gordon, late Censor of Christ Church, was appointed in his place—not by any means so influential a personality. Dean Goulburn, recounting the event in his *Life of Burgon*, speaks of it as 'creditable to himself, as showing the equanimity with which he submitted to what must have been, to one who loved Oxford as he did, a very keen disappointment.' He adds dryly: 'It is to be wished that it was equally creditable to the Government' (vol. ii., p. 136).

Burgon's loyalty to his Church was shown by his serving her in every way in his power, and in particular by resisting the Romeward tendency and Ritualistic extravagances which grew out of the

7

break-up of the Tractarian party. Against these he preached, lectured, declaimed, taught, and argued. ' For,' says Dean Goulburn, 'he adhered through-out his life to the views that the Church Move-ment, as originated by the primitive Tractarians, had nothing in common with that efflorescence of Ritual, which indeed succeeded it historically, but which he held to be merely its running to seed and degradation ' (p. 188). ' In the second sermon, " taking up a position directly hostile to many of my personal friends," he launches out with his usual plain-speaking and intrepidity against the Romanizing practices and tenets which were being introduced and inculcated ; against the representing Tradition as an unwritten Word of co-ordinate authority with the written; against Saint-worship and Mariolatry ; against en-forced Auricular Confession ; against Transubstantia-tion and all the observances and ceremonials which are grouped round Transubstantiation, such as the Vestments, the Eastward Position, Fasting Com-munion, and Non-communicating Attendance, as well as the phraseologies unknown to our own Book of Common Prayer, such as High Mass and Low Mass ; he will not allow of a localized Presence ; Christ is present in the heart, *not in the hands*, according to the words of the author's last edition of *The Christian Year*—words which were tampered with after his death' (*ibid.*, p. 86). When Dean Lake and others presented to the Archbishop an address in favour of toleration of Ritualistic practices, Burgon published letters to the Archbishop, and Dean Gregory, depre-cating 'a proposal that indiscriminate license should henceforth be the law of the Church,' or that ' a clergy-man ought to be at liberty to violate the law, provided only that his congregation will go along with him in his lawlessness,' which was 'the principle of the veriest Congregationalism.'

Burgon's battle for Christianity was partly defensive
—partly aggressive—defensive of God's Word, aggressive towards rationalism.   Rationalism was already
beginning to take the form of Biblical criticism, and
his method of opposing it was to devote himself to the
study and maintenance of the text of Scripture and
of the truths that it contains.   His first work in this
sphere was his vindication of the genuineness of the
last twelve verses of St. Mark's Gospel, thrown into
the form of two dissertations read by him as an exercise in taking his degree of Bachelor of Divinity in
1871.   As soon as the Revised Version of the New
Testament was published, Burgon made a fiery and
impetuous attack upon it in the *Quarterly Review*,
which, being supported by the arguments of Scrivener
and Cook, struck a blow at the Revised Version from
which it has not recovered ; for the assailing party
showed that a fundamental error was adopted by the
Revisers which has vitiated many of their conclusions
—namely, that the authority of the Vatican and Sinaitic
codices outweighs that of all the other MSS., when
those two codices agree, which they naturally do most
commonly, as they are contemporaneous, and are
probably two of the MSS. prepared by Eusebius for
Constantine.   For twenty-five years Burgon devoted
himself to the study of the text of the New Testament.
But he died before his great work was accomplished,
and it has not seen the light.   In his last illness he
begged that the portfolios containing the notes and
MSS. for this work might be brought and placed
within his sight.   ' When a man is dying,' he said, ' he
wants to say good-bye to his favourite child.'   In 1876
Burgon became Dean of Chichester, but he longed to
return to Oxford, and on Mozley's death hoped to be
appointed Regius Professor of Divinity, that he might
carry on the teaching and training of young men,
which he had begun while residing at Oriel, as Vicar

of St. Mary's, in which post he had succeeded the Rev. D. P. Chase, who followed Charles Marriott. At his death he left ready for publication *The Lives of Twelve Good Men*, each of which lives is the model of a short biography. The twelve men are Dr. Routh, Hugh James Rose, Charles Marriott, Edward Hawkins (Provost of Oriel), Samuel Wilberforce, R. L. Cotton (Provost of Worcester), Richard Greswell, H. O. Coxe (Bodleian Librarian), H. L. Mansel, W. Jacobson (Bishop of Chester), C. P. Eden, and C. L. Higgins.

Burgon was always a favourite with undergraduates. In the early part of his academic life he became Librarian of the Oxford Union Society. It is the office of the librarian to propose the books that are to be bought by the society, and it is usual for him to put on his list any books recommended by a considerable number of members. Dean Stanley had just published one of his books, and his admirers desired to introduce it into the library, and strongly recommended it to the librarian. Burgon would not propose it. He said airily that there were other books of greater value, which he therefore proposed in preference. Stanley's friends grew angry, and moved a vote of condemnation on Burgon. The votes given on such occasions were more tests of the popularity of the person assailed than calm judgments on the matter in hand. Burgon carried the day triumphantly.

A similar event happened to myself. The secretary of the society, in reporting the debates, was bound to state only the subject under discussion, the names of the speakers on each side, and the result of the voting. On one occasion, in 1848, I introduced a descriptive account of a scene of confusion that had occurred, in order to explain why there had been so few voters. I had clearly transgressed the rule, and the opposition determined to impeach me. Great preparations were made on both sides. A Balliol man, Mr. Stanton, who had lately gone to London, and was studying for the Bar, was brought down to prosecute me, and canvassers were appointed on both sides for each college. An overflowing house met for the debate, and, like Burgon, I met with a triumphant vindication of my action, as being in accordance with the spirit, though not with the letter, of the society's laws.

I was frequently in the habit at this time of dining at the high table in Balliol, where I met two men of the Liberal school : Henry Halford Vaughan, whose lectures on Modern History were more appreciated by the ladies of Oxford than by the undergraduates ; and Benjamin Jowett, who was the chief representative of the sceptical school at Oxford. He was now Fellow and Tutor of Balliol, and strange tales were told of the things that he would say in his lectures, suggesting doubts and hinting at insoluble difficulties, while directly denying nothing. In 1855 he published a commentary on the Thessalonians, Romans and Galatians, together with some essays in which the doctrine of the Atonement and other articles of the faith were contravened. This was regarded as a challenge to the orthodoxy of Oxford, or at least an assault upon it, which had to be met. Dr. Cotton, Provost of Worcester, one of Burgon's twelve good men, was Vice-Chancellor, and he felt his responsibility very deeply towards the young men under his charge. ' If ever pious zeal for the glory of God and charitable interest in the spiritual comfort and salvation of mankind called for great efforts, surely this is the case at the present crisis,' he said. It was not thought wise to invoke authority to condemn the book or to deprive Jowett of his tutorship, the last of which could only be done by the Master of Balliol, Dr. Scott (afterwards Dean of Rochester), who would have been indisposed in any case to act in so peremptory a manner, and was still more unwilling in the present case because Jowett

had been candidate for the Mastership in opposition
to himself in 1854. During Lent the nominations of
Preachers before the University is in the hands of the
Vice-Chancellor, and Dr. Cotton determined to make
use of this power to nominate Preachers who should
deal with the doctrines that had been denied. Accordingly, he appointed Dr. Pusey, T. D. Bernard
(afterwards Canon of Wells), S. J. Rigaud (Bishop of
Antigua), S. Wilberforce (Bishop of Oxford), C. A.
Heurtley (Margaret Professor of Divinity), E. M. Goulburn (afterwards Dean of Norwich), Charles Baring
(afterwards Bishop of Durham), and myself (at that
time Fellow and Tutor of Trinity College). Dr. Pusey's
subject was 'Faith,' Canon Bernard's 'The Exclusion
of Wisdom,' Bishop Rigaud's 'Inspiration,' Bishop
Wilberforce's 'Our Reception of Christ's Message,'
Professor Heurtley's and Dean Goulburn's 'The Atonement,' Bishop Baring's 'The Propitiatory Sacrifice of
Christ,' and the title of my own sermon was 'God's
Revelation and Man's Moral Sense considered in reference to the Sacrifice of the Cross.'

My argument was that the moral sense, to which
Jowett had appealed as justifying his denial of the
Atonement and of the Propitiatory Sacrifice, was not
the final arbiter to which we could refer in matters of
revelation, for God's nature must be incomprehensible
to us owing to the limitations of our faculties, which
caused things not contradictory in themselves to appear
to us contradictory. God has two attributes—infinite
justice and infinite mercy. How are we to represent
such a Being to ourselves? As infinitely just? Then,
according to our conceptions, He cannot be merciful.
As infinitely merciful? Then we cannot see how He
can be just. As one whose justice is limited by mercy?
Then He is not all-just. As one whose mercy is limited
by justice? Then He is not all-merciful. Therefore,
whatsoever revelation of Himself and His acts God

might vouchsafe to man, it must be open to cavils brought against it in the name of man's moral sense. And, consequently, when the doctrine of the Sacrifice of the Cross was objected to in the name of the moral sense, as 'inconsistent with the Divine attributes,' as 'sullying the mirror of God's justice' and inferior to a free forgiveness (Jowett, ii. 472, 480), all that was proved was the weakness of our powers of comprehension, which cannot reconcile attributes which, however, admittedly are not contradictory—the attributes of justice and mercy.   The sermons were published separately, and afterwards were collected by the Vice-Chancellor into a volume, to which he prefixed a preface and added an appendix.   The name that he gave it was *Christian Faith and the Atonement : Sermons preached before the University of Oxford in Reference to the Views published by Mr. Jowett and others* (Parker, 1856).

Some of the Masters of Arts, specially those who, being college Tutors, had pupils in whose weal they were interested, thought that something more was needed, but it was difficult to know what that should be.   Consequently a meeting was held in the rooms of Lewis Gilbertson, of Jesus College, to consider the matter.   Dr. Pusey attended it, and of course was asked to take the chair.   The Rev. Thomas Chamberlain, student of Christ Church and incumbent of St. Thomas's, Oxford, began by saying that he had understood that I had something to propose respecting a brotherhood.   I shook my head, and then was asked if I had any other proposal to make.   I said 'Yes.'   I thought that sermons might be preached at St. Mary's Church on Sunday evenings (there were none at that time), of a non-controversial character, but dealing with the points of faith that had been impugned. After discussion the suggestion was adopted, and Dr. Pusey, drawing an old envelope towards him and taking up a pen, said: 'Then we had better put down on paper the subjects that we wish for, and the preachers of the first series during the Lent term.' This was done, and, as I happened to be going to see Bishop Wilberforce the next day at Worcester College, where he was staying, I was asked to take the proposal and the names and the subjects to him, and ask for his authority for the scheme, as it was to be a diocesan, not a University, matter. The Bishop listened gravely to me, read the list of subjects and preachers deliberately, and then looked up and said in a decided voice: 'Yes, it is a good plan. I will give it my authority, and will write to the persons proposed and ask them to preach on the suggested subjects. The plan had better not drop after one year. Next year I will invite a similar set of preachers.' This was the origin of the evening Lent sermons at St. Mary's, at which men of name, not resident in the University, have preached for many years, to the great benefit of the undergraduates.

Jowett's Greek scholarship was not so pre-eminent as to justify his appointment as Regius Professor of Greek, but it was adequate. When Dr. Scott—author, with Liddell, of *Liddell and Scott's Lexicon*—became Dean of Rochester in 1870, Jowett was elected Master of Balliol. His vague scepticism continued to the end of his life, not rising into belief, and not sinking into unbelief.

I made acquaintance with Mark Pattison at the time that he was in a transition state from Tractarianism, for which he had been a diligent subordinate worker, to scepticism, which finally proceeded to unbelief. He came up to Oriel, a rude and unlicked boy, in 1832. He was quizzed unmercifully by his companions, which, he says, 'developed a self-consciousness so sensitive and watchful that it came between me and everything that I said and did.' The wholesome discipline that he received from his comrades was probably the best treatment that his self-love could have received; but he did not get enough of it. He did not learn to bear a reverse with dignity or to trace his failures to his own deficiencies; they only threw him into a state of misanthropy and sulkiness. This was the effect of his failure when he stood for the headship of Lincoln College in 1851. He has given us a history of that event himself, and it is strange that any man should have written it down. When the Rector of Lincoln died in 1851, the senior Fellows selected for their candidate Dr. W. Kay; the junior Fellows, Pattison. The votes were nearly even, and all depended on the vote of a Fellow named Kettle. Kettle, though a strong Liberal, determined to vote for the Conservative candidate Kay. Hereupon Pattison and his party went to one and another of Kay's supporters and offered him their votes if he would vote for himself. The first man so applied to was a gentleman, and refused. The second acquiesced. The result was that Dr. Thompson was elected by his own vote and those of Pattison and his followers, although he had promised to support Kay. If Pattison had thought Thompson better than Kay, this sharp practice might possibly have been condoned. But he did not. 'Thompson was the very last man I should have wished to see elected,' he has written (*Memoir*, p. 287). 'It was impossible to say anything in defence of Thompson, who was a mere ruffian' (p. 288). Yet for this man, whom he called a ruffian and other opprobrious names, Pattison and his friends voted. It was a pure act of spite. The college would not have Pattison, so they should have the man whom Pattison judged would make the worst Rector of his college. When the election had taken place, Pattison gave himself up deliberately to sulk year after year, and then he published to the world in his *Memoir* his unhealthy moanings. No man could yield himself to such influences as Pattison did on this occasion and come out unscathed. Pattison had been brought up in a religious home—Sister Dora was his sister—by a father of Evangelical sentiments, which the son in later years took every occasion to scorn at. This religion clung fast to the young Oxford lad, and was expanded by the Tractarian Movement, which carried him away. But his sympathies were never those of an English Churchman. He was brought up as a Liberal, and 'I could never bring myself to sympathize with Charles the Martyr' (*Memoir*, p. 253). He belonged to the body, not to the soul, of the religious movement which Keble had originated in Oxford. When Newman went over to the Church of Rome in 1845, he stopped still and thought. ' Romanism is false and bad' was his syllogism; 'Tractarianism' (he ought to have said Newman's Tractarianism) 'leads to Romanism: I will have none of it.' But this was not all. He not only cast behind him Newman's teaching, which his argument justified him in doing, but also his faith in Christianity received a great shock. Had his religion, however, been ever so earnest, it could not have survived the years of misanthropical misery and bitterness into which he voluntarily plunged himself after his non-election to the rectorship of Lincoln in 1851. He awoke out of what he calls his 'passive wretchedness,' to despise his previous emotions as superstition, ecclesiasticism, fanaticism. It was not the peculiarities of any one school of religious thought which offended him. He became more than a sceptic. On the death of Thompson, he obtained the coveted post of Rector of Lincoln College ; but this success did not seem to sweeten him. He spent much of the rest of his life studying in the Bodleian Library, and writing books as the result of his studies. He was not, as has been thought, a scholar, or a theologian, or a University reformer, or a philosopher, so much as a bookworm, and he would have found his right place if he had been an assistant-librarian in the Bodleian Library instead of the Head of a college. The *Memoir* that he left behind him at his death is written, not with ink, but with gall. His widow married Sir Charles Dilke.

Between the time of my election to a Fellowship at Trinity College and of my appointment as Tutor (1847-1851), I had some leisure at Oxford, which I devoted to the study of theology, and for this purpose attended the lectures of Robert Hussey, Regius Professor of Ecclesiastical History, on Eusebius and Socrates and Bede, and of William Jacobson, Regius Professor of Divinity, on Arnobius and Lactantius, as well as the latter's public lectures, at which all candidates for ordination had to be present. Professor Hussey was a learned and grave divine, very seldom seen to smile, devoted to his work of teaching and of study, and bearing the reputation of great firmness and imperturbability. A myth about him was current in the University, that a surgeon telling him that one of his toes must be cut off, he replied: 'Very well, cut it off; but be good enough not to disturb me by any remarks while you do it, as I have to prepare my lecture.' He was an able preacher, and he wrote a valuable manual on the Papal Supremacy, a tenet which, after balancing the facts and arguments on each side, he pronounced to be a falsehood, a fiction, and a fraud.

Dr. Jacobson was the son of a Churchman, but was educated by a stepfather as a Dissenter. As soon as he came to Oxford he exhibited himself as the soundest of Churchmen. He was so careful not to speak hastily that he earned the character of never giving an opinion on any controverted subject, and delightful stories to that effect were told of him both before and after he was Bishop. 'What do you think, my lord, of the Bennett judgment on the doctrine of the Eucharist ?' asked an acquaintance who was making conversation on the day that it was pronounced, expecting a theological statement of the Bishop's views. 'I think it has been a very long time in coming out,' replied the Bishop. But had the man's heart been in the question the answer would have been very different. Occasionally in one of his lectures I asked him a question which required an answer on some burning question of the day. He would look quizzically at me out of the corner of his eye, and say: 'Ah! come to breakfast to-morrow, and we will consider that point.' After the breakfast he would discuss the point fully, and give a clear judgment of his own upon it.

He was the least self-asserting of men. On one occasion he was standing at the door of the Regius Professor's house in the Tom Quadrangle, Christ Church, without a hat, when a party of trippers came by, and, one of the party, taking him for the butler, asked him to show them the hall. 'With all my heart,' said Jacobson, with his quaint smile of amusement, and putting on his college cap, which betrayed their mistake to the trippers, he led them up the staircase and conducted them round the hall of Christ Church, pointing out to them what to admire, and sent them on their way congratulating themselves that their mistake had turned out so well. I made a mistake myself once which was received as merrily. At one of the Commemorations, T. L. Claughton, as Professor of Poetry, had delivered the annual Latin oration, short, clear, and well heard. Walking away with Jacobson, I said: 'What an excellent oration! I wish we always might have such orations.' 'Yes, indeed,' said Jacobson heartily; 'but' (regretfully) 'that is not likely, because' (dryly) 'I am Public Orator, and shall have to deliver the next oration—and' (lingering on the words) 'you remember that I delivered the last.' He received my assurance that I had not been present on that occasion with a twinkle in his eye and his curious curve of the lip, which showed that he was enjoying my discomfiture.

During the year of my proctorship (1857) the Hebdomadal Council, of which Jacobson was a member, formally requested the Proctors (Dr. Tufnell, afterwards Bishop of Brisbane, and myself) to make an effort to restore a more common use of the academical dress by undergraduates, and more particularly to put a stop to their going about the streets with their gowns wrapped round their throats instead of being worn properly. Jacobson happened to be sitting next me at the time that the matter was discussed. The same evening I was walking in the High Street, with the marshal and one of the 'bull-dogs,' as it was growing dark, and someone passed me with his gown wrapped round his neck. As I passed, I said : 'Will you put your gown on, sir, if you please ?' Looking back, I saw that he had not done it, so I said to the marshal : 'Stop that gentleman.' He ran back and did so, with the Proctor's compliments. As I walked back, I heard a gruff voice saying, 'I think Mr. Meyrick will let me go by.' On my coming up Jacobson unfolded his gown. ' It was very wrong of me, my dear Proctor, very wrong ; but please forgive me this time. It was very cold.' 'It is not everyone,' I laughed, ' who can boast of proctorizing the Regius Professor of Divinity.'

I was proctorized myself for being in the High Street without my gown by W. E. Jelf, of Christ Church, who was Proctor when I came up as an undergraduate. I had been walking on Shotover Hill with Henry Coleridge ; and Jelf, who was riding, overtook us and joined us for about ten minutes. We turned to go home about the same time, and, as he was riding, he naturally got back before us. Having gone to his rooms and put on his Proctor's gown, he emerged from Oriel Lane just at the moment that we were walking in that part of the High Street (between St. Mary's and All Saints' Churches) which he had ruled was to be kept sacred to caps and gowns. He could not help stopping us, which he did with a laugh, telling us to go to our college, which we were already doing. This was the only occasion on which I was proctorized during my undergraduate life. At a later time I became an intimate friend of W. E. Jelf, and we acted together as examiners. He was a man of strong will, and he had resolved, when he became Proctor, to put a stop to the slovenly dress which was becoming customary, by insisting on the use of the cap and gown. In other respects also he drew the reins of discipline tight. In consequence he was very unpopular with the noisy set in the University, and in the Commemoration preceding my residence they had created so much disturbance that the proceedings could hardly be carried on. ' What are they doing now ?' said one of the strangers, who had come for an honorary degree, to Jelf. ' Hissing me,' said Jelf with equanimity. A Proctor who does his duty looks on a certain amount of hissing in the theatre as his due. A body of men, one of whom I had rusticated, conspired to hiss me. For some half-minute they were successful, but the other undergraduates, with whom I was popular, rose to the occasion and overwhelmed the hissing with plaudits which almost made an ovation.

Jelf was thoroughly kind-hearted and a man of ability. He wrote some *Notes on Aristotle's Ethics*, and preached a course of Bampton Lectures on *Christian Faith—Comprehensive, not Partial ; Definite, not Uncertain.* He also published twelve of the sermons that he preached at the Chapel Royal, Whitehall.

A few months before he died I received, in 1854, a letter from Martin Joseph Routh, President of Magdalen College, which I keep as a curiosity, for it was written when the President was nearly 100 years old. I had had several interviews with him, for he was much interested in the proposal to make the doctrines of the Anglican Church better known on the Continent, with a view to the various European Churches reforming themselves on like principles with those of the English Church. On the occasion of one of these interviews we spoke of the doctrine of the Holy Eucharist. 'The right view, sir,' he said, 'is that of a Cambridge divine, I think, sir—I have forgotten his name [no doubt, Cudworth]—who has taught that it is not a sacrifice, but that it is a feast upon a sacrifice ; that is, that we feed our souls on Christ upon the cross, re-calling all the benefits which we derive from His death, and humbly seeking and, if we are worthy, receiving grace.' Stating his opinion in writing to his friend, Dr. Ogilvy, he expressed himself as follows : 'In confidence, I will submit to your consideration the following brief result of my humble inspection of St. John's sixth chapter, the account of the other Evangelists of the institution, and of St. Paul in 1 Cor. xi. and Heb. ix., xiii.: " Take this Bread, representing the Bread which came down from heaven and the Body which was crucified and broken for thee. Feed on that life-giving Sacrifice by faithfully believing in, and thankfully remembering, the Lord's death." '

These words are of great importance, coming from so learned a divine, of whom Dr. Newman said, in the dedication of one of his volumes to him, that he was 'reserved to report to a forgetful generation what was the theology of their fathers.' He was born in 1755, and died in December, 1854. He was elected to the headship of his college in 1791. His appearance in

his later life was that of a man of a previous generation. He always wore his academical gown, even
when in his study, and there he sat surrounded by his
books as his intimate friends. It was reported that
he died at last by his having mounted a ladder to
reach a large folio which fell upon him. This was not
altogether true, but it was true that some years previously he had severely injured his leg in this manner.
In giving an account of the accident to his medical
man, the President pathetically complained that the
injury had been done by 'a worthless book, sir—a
worthless book,' as though, says Burgon, 'he would
not have minded if it had been done by a volume of
Chrysostom or Augustine.'

He published two valuable works containing short
treatises of the earliest Fathers. The first of these was
called *Reliquiæ Sacræ*, and the other *Scriptorum Eccle-
siasticorum Opuscula*. He was buried in the college
chapel, of which he had been President for sixty-three
years, on December 29, 1854. Dr. Mozley, a Fellow
of Magdalen, wrote : ' The majestic music and solemn
wailings of the choir seemed to mourn over some great
edifice that had fallen and left a vast void, which
looked quite strange and unaccountable to one.'

One of the ablest men of my acquaintance in the
academic generation senior to myself was William
Sewell, Fellow of Exeter College. He was Tutor of
his college, and introduced a style of lecture which
was rather that of the Professor than that of the Tutor.
He was one of the first men who appreciated Plato's
philosophy, and led to his *Republic* being adopted
as one of the books to be taken up by candidates
for a first class in the University. He was so fond of
using Plato in illustration of his lectures that it was
said that his class did not always know whether he
was lecturing on St. Paul's Epistles or on Plato's
Dialogues. When the first symptoms of disloyalty to

the Church of England began to exhibit themselves, he preached and spoke very strongly against such tendency, and this led him to be attacked very unjustly by the admirers of Dr. Newman. He was an able writer, and it is said that an article of his in the *Quarterly* staved off the Parliamentary reform of Oxford for a time. He was deeply interested in the question of education, and, though a poor man, he contrived to establish two colleges or schools—St. Columba's in Ireland, and Radley near Oxford—where boys should be brought up on the principles and in the way in which he thought that education should be imparted. For some years he took charge of Radley himself. Both of the schools were to be conducted in such a way that the boys might be brought up as intelligent and attached members of the Church of England, as well as good scholars. Dr. Sewell's home was in the Isle of Wight, where I became well acquainted, not onl, with him, but with his brothers and sisters. One of his brothers, Dr. Edwards Sewell, when I came up as an undergraduate, was a Fellow of New College, and he afterwards became Warden. He lived to a great age, and was always in his place in the college chapel, and after morning chapel took a walk round the parks when he was nearly ninety years of age. One of his sisters was Miss Elizabeth Sewell, who shared with Miss Yonge the honour of having provided wholesome and attractive reading for girls of the upper and middle classes. Her first work was *Amy Herbert*, which, when she found publishers unwilling to take it, she published at her own risk and to her great advantage. It was followed by a long series of tales which have been of incalculable benefit to many readers. Neither she nor Miss Yonge ever gave herself the slightest airs as a popular author. Both lived simple lives, both were warmly attached daughters of the English Church, and many heads of

8

Christian families, looking at the tone of publications which have of late invaded their homes and found a place in the schoolroom and drawing-room, have risen up and called them blessed. I first made acquaintance with Miss Yonge in Judge Coleridge's house at Ottery St. Mary, in Devonshire, in 1844. Miss C. Coleridge, in her *Life of Miss Yonge*, has published the record of a conversation, made at the time by Miss Yonge, that took place there on the merits of Miss Sewell's books, in which I took a humble part.

Isaac Williams, author of a devout commentary on the Gospels, and of several books of religious poetry, was Fellow and Tutor of Trinity College at the time of my election, but ceased to reside the same term that I came up to the college. I made his acquaintance afterwards, when he was living at Stinchcombe. Mr. Williams's character was formed on the model of Keble's. The latter took him, with R. Isaac Wilberforce and Hurrell Froude, on an Oxford reading-party, while he was still an undergraduate; and Williams, becoming much attached, gave himself up to be moulded by him. A little later he came to know J. H. Newman, who at that time belonged to the school of the Church Missionary Society, with a dash of Archbishop Whately's Liberalism. After his ordination, when Newman had now come under the influence of Keble, Williams became Newman's curate, but from the beginning of his connection with Newman he felt a strong difference between him and the Kebles. 'Newman,' he writes, 'was looking for effect, for what was sensibly effective, which from the Bisley and Fairford School I had been long habituated to avoid. I had been taught there to do one's duty in faith, and leave the effect to God, and that all the more earnestly because there were no sympathies from without to answer.' Again, speaking of Newman, he says: 'We lived daily very much together; but I had a secret uneasiness, not from anything said or implied, but from a want of repose about his character, that he would start into some line different from Keble and Pusey, though I knew not in what direction it would be. But at all times there was a charm about his society which was very taking, and I do not wonder at those being carried away who had not been previously formed, like myself, in another, or at all events earlier, school of faith.'

When Newman had once said definitely that he held Rome to be right and England wrong, Williams withdrew from him, and so, too, did Keble, not without great distress of mind. 'Now that I have thrown off Newman's yoke,' said Keble to Williams, 'these things appear to me quite different. . . . I have now returned to my old views which I had before.' Had Williams lived longer, his influence would have served as some counterpoise to that of Newman. No doubt he would have been too acquiescent in failure, as being the lot of God's servants, and too much resigned under it, to have moved the world as a party actuated by Newman's spirit could do ; but he represented an element which was most valuable, and, had it been stronger, might have prevented a widespread mischief. During his last illness he wrote an autobiography, since published by his brother-in-law, Sir George Prevost, which throws much light on the history of the Oxford Movement. It was retained in manuscript for a number of years by W. J. Copeland because too little favourable to Newman for Copeland to make public. The extracts given above are taken from it.

Richard Cobden paid a visit to Oxford during the time of my residence—in, I think, 1851. He came partly to see a cousin, J. E. Thorold Rogers—at that time resident in Magdalen Hall, who afterwards exchanged the academical and clerical life for that of

8—2

a Radical M.P.—and partly to learn what political effect Tractarianism and the example of Mr. Gladstone would have on the young generation of clergy. Rogers asked a certain number of representative men to meet Cobden, and after dinner he propounded his question. Sir Robert Peel, he said, and the Conservative party in general, had rested for their support upon the Church; he desired to know whether this alliance between Churchmen and Conservatives was likely to continue. We replied that Tractarians as such were not attached to any political party, that many of them would be found in the Liberal ranks, and that Mr. Gladstone's example would have a Liberalizing effect upon the clergy; but that, nevertheless, as the Church was a great institution of the country, Tories would naturally be disposed to support it, and their support would as naturally create a disposition in the Church to support the Tory party in return. The result on the whole would probably be to add some Churchmen to the Liberal party, but not to withdraw the support given to the Tories by the Church, though that support would probably be given, not solely on account of the Church's establishment, but for other reasons as well.

Max Müller on his first visit to Oxford brought a letter of introduction to me. He was at that time uncertain whether he should settle in London, near the British Museum, or in Oxford, near the Bodleian. He had been disappointed with the coolness of his welcome to Oxford, which he had expected would receive him with open arms as a scholar in a sister University. I told him that we were all so busy in either teaching or being taught that we were (perhaps too much) engrossed each in his own work, but that if he came to reside among us he would not have to complain of any want of warmth in his recep-

tion.   He asked me to tell him what books I thought
that he should read in order to put him abreast with
English literature.   Early in the list that I gave him
I put Butler's *Sermons*.   'Sermons,' he said, 'are not
the sort of books that I desire; they are generally
ephemeral, and appeal to the feelings, whereas I want
books of permanent value in the history or literature
of the country.'   I assured him that he would not find
Bishop Butler's sermons ephemeral or superficial, in
spite of their being called 'sermons,' but that they
contained the best system of ethical philosophy which
was to be found in the English language.   Accordingly, he wrote down the name in his list as a book
to be studied by him.   Max Müller settled in Oxford,
and became, though a foreigner, one of the most
popular men in the University.   He was much disappointed at not being elected Professor of Sanskrit,
and at the preference given to Monier-Williams.   It
is probable, however, that the University acted wisely
in the decision to which it came, as Mr. Monier-
Williams was better suited to carry on the instruction of individuals than Max Müller, who rather
addressed himself by his publications to the whole
world.

CHAPTER V

Dr. Pusey—Bishop Stubbs—Bishop Samuel Wilberforce.

Soon after I had taken my degree I was urged very strongly by Charles Marriott to learn Hebrew, and with that end to attend Dr. Pusey's lectures as Professor of Hebrew. Having first learnt something of the language from his assistant or deputy, William Kay junior, of Lincoln College, I accordingly went to Dr. Pusey's lectures. This was not the occasion of my first making acquaintance with Dr. Pusey. Canons of Christ Church and University Professors had generally lived in a sphere separate from undergraduates, but Pusey was accessible to anyone who needed his advice or help ; the barrier between Dons and young students was in his case done away, and the kind smile and ready attention which he gave might lead the man who sought his counsel to think that he had nothing to do but to listen to him. In my early undergraduate days a brother undergraduate had come to me for counsel on a matter involving such serious moral difficulties and perplexities that, not feeling myself competent to deal with the case, I had taken it and him to Dr. Pusey, that he might resolve them. In like manner, a little later, a man in the position of a gentleman having stolen some of the books belonging to the Union Society at the time that I was treasurer, and having been sent to prison (not on my prosecution, but on that of a bookseller whom he had also defrauded), I thought it right to visit him. He professed deep penitence (in which I did not quite believe), and begged to see a clergyman for his spiritual comfort. I mentioned the facts to Dr. Pusey, and he at once undertook to visit the prisoner.

Having spent one term in learning the elements of the Hebrew language from Dr. Kay, I went to Pusey's lectures. They were not anything remarkable. Evidently the Professor had not had time to make much preparation, and his method was to draw one folio after another to him and read to us the comment made by the authors on the text of Scripture under discussion. Still, in the end he always gave us a clear notion of its meaning, and the reverence with which he dealt with Holy Scripture was a lesson to us all, as well as the patience which he exercised towards indifferent Hebrew scholars in his class.

Pusey's Oxford life may be divided into four parts of almost equal lengths. The first was from 1834 to 1845, when at first tentatively, afterwards enthusiastically, he threw himself—already a Canon of Christ Church and Professor of Hebrew, and with a reputation for great learning—into the thick of the battle initiated at Oxford by Keble, which came to be known as the Tractarian Movement. He had placed his initials after one of the Tracts that he had written, with the intention of limiting his responsibility to his one Tract, as he was not yet perfectly in sympathy with the other contributors to the series. But his name, becoming thus known, was seized upon by the opponents of the movement, and attached to the Tractarians, who were thence called Puseyites. Henceforward Keble, Pusey, and Newman formed a triumvirate which directed the action of the Tractarian party. That action was in some respects far from wise. The Hampden controversy had better have been let alone (how mild does Hampden's unorthodoxy, into which he was led blindfold by Blanco White, look now!); an opposition raised to the erection of the Martyrs' Memorial was narrow-minded in the extreme; and an attempt to veto the appointment of Dr. Symons, Warden of Wadham, as Vice-Chancellor was impolitic and reprehensible. On the other hand, much valuable work was done. The aggressions of the State were beaten back; the character of the Anglican clergy was deepened by the more religious character given to the Universities (which had not then been secularized); the 'Library of the Fathers' and the 'Anglo-Catholic Library' were issued, opening sources of information that had not been readily accessible.

The next ten years were a period of loneliness and distress to Pusey. Newman had deserted him, and Dr. Pusey had thus not only lost a loved associate, but a change had come over the University. Men felt that they had to take their choice between four courses—either following Newman to Rome, or starting back and withdrawing farther and farther from the verge of the precipice, or casting off all thought of religion, or remaining as nearly as possible as they were. Pusey took the last of the four alternatives. He would not join the Church of Rome; he was kept estranged from her by her Mariolatry, her Masses for the dead, her Indulgences, and her denial of the Cup; but he would not join in any condemnation of what was now Newman's home. Many men and women, disturbed by Newman's act, came to Pusey in distress of mind, and he confirmed them in faithfulness to the Church of England on the ground of her catholicity; but he refrained from basing his argument on the character of the dogmas and practices of the Church of Rome. In consequence, those who were retained in spite of their attraction to Rome were retained rather by the personal influence of Pusey than by a conviction of the superiority of the Anglican to the Roman position. This answered better with women than with men. Maskell, Allies, H. Wilberforce, Dodsworth, Manning, James Hope, R. Wilberforce, all fulfilled their courses. Still, the very fact of Pusey's standing firm himself had a widespread effect in calming disquiet, though he did not speak with the decision of Andrewes, or Laud, or Cosin, or Bull.

It was during this period that great trouble took place in connection with St. Saviour's, Leeds. It had been built by Dr. Pusey, who therefore had the nomination of the incumbent. In exercising this privilege Pusey was most unfortunate. Two sets of incumbents or curates went over to the Church of Rome one after the other, the best known of whom were R. G. Macmullen and John Hungerford Pollen. After the second secession in 1851, Pusey was anxious to find an incumbent who should satisfy Dr. Hook and Bishop Longley, and he asked me to take the post, though I was then only a deacon. I could not take it, and it was filled by a most devout and excellent man, J. W. Knott, who after holding it for some years gave himself up to missionary work. From the time of his appointment there was peace at St. Saviour's, Leeds, for Knott, though a mystic, was no Ritualist.

In the decade from 1855 to 1865, Dr. Pusey rose from the controversies of the day to be the champion of no lesser thing than revealed truth against rationalism, and the representative of no narrower body than that of Christian believers in their struggle against scepticism. Dr. Jowett's commentary on the Romans, which cast a slur on the authority of Scripture and denied the Atonement, was the first indication of rationalistic aggression at Oxford. That was in 1856, and I have already pointed out the active part taken by Dr. Pusey in opposition to it. Then followed the

Essays and Reviews in 1860. Five of these, written by Rowland Williams, Baden Powell, H. B. Wilson, C. W. Goodwin, and Professor Jowett, were sceptical and rationalistic. Pusey felt that this was a matter in which High Churchmen and Evangelicals might work together, and he wrote to the *Record* suggesting common action. Lord Shaftesbury responded : ' For God's sake, let all who love our Blessed Lord and His perfect work be of one heart, one mind, in our action on this great issue, and show that, despite our wanderings, our doubts, our contentions, we yet may be one in Him. What say you ?' Pusey answered : ' This soul-destroying judgment [acquitting R. Williams] may, with, I fear, its countless harms, be over-ruled by God's mercy to good, if it bind as one man all who love our Blessed Lord in contending for the faith assailed. I have ever loved the (to use the word) Evangelical party (even while they blamed me), because I believed that they loved our Redeeming Lord with their whole hearts.' ' What I am most anxious about for the present,' wrote Bishop Wilberforce to Dr. Pusey, ' is that you should do your utmost to weld together the two great sections of the Church—High and Low.' A committee representing High Churchmen, Low Churchmen, and men that were neither one nor the other, was formed in Oxford, and a declaration was framed maintaining the doctrines of the inspiration and authority of Scripture and of everlasting punishment. Mr. F. D. Maurice angrily assailed it in the *Times*, and Dr. Pusey replied to him. The Declaration was signed by 11,000 clergy, and presented to the Archbishop in 1864.

A common opposition to Bishop Colenso's tenets, as well as to those of the *Essays and Reviews*, seemed still more to make the Evangelical party forget their antagonism to Dr. Pusey, whose *Lectures on the Book of Daniel* were published in the autumn of 1864 as an apologetic. 'The exposure of the weakness of criticism, where it thought itself most triumphant, would, I hoped, shake the confidence of the young in their would-be misleaders' (Preface, p. vi). In addition, Pusey at this time invited Bachelors of Arts and undergraduates to meetings at his house, at which any present had the right of propounding difficulties, which were dealt with at the next meeting. In this way the Mosaic account of the Creation, the Deluge, the ten plagues, the influence of Egypt on the Mosaic system, Colenso's *Pentateuch*, and other subjects, were discussed. His University sermons at this period all had the same end in view. He preached on the evidences of Christianity, on God as the Source of knowledge, on the predictional element in the Old Testament, on the Atonement, on eternal punishment, on prayer. One day I was walking with him, when he stopped, and, with that catch in the voice which he used when much interested, he said: 'The battle of the coming generation will be for Holy Scripture. It was impending thirty years ago, but the controversy on the Tracts deferred it. Now it is close upon us, and it will begin by an assault on the authorship and dates of the books of the Old Testament, whence it will extend to their subject-matter and to the New Testament.'

Confidence in Dr. Pusey as a representative Churchman grew more and more, and it was exhibited most clearly at the Norwich Church Congress of 1865. This was the zenith of his popularity in England, when he reached a height of reputation from which he soon after declined, and to which he never again attained. The Congress of 1865 was perhaps the most remarkable of the Congresses of the Church of England. Dr. Pusey, Bishop Wilberforce, and Dean (afterwards Bishop) Harvey Goodwin, who formed a host in themselves, were supported by Archdeacon

Denison, Sir Robert Phillimore, Mr. Beresford Hope,
Lord Arthur Hervey, Dean Alford, the Earl of
Harrowby, Canon (afterwards Bishop) Claughton,
Bishop Charles Wordsworth, Dean Howson, Canon
(afterwards Bishop) Mackenzie, Dr. (afterwards Dean)
Goulburn, Mr. Joseph Napier, Dr. Salmon, Bishop
Cotterill, and other good speakers. At this meeting
Dr. Pusey was received with an extraordinary outburst of enthusiasm. He had won the goodwill of
all parties in the Church and of all members of the
Church, with the exception of semi-rationalists, who
then were few. His paper on 'The Spirit in which
the Researches of Learning and Science should be
applied to the Study of the Bible' increased the
enthusiasm in his behalf, and it remains a valuable
Eirenicon between the claims of Holy Scripture and
the physical sciences at this day. It avoids both the
ecclesiastic's temptation of claiming too much for
revelation and allowing too little to human research,
and the timid man's error of giving away what
cannot be yielded without imperilling the whole.

Dr. Pusey went away from the Norwich Congress
the most popular man in the Church of England, and
he passed from Norwich direct to France, and forthwith destroyed that popularity and sharpened against
him afresh the blunted weapons of his old antagonists;
for now, at the beginning of his fourth decade, he set
forth on the *ignis fatuus* pursuit of union with Rome.
Dr. Manning had assailed the position of the English
Church, and Pusey began an apologetic reply; but
when he had proceeded a little way with it, he changed
its character and made it an Eirenicon, in which he
proposed terms of union with the Roman Church
under certain conditions. The Eirenicon appeared in
three parts; the first was addressed to Mr. Keble, and
called *The Truth and Office of the English Church*.
Its proposal was that Rome should draw a sharp line

of distinction between her authorized doctrines and the religious system working in the hearts and lives of the people attached to her. The idea was an impracticable one, as Newman more than once pointed out to him. 'It is quite true that I said, and I should still say, that it is a mere doctrinaire view to enter a Church without taking up its practical system, and that as represented by its popular catechisms and books of devotion. In this sense I hold by the system of St. Alfonso Liguori' (*Apol.*, p. 127). Rome will not, cannot, distinguish between her more and less superstitious doctrines and practices, for they all belong to her; and if she could and would, it would not bring about union with her, for we have no right to endorse her less superstitious any more than her more superstitious tenets. That they are superstitious is sufficient. Still, the first part of the Eirenicon did not give serious offence in England. Pusey's reputation stood at the moment so high, its title was so harmless, it was addressed to Mr. Keble, and it severely condemned some of the Roman practices. But the necessary consequence of its moderation ensued. It did not satisfy the other side. Newman was 'disappointed,' and he invented the clever saying that Pusey 'discharged his olive branch as if from a catapult.'

Pusey could not bear to hurt Newman's feelings. Most of all was he anxious to set himself right in Newman's estimation, and to do this he must be less aggressive — *i.e.*, defensive, and more yielding to Roman arrogance. He took two ways of soothing his offended friend. He republished Tract XC., with a preface condoning and defending the sophistical mode of dealing with the Articles, by which Newman had brought the series of *Tracts for the Times* to an end in the midst of an outburst of honest indignation. Then he turned again to the Eirenicon. Keble had died, and Pusey, when he had written the second part of the Eirenicon, addressed it 'to the Very Rev. J. H. Newman, D.D., and in it he mildly suggested that the Bull *Ineffabilis* on the Immaculate Conception needed explanation. But Newman was still dissatisfied. Pusey resolved upon writing a third part of the Eirenicon in the shape of a second letter to Newman, and it was published under the title *Is Healthful Union impossible?* In it he enumerates 'the most common causes of dread among us, in case of union with Rome,' and 'suggests some way of agreement, where possible.' This letter formed a book of 350 pages, and being published in the early part of 1870, when the Vatican Council was on the point of assembling, it dealt largely with the Papal claim to Infallibility. By Newman's advice, he sent a copy of the work to several of the Bishops about to take part in the Council : among others, to Dr. Clifford, Roman Bishop of Clifton, and Monseigneur Dupanloup, Bishop of Orleans. But both prelates sent back their copy with ' Refused' written upon it. Pusey, who had visited Dupanloup at Orleans, was naturally hurt. But it was the idlest dream that the Vatican Council would take into consideration theories of reunion proposed by heretics. Before it met, Pope Pius had given his sanction to a decree of the Supreme Congregation ordering a correspondent of Dr. Pusey and Bishop Forbes, named De Buck, 'to desist entirely from discussing the subject of reconciliation with some heterodox Anglicans.' Pusey soon saw that his efforts were doomed to the disappointment which they deserved. 'I can only turn away sick at heart.' 'I have done what I could, and now have done with controversy and Eirenica' (August 26, 1870). At length he was aware of his error, and after Papal Infallibility had been adopted on July 18, 1870, he altered the title of the third part of his Eirenicon, and in later editions, instead of *Is Healthful Union impos-sible ?* adopted the title *Healthful Reunion, as conceived possible before the Vatican Council.*

A result of his dealings with Rome was that Pusey would have nothing to say to the Old Catholics. These were representatives of the Catholic element in the unreformed Churches, as distinct from the Papal or Ultramontane element. They had been thrust out of the various Churches subjected to Rome because they would not accept the dogmas of the Infallibility of the Pope and his Universal Bishopric. Pusey was invited to the Old Catholic Congress at Cologne in 1872, and he hesitated as to accepting the invitation, but finally declined it. With the first Bonn Conference of 1874 he had nothing to do, nor was he present at the second, held in 1875, in both of which, however, a very active part was taken by his lieutenant, Dr. Liddon. In 1875 the Conference proposed a form which members both of the Eastern and Western Churches might accept in reference to the doctrine of the Procession of the Holy Ghost. This formula was drawn up and agreed to by a committee, consisting of Dr. v. Döllinger and two other Old Catholic theologians, the Archbishop of Syros, Arch-Priest Janyscheff and three other Oriental divines, Dr. Liddon, Dr. Nevin, and myself. It was then approved by the Conference and remitted to England, St. Petersburg, and Constantinople, for the consideration of the authorized organs of the Churches of England and the East. Accordingly, on the petition of the members of the Conference on their return to England, the formula was submitted to the Convocation of Canterbury, and a committee was appointed, which declared it to be in all respects orthodox.

But Pusey was strongly opposed. He was absolutely resolved not to admit the recurrence by the Church of England to the original form of the Niceno-

Constantinopolitan Creed, because it would be widening the chasm between the Church of England and Newman's communion, which, in spite of his own efforts at union having come to naught, he could not bear. Correspondence on the subject between Dr. Pusey and myself continued in the *Times* for the whole of January, 1876, and Pusey published a treatise against the Bonn proposal in July of the same year. His influence was so great in the English Church that the favourable report of the committee of Convocation in respect to the Bonn propositions was allowed to remain without effect, and the question was not submitted to, or considered by, the House. Dr. v. Döllinger was so much disappointed and hurt by Pusey's opposition to his scheme of reunion that he gave it as the chief reason for not summoning a third Conference at Bonn. Then, as now, sympathy with a scheme of reunion with Rome was found incompatible with sympathy with those who had been excommunicated by Rome.

Pusey never regained the confidence of the Evangelical party which he enjoyed in 1865 and forfeited by his futile attempt at union with the Roman See. For the rest of his life he was deeply respected for the work that he had done, and idolized by his immediate followers; but he was the head of a party, not the representative of the Church, as he was in 1865, and might have continued to be.

Dr. Pusey died in 1882, and was buried at Christ Church, in the cathedral where for so many years he had worshipped God.

Next to me in the list of the Fellows of Trinity College was William Stubbs. He was elected the year after myself, and we were thenceforth companions and friends. The last communication that I had from him was a letter in which, 'with love,' he declared himself unequal to the exertion of travelling into Norfolk to officiate at the marriage of my daughter, as I had asked him to do. His death occurred soon afterwards. He was originally a 'servitor' at Christ Church, and, being a man of great industry as well as ability, he gained a first class shortly before his election at Trinity College. He had an extraordinary amount of learning on out-of-the-way points of history. For example, I said to him once : 'Stubbs, I want to know how the Visigoths of Spain behaved to their slaves.' 'Go to the Bodleian,' he replied immediately, 'and consult the *Leges Barbarorum.*' He was very kind-hearted, and also had a strong sense of humour, as in later days unwise young curates found to their surprise when they did or said some foolish thing. He took the college living of Navestock, and then returned to Oxford as Professor of Modern History. He was also appointed Librarian of Lambeth Library by Archbishop Longley. Mr. Gladstone nominated him to the See of Chester, whence he was translated to Oxford. His works are marked by an extra-ordinary accuracy, the result of a never-failing industry and a remarkable memory.

In 1850 I was ordained deacon, and in 1852 priest, by Samuel Wilberforce, Bishop of Oxford. In the previous generation it had been usual for the Bishop of Oxford to take the qualifications of Fellows of colleges for granted, and not to subject them to any examination, except such as could be passed in their own rooms by a little paper-work. That was, of course, now changed. Bishop Wilberforce received all the candidates, between thirty and forty, in his palace —a custom now universal, begun by Wilberforce.

The two weeks thus spent were as happy as any in my life. Not an hour was allowed to be lost ; papers, chapel services, exercise, meals, all had their allotted time. In the chapel we listened to the Bishop's ordination addresses, afterwards published, and even

9

at mealtimes the conversation, led by Wilberforce and his chaplains—Archbishop Trench, Archdeacon Randall, Archdeacon Clerke, Archdeacon Pott—was not a little instructive to the young candidates for the ministry. No one ordained by Wilberforce will ever forget those happy days at Cuddesdon.

On looking back on the men whom I have known, and comparing them in respect to ability, I put Wilberforce first, regarding him and them from all points of view. In his special sphere as a Bishop he stood before and above the prelates who were his contemporaries, and there was in him so great a reserve of power and such versatility of mind that he gave the impression of there being nothing in which he would not have surpassed competitors, had he laid aside other matters and given himself to that special study and work. A still more striking characteristic in one so universally gifted was that he held his intellectual powers well under control, and did not allow himself to be hurried away on any abnormal path from a consciousness of being able to surmount its difficulties. He was a great preacher, greater than Magee, who could alone be compared with him. He was called upon to speak in public, and he surpassed the then Lord Derby and Mr. Gladstone. He was thrown by circumstances into the midst of English social life, and he outshone in it those that made it their chief pursuit to shine. Had he been a politician, he must have been Prime Minister. Lord Aberdeen regretted that he could not make him Lord Chancellor. Had he devoted himself to law, philosophy, history, poetry, he has shown that he would have excelled in each. It is his great glory that, having been so gifted, he subordinated every other study and pursuit to that of being, in the most perfect manner of which he was capable, a Bishop of the Church of Christ.

There is a remarkable unity in the life of this

versatile man.   Possessed of sympathies both wide and intense, he touched every school within the Church of England and in the English nation, and appeared to draw nearer, now to one, and now to another, of them ; but throughout his whole career he was essentially an Anglican of the old historical Anglican type.   It is perfectly true that at one time of his life he held himself consciously, deliberately, and of set purpose, external to the knot of earnest men who came to be known by the name of Tractarians, a position which he held in common with many other sound Churchmen, and tried to recall them to more sober views.   It is true, also, that he took into his own hands in later years the organization and consolidation of the younger generation of Churchmen, many of whom looked up to the early Tractarians as their teachers. But there was no inconsistency in this ; it was not the Tractarian party that he was thus reconstructing, but it was the old historical High Church school, which, as a Bishop, himself belonging to that school, he guided, directed, and led.   As in his early life he re-sisted 'Tractarian extremes,' so in his later years he discountenanced 'Ritualistic extravagancies,' 'those coruscations,' as I remember hearing him describe them, 'which lift themselves up in fantastic shapes over the stream of good metal flowing beneath.'   In either case he was ready to give, and he gave, the warmest sympathy to zeal, earnestness, and a desire after holiness ; but he was not carried away to be a partisan of anything narrower than the great school of thought represented by Hooker, Andrewes, Laud, Cosin, Taylor, Sheldon, Pearson, Ken, Bull, Wilson, Waterland, and Hook.

His many-sidedness necessarily laid him open to misrepresentation.   When a man whose sympathies were confined to a narrow school or clique found him-self in sympathy with Wilberforce, and soon after saw

Wilberforce co-operating with a school to which he was himself opposed, he charged Wilberforce with insincerity, when the latter was perfectly sincere, the explanation of his conduct being that he touched the partisan on this side with one hand, and the partisan on that side with the other, taking up into himself the different aspects of the truth which they each held, and combining them without the sacrifice of either.

The Bishop's life falls into three acts of a drama : the first ending with the year 1848, a period of success and popularity ; the second ending with 1860, a period of struggle and conflict ; the third with 1873, during which period he was, without question, the foremost man of the English Episcopate, of the English Church, of the Anglican Communion. He began his clerical life at Checkendon, but within two years was appointed, by the Bishop of Winchester, to the rectory of Brighstone in the Isle of Wight. Here he remained ten years, when he became Rector of Alverstoke as well as Archdeacon of Surrey. Alverstoke retained him only five years, when he was made Dean of Westminster, and within a few months Bishop of Oxford. Two great sorrows — one belonging to his earlier life, the other to his later life—supplied elements of character which might otherwise have been lacking in one who seemed made to be the favourite of fortune and the idol of his friends and contemporaries.

The first of these griefs was the death of his dearly-loved wife in the year 1841. The following exquisite lines were written nearly eight years after his loss :

> ' I sat within my glad home, and round about me played
> Four children in their merriment, and happy noises made ;
> Beside me sate their mother, in her loveliness and light ;
> I ne'er saw any like her, save in some vision bright.

> ' It was in life's young morning that our hearts together grew,
> Beneath its sparkling sunlight, and in its steeping dew ;
> And the sorrows and the joys of a twelve years' changeful life
> Had drawn more closely to me my own, my blessèd wife.

' Then at our door One knocked, and we rose to let Him in,
For the night was wild and stormy, and to turn Him thence were
  sin :
With a " Peace be to this household " His shelterers He blest,
And sat Him down among us like some expected guest.

' The children's noise was hushed, the mother softly spoke,
And my inmost spirit thrilled with the thoughts which in me woke ;
For it seemed like other days within my memory stored—
Like Mamre's tented plain or Emmaus' evening board.

' His form was veilèd from us, His mantle was not raised,
But we felt that eyes of tenderness and love upon us gazed :
His lips we saw not moving, but a deep and inward tone
Spake like thunder's distant voices unto each of us alone :

' " Full often ye have called Me, and bid Me to your home,
And I have listened to your words, and at your prayer have come ;
And now My voice is strange to you, and ' Wherefore art Thou
  here ?'
Your throbbing hearts are asking, with struggling hope and fear.

' " It was My love which shielded your helpless infant days ;
It was My care which guided you through all life's dangerous ways ;
I joined your hearts together, I blessed your marriage vow,—
Then trust, and be not fearful, though My ways seem bitter now."

' We spake no word of answer, nor said He any more,
But as one about to leave us He passèd to the door ;
Then, ere He crossed the threshold, He beckoned with His hand,
That she who sat beside me should come at His command.

' Then rose that wife and mother, and went into the night ;
She followed at His bidding, and was hidden from our sight :
And though my heart was breaking, I strove my will to bow,
For I saw His hands were piercèd, and thorns had torn His brow.'

It would not be true to say that he was crushed by
this great blow, but his ambition was crushed out of
him ; and while he gave up the joyousness of life, he
devoted himself more earnestly to its work. He
poured life into his diocese, life into his clergy, life into
the Colonial Churches, life into the great missionary
societies, life into the whole Anglican communion ; he
changed the character of Confirmations, ordinations,
ministrations, sermons ; he intensified and expanded

the previously entertained conception of the pastor's work; he revived Convocation and gave vigour to Church Congresses; he encouraged the institution of new societies for new Church needs; he watched over the interests of the Church as a vigilant guardian in Parliament, giving the word, with unerring judgment, where to resist and where to give way.

Dean Burgon, in his *Lives of Twelve Good Men*, justly attributes to him the remodelling of the Episcopate in England. Men of a previous generation looked on with surprise and disfavour at his activity and ubiquity. ' I saw,' said T. Short of Trinity College—' I saw Sam riding unattended into Oxford to-day; Bishops of Oxford used not to appear here except in a carriage with four horses and footmen.' He rode a powerful horse which soon bore him from Cuddesdon to Oxford and back. Occasionally his brother-in-law, John James, would ask to accompany him on his return. ' Delighted, my dear James ! but I have an engagement at six o'clock, so I must gallop.' ' Oh yes,' said James, and scuttled after him on his pony, generally half a horse's length behind. After some miles he turned back, bespattered with mud, but quite content and very happy. Men would walk miles for the mere pleasure of looking the Bishop in the face and shaking hands with him.

His industry was marvellous. On one occssion when I was staying at Cuddesdon, I was assigned a bedroom which had its own staircase into the garden. After other guests had gone to bed, Arthur Gordon (Lord Stanmore) came to sit with me, and we went on talking till nearly three o'clock. When Gordon turned to go away, we found that the servant had locked the door, leading into the rest of the house, for the night. We went down into the garden, and, walking round the house found a light still burning in the Bishop's bedroom. Gordon threw up a pebble; immediately the

Bishop appeared, with the words, ' Who walks so late by night ?' Learning our plight, he let Gordon in, and he and I went to bed. The next day, which was Sunday, the Bishop confirmed some of the boys at Radley School, making them a striking address, preached to the country folk in Radley Parish Church, and delivered a powerful sermon before the University of Oxford, returning in the evening to Cuddesdon with us, who had accompanied him. On another occasion, when four Oxford men came half an hour too soon for dinner, 'You are just the men I wanted,' said the Bishop, and, sitting them down, he dictated four letters, sentence by sentence in turn to each of them. On the occasion of my ordination I was deputed to ask the Bishop that a sermon preached to us might be printed. 'Ask the Bishop,' said Archdeacon Pott, 'as soon as he has left the room,' where he was talking to the newly ordained as if he had nothing to do except to talk to them. On my following him into the passage, he was not to be seen. Pott laughed. ' Come along,' he said ; 'we shall find him.' Immediately that he had closed the door the Bishop had run off full speed to his dressing-room at the other end of the house, and we found him with his dress half changed, about to start in two minutes for the train to take him to London to attend an important meeting. He replied to my request, said good-bye, and was off.

The Bishop was kept up amid his incessant work by a strong sense of humour and a power of finding amusement. Before the trials of life came to temper his original disposition, he was full of merriment, and he never altogether lost that quality. When he had time for it, no one was fonder of a jest which would not give pain to others. On one occasion a large party of Oxford men had come to Cuddesdon to dinner at Christmastide. After dinner, as we were sitting in the drawing-room, the Bishop stood up and said in a loud and joyous voice, 'It is Christmas, and we must all sing a Christmas carol.' We had gathered round the piano, when the Bishop saw that Archdeacon Clerke was still sitting in his chair. The Archdeacon, with many excellencies, had a voice like a badly-creaking door. 'Come, Archdeacon!' said the Bishop. 'Oh, but I can't sing,' he replied. 'No excuses! Come along!' cried the Bishop, and, striding across the room, he took him by the arm and brought him to the piano. 'Now what carol shall we sing?' Someone suggested 'King Wenceslaus,' and, it appeared, one of those present could play the accompaniment. 'Remember, Archdeacon,' said the Bishop, 'that we all hang upon you. Now let us begin.' We got through the carol, led chiefly by the Bishop. 'There, Archdeacon,' he said, 'see how much we owe to you!' At the same time, lest the dear old man should be hurt, he kept his own arm affectionately linked with his on the pretence of not allowing him to run away. The Bishop's manner towards anyone on whom he seemed to be passing a joke was such as to make it impossible for him to be hurt by it.

The Bishop's second great grief was the secession of his brother, Robert I. Wilberforce, and of his dearly-loved daughter, to the Church of Rome. The following are extracts from the Bishop's diary when the news came of the last step having been taken: 'H. and E. have joined the debased communion. Utterly crushed.' The next day, 'A pain at my heart by night and by day for beloved E. and for H.' The next: 'Ever the pain in my heart for E.' And again: 'As if I could see H. and E. bartering away their birthright of Gospel freedom and eternal truth.' At the same time he wrote to Sir Charles Anderson: 'The insult to our Church from one so near to us, the reproaches I shall have personally to bear from those who little know how I have striven, guarded, and prayed against this in all its most distant approaches, the separation from my child, and the fear for their souls, all together press upon me more heavily than I am well able to bear.' And to his son Ernest : ' The whole thing lies so clearly before me that I am for ever needing to discipline my spirit not to feel unkindly to one who has robbed me of my only daughter in blood, and brought reproach on the Church which I have, however imperfectly, ever endeavoured to serve. As to the Papistry itself, I only more than ever see it to be the great cloaca into which all vile corruptions of Christianity run naturally, and loathe it.' The charge of Romanizing brought against Wilberforce, as it was brought against Laud, was utterly false, but in both cases it served the purposes of the opponents of the two prelates.

How little Wilberforce sympathized with the disloyal developments of Ritualism may be seen by his latest public utterance, addressed to the Rural Deans of his diocese four days before his death : ' There is a growing desire to introduce novelties (such as incense, a multitude of lights in the chancel, and so on). Now, these and such things are, honestly and truly, alien to the Church of England. Do not hesitate to treat them as such. All this appears to me to indicate a fidgety anxiety to make everything in our churches assimilate to a foreign usage . . . as if our grand old Anglican communion contrasted unfavourably with the Church of Rome. The habitual language held by many men sounds as if they were ashamed of our Church and its position ; it is a sort of apology for the Church of England as compared with the Church of Rome. Why, I would as soon think of apologizing for the virtue of my mother to a harlot ! I have no sympathy in the world with such a feeling. I abhor this fidgety desire to make everything un-Anglican. This is not a grand development, as some think. It is a decrepitude. It is not something very sublime and impressive, but something very feeble and contemptible.' He went on to condemn auricular and habitual confession—'one of the worst developments of Popery'; the 'new doctrine' of fasting Communion—'a detestable materialism'; non-communicating attendance—'the substitution of a semi-materialistic presence for the actual presence of Christ in the soul of the faithful communicant,' which is 'an abomination,' 'a corollary on the practice of fasting Communion': 'the sacrificing priest stands between your soul and your God, and makes atonement for you.' With these his final words before them, it is strange that any should venture to charge Bishop Wilberforce with disloyalty to the English Church. 'I am said to be unfaithful to my own Church, and a concealed Papist. I cannot say that I do not feel such attacks. It is impossible not to be pained by them. It is hard to bear. But, after all, it is nothing when weighed against the testimony of one's own conscience; it is nothing to make one recede from the course which one believes to be right, or to shake one's resolutions, by God's help, to maintain it.' These, too, were some of his last words.

When the news of the accident whereby Wilberforce's life was sacrificed on the Surrey Downs on April 19, 1873, became known, a thrill passed through the Church and through English society such as is seldom felt. The following lines, made public at the time by Mr. Stone, will recall something of the feelings which then prevailed:

> 'Another beacon light gone out above us;
> Another buoy-bell stilled upon the sea;
> Another pilot, of the hearts that love us,
>   Passed from our company!

> *   *   *   *   *

'An hour ago, and at the helm serenely,
　His steadfast eye upon the steadfast star,
We saw him stand, and, lovingly as keenly,
　Steer for the haven far.

　　*　　　　*　　　　*　　　　*　　　　*

'Still do we see—not now the changeful splendour,
　Lambent or sparkling, leaping through the night ;
But the abiding glow, most deep, most tender—
　A great life's lasting light.

'Still do we hear—not now the silvern laughter
　We loved to catch 'mid many a mightier tone ;
But this—the golden cadence that hereafter
　All memory shall own.

'Still do we hold—not now the presence human,
　Kind, fearless eye, frank hand, and vigorous form ;
But closer yet, the inner and the true man,
　That steered us through the storm ;

'To guide us still who loved him ! cheering, warning,
　Past rock and shoal and through the blinding foam—
Until the homeward-bound at the clear morning
　Shall be at last at home.

'Ah, Saint, there are who in the heavenly places,
　After the vision of the Form Divine,
Shall greet not one among the blissful faces
　More wistfully than thine !'

It was the custom of Bishop Wilberforce at his ordinations to invite someone whose life or power of conversation might interest the young men gathered in Cuddesdon Palace. At the time of my ordination his guest was Bishop Whittingham of Maryland. He and his chaplain, who accompanied him, had lately been on the Continent, and were much interested by Dean Hirscher's proposals for a reformation, which Bishop Cleveland Coxe made known to English readers in his *Sympathies of the Continent*. They had also just read the *Practical Working of the Church of Spain*, a book which I had published, containing the experiences of myself and my brother and sister in

the Peninsula. 'I make two demands,' said Bishop
Whittingham at the Bishop of Oxford's table, 'in the
name of my countrymen, of the Church of England.
We have a right to ask of you, surrounded as you are
with magnificent libraries, and having opportunities
for learned leisure, to publish a critical edition of the
first four Œcumenical Councils in Greek, Latin, and
English; and we ask that measures be taken for
exhibiting the true character of the Anglican Church
to those who are ignorant of it, and we call on the
English Church to take the lead in such an effort.'
His second demand was partially accomplished by the
institution, two or three years afterwards, of the
Anglo-Continental Society, of which Bishop Wilberforce, Bishop Charles Wordsworth, and Bishop
Whittingham became the first Episcopal patrons.
Bishop Whittingham's first suggestion to the new
society was that of the republication of Casaubon's
letter to Cardinal Perron, a suggestion that was
carried out in the year 1875, when a Latin edition
of the work, with a preface by Bishop Christopher
Wordsworth, was brought out in England by the
Anglo-Continental Society, while at the same time
an English edition of it was issued by himself in
America.

This treatise of Casaubon was Bishop Whittingham's
favourite theological work. When about to reprint
it, he declared that it contained in the choicest and
most scholarly language his fatherly counsel and
advice on the topics therein treated, and he said that
he preferred reprinting it to writing anything new
himself, or adopting the words of any living author,
because of Casaubon's known theological learning,
and also because his work had been revised by the
great Bishop Andrewes. Few men of the present
generation had so wide an acquaintance with theology
as Bishop Whittingham had; his library consisted

of 16,000 volumes collected by himself, containing every work of importance on the controversy with Rome. This library he left as an heirloom to his successors in the See of Maryland.

In 1872 the Bishop repaired to Europe partly for the sake of recruiting his health, partly to represent and act for the American Church in the crisis of the Old Catholic revolt against Rome. In the latter capacity he attended the Old Catholic Congress at Cologne, where he met Bishop Harold Browne and Bishop Christopher Wordsworth. Here he took an active part with those prelates in formulating a basis of intercommunion, which was adopted at a meeting of a committee appointed, on the motion of Bishop Reinkens, with a view to the restoration of unity.

The action of this committee led naturally to the Conferences of Bonn, and resulted in bringing about a fellow-feeling between the Anglican and Old Catholic Churches.

Bishop Whittingham was a typical Anglican Church-man of the school of Andrewes. An Anglican, not a Gallican, he had sympathy with everything that was primitive and with nothing that was mediæval. To him Popery was one thing, Catholicism was another. Popery was the corruption of Catholicism; Catholicism was pure Christianity not yet corrupted by Popery, or having happily rid itself of Popish corruption. 'He regarded Romanism,' said Bishop Atkinson of North Carolina, 'as an innovation on the primitive Church doctrine and polity; as the original cause for the divisions of Christendom, which he so deeply deplored; and as the author of additions to the primitive faith, which Cardinal Newman and others called developments, but which he rejected as excrescences and corruptions.' 'He disliked mediævalism,' says his biographer, 'because he knew the old to be far better.'

Bishop Whittingham took a leading part in a great crisis of the American Church, with the happiest results. The Southern Bishops had sided with the Confederates in the war between the North and the South, and when the war was over they did not know how they should be regarded by their brethren of the North. A General Convention of the Church was held in Philadelphia in 1865. The Southern Bishops were doubtful of recognition, and sent to inquire in what spirit and on what terms they could resume their seats. Bishop Whittingham sprang to his feet. ' Tell those Bishops,' he cried, ' to come in, and to trust to the love and honour of their brethren !' As they filed in, he greeted the foremost of them with such an embrace as Anglo-Saxon temperaments and manners would permit, and the other Northern Bishops followed his example. No word of politics was spoken, and a threatened schism was averted by the spirit of brotherly love.

Soon after my return to Oxford from travelling on the Continent with Lord Lothian, I received a request from Lord Panmure, afterwards Lord Dalhousie, to travel with his ward, Lord Abercrombie. It was a tempting offer, but it was made upon the condition of my accepting it for five years. I did not feel that I should be justified in doing this unless I resigned my Fellowship, and that involved giving up my Oxford life, which I dearly loved. On my declining it, Lord Panmure asked me to recommend to him a suitable tutor for his ward, saying that, owing to circumstances, he wished him to be a High Churchman, but with no inclination to the Church of Rome. Walking with E. S. Foulkes, Fellow of Jesus College, a few days after receiving Lord Panmure's letter, I mentioned it to him, and he at once asked me to recommend him : ' for,' he said, ' you know nothing could induce me ever to join the Church of Rome.' Mr. Foulkes was appointed,

and went with Lord Abercrombie to Paris. There he
fell in with Archdeacon Robert Isaac Wilberforce, and
by his persuasions, added to a personal disagreement
with Lord Panmure, he forthwith joined the Church
of Rome. At the same time he wrote a pamphlet
stating the cause of his conversion, and saying he
intended to travel in Greece. I sharply reviewed the
pamphlet in the *Christian Remembrancer*, and added
that I hoped that while traversing the Grecian isles
he would be enabled to find the herb ' moly' there
growing, which might restore him to his original
estate. A few years passed and he found his ' moly';
and having duly digested it, he returned to the Church
of England, clothed and in his right mind : for, on
close examination, he saw that the piety and belief of
the Roman Church was inferior in type and in purity
to those of the Church of England. After his return,
he said that one of the points that had much affected
him was the memory of the English parsonage, and
particularly that of Mixbury, with which he was well
acquainted. There he had seen the patriarchal Mr.
Palmer, a man of cultivation and a fine scholar, perfectly contented with the care of his few village sheep
and with training his children to lead noble lives.
Three of his sons he gave to the service of the Church
(William, Edwin, Horsley), and one to the State
(Roundell, Lord Selborne), and his daughters did the
work of Sisters of Mercy, without the title, dress,
or paraphernalia of enrolled Sisters. There was
nothing abroad to compare with such a household :
not the priest's establishment, with its one maid-
servant, a source of scandal not of honour; not the
seminary, which inculcated its petty rules and its cut-
and-dried dogmas, without encouraging thought ; not
the nunnery, into which Liguori allows that the
majority of occupants enter without any call to such a
life ; not the sisterhood, each member of which regards

herself as responsible to her own Superior, instead of
to the parish priests. Another thing that made it
impossible for him to continue in the Roman communion was his knowledge of Church history, acquired
before the duty of looking at the past and present
through none but Vatican spectacles had been felt,
and impossible to be afterwards obliterated. Yet it
requires courage to acknowledge an error, and this
natural cowardice may account for there being so
few footsteps directed back by those who have been
bitterly disappointed at what they found as the goal
of an enthusiastic search. Mr. Foulkes ended his life
as Vicar of St. Mary's, Oxford.

CHAPTER VI

The South of Spain—The Alhambra—Cordova—Seville.

THOUGH unwilling to engage myself for five years, I accepted an offer of the Duke of Buccleuch to travel in Spain with his son, Lord Henry Scott, now Lord Montagu, for some weeks in the spring of 1851. We landed at Gibraltar, and, buying our horses, rode on them by Ronda to Granada, and thence to Cordova and Seville. Arriving at Granada shortly before Easter, I read the prayers of the Church of England for the English residents in that city, by which I exposed myself to the liability of immediate expulsion from Spain. We spent a week at Granada, the greater part of which was devoted to wandering among the halls of the Alhambra. At this time the paint had not been added, which I believe has now been supplied, and I am glad of it. The purpose of the paint is to restore the walls and ceilings to their old appearance, but the faded remnants of colour were far better adapted to produce the impression of dreamy beauty than any restoration could be. The Alhambra must always be the most graceful and beautiful of palaces, but its dreaminess must be lost in its restored brilliancy. Anyone desirous of seeing the patios in their faded glory should turn to the representations of Owen Jones and Murphy; and anyone who would understand the fascinations of the place must read and re-read Washington Irving's *Tales of the Alhambra*.

The Alhambra was the work of the Arab dynasty in its decay; the Mosque of Cordova belongs to an earlier part of their history. This is the strangest, though not the most beautiful, building used for religious worship in Europe.

The space occupied by the mosque is a parallelogram, measuring from north to south 410 feet, and from east to west 440 feet. Above this space stretches a flat roof only 35 feet from the ground, supported by rows of pillars, which divide the 440 feet into nineteen aisles, running from north to south, while the narrower aisles from east to west are no less than thirty-one. Small as is the distance between roof and floor, the horseshoe arches over the aisles are double, the lower arch being a few feet below the upper arch. Like other Mahometan religious buildings, the mosque had a sacred point representing the direction of Mecca, actual or conventional. This was formed at Cordova by an octagon chapel, still remaining, entered by a horseshoe archway, the sides of which are adorned by flashing, glistening mosaic, more brilliant than that of Constantinople, Venice, Rome or Sicily. The mosque was begun in the eighth and finished in the eleventh century.

The date on which I visited Cordova was the month of May, 1851. Exactly a thousand years earlier, and in the same month, there burst out the persecution, in which there suffered those known as the Martyrs of Cordova. The Mozarabs, who lived in the magnificent capital (then containing a million inhabitants) of the splendid Ommiad Caliphs, were tempted to forget their faith and embrace Mahometanism. Two men, Eulogius and Alvar, set themselves to resist this tendency, and under their teaching a sharp feeling of antagonism sprang up between the Arabs and the Christians. The Moslem populace seized two Christians, Perfectus and John, and they were beheaded.

This led to an extraordinary outburst of zeal on the part of the Christians. One and another presented themselves before the Kadi, declared themselves Christians, and reviled Mahomet. They were at once beheaded, and their bodies were tied to stakes planted by the side of the Guadalquivir. Eight bodies were standing together in a ghastly row by the side of the river just a thousand years ago. In the year 851 thirteen martyrs died, in 852 eleven, in 853 six more, and so on. In 857 Eulogius was himself apprehended for concealing a girl converted by him whom the Moslems regarded as a renegade. A friend who was on the Council of Judges besought Eulogius to temporize, promising him safety and future liberty of action. Eulogius smiled, and, putting his friend aside, preached Christianity to the Council. He was beheaded, together with his convert Leocritia. This was the last flash of light that emanated from the Mozarabic Church, soon to be swallowed up by the new Church of Leon and Castile, which superseded and took the place of the old Spanish Church, acknowledging an authority in the Bishop of Rome never till then admitted by Toledo.

I determined before leaving Spain to test some of the peasantry, to learn what they practised and what they believed, remembering at the same time that such a test could not but be inadequate. The subjects which I selected were the Bula de la Cruzada and the worship of St. Mary. The Bula is a square piece of paper emanating from the Pope, and sold to every Spaniard and Spanish woman who will buy it; and its effect is to enable the purchaser to enjoy indulgences (which without it he cannot do), and to excuse him from all fasting except on a few days of the year. The ordinary price of the Bula is 5d. A rich man is charged 7½d., or even 10d. It was calculated that till of late years the Pope and the Spanish Church earned

£200,000 a year by the sale.   The Bula is the joy and
the supposed safeguard of every religious Spaniard.
'Have you got your Bula ?' is the first question asked
by the priest at a death-bed, and to the living it gives
an extraordinary sense of spiritual security.   Cart-
loads arrive every year, and are deposited at various
churches, where they may be bought ; and their
arrival each mid-Lent is celebrated, says Blanco
White, by some curious children's sports, in which
the old Bulas (no longer of use) are made up into hats
for the boys and girls, and they dance round the
figure of an old woman, which represents Lent and is
sawn in two to the cry of ' Saw the old hag asunder !'
('Asserrar la vieja la piccara pelleja !')   The three men
whom I first questioned were Roqué, Nicola, and
José.   The first of these was an ordinary yokel, the
second a shrewd, non-religious man of ordinary intelligence, the third a warm-hearted believer in all
that his priests told him to believe.

'Have you the Bula, Roqué ?'

'No, señor '—with a face showing a consciousness
of neglect.

'Have you the Bula, Nicola ?'

'No, señor ; that is bought by the women more than
the men now.'

'But you can have no benefit from indulgences in
that case.'

'No, señor '—with the most perfect indifference.

'Do you fast on Friday and other fast-days ?'

'No, señor.'

'Are you not bound to do so if you have not the
Bula ?'

'Why, señor, we say if these indulgences and
dispensations are of any avail when we have paid fivepence, or, if we [wanted a double quantity of indulgences, tenpence, they will be of avail without it.   And if
I may eat meat without sin when I have paid fivepence

for a piece of paper, it can be no great sin to eat it whether I have paid the fivepence or not.'

' Have you the Bula, José ?'

'Yes, señor; I bought it at such and such a church for fivepence.'

' And what good will it do you ?'

' I shall be able to get indulgences.'

' And what good will they do you ?'

' They will take me out of purgatory, and make up for my not having done penances.'

' And you don't fast ?'

' No, señor; I have my Bula.'

' Which do you pray to most, José—Our Lord or Our Lady ?'

' As much one as the other, señor.'

' Nicola, to which of the two do Spaniards most commonly pray ?'

' Some to one, some to the other.'

The statements of José and Nicola were singularly moderate. In the last Spanish church that I entered, at Cadiz, I counted the images and pictures that it contained, and found fifteen of Nuestra Señora, five of Nuestro Señor, a very conspicuous one of S. Philomena (a saint made out of a broken stone's inscription and a Jesuit's much-needed interpretation), and several of other saints. The relative number of pictures represented, it seemed to me, the relative number of worshippers of our Lord and our Lady in Spain. Some years ago, when the Carlists were in the ascendant, during the procession of Nuestra Señora de las Angustias to the Cathedral of Granada, cries were raised : ' Viva la santisima Maria, y muerte a todos los dios !' (literally) ' Live the most holy Mary, and death to all the gods !' meaning, ' Hurrah for most holy Mary ! we want none other gods but her.'

' Do those who worship St. Mary count her to be a woman, or something more than a woman ?'

'She is generally considered far above a woman.'

'But,' said José, 'I consider her to be no more than a woman.'

'And yet you pray to her?'

'Si, señor, certainly.'

Another Spaniard, Antonio, was a man who, unlike Nicola, had a bitter hatred of the Spanish Church. Going into a church with me on Good Friday, he said: 'Señor, you will not object to go through the superstitious ceremony of crossing yourself? Do as I do.' He knelt down, crossed himself, and appeared sunk in devotion, and on coming out of the church made a low genuflexion to the altar, knelt down, crossed himself, and retired. 'Did you go through the foolish, superstitious ceremony, señor?' he asked as soon as we were outside. I asked him how he could be guilty of such mockery. 'Ah, señor,' he answered, shrugging his shoulders, 'you do not know Spain. Everybody here must be a *puro Cristiano* — that is, a Roman Catholic—and they dare not express themselves freely. A little while ago they would have been thrown into the dungeons of the Inquisitions. I myself was brought before the Bishop of Malaga because two Englishmen, with whom I was, did not kneel at the Elevation, and no one knows for what he may find himself in the prisons of the State.' This led him on to a denunciation of the lives of the clergy.

The indifference, unbelief, and superstition prevalent throughout Spain point to the necessity of such a reform as that which has been organized under Bishop Cabrera. Already there were indications of the movement connected with the name of Bishop Cabrera, though he himself was, I believe, at this time a student in the Escuelas Pias. Archdeacon Burroughs showed to me two letters written by a Canon of one of the Southern cathedrals praying for the help of the Anglican Church in bringing about reformation.

Being asked to state his demands more definitely, the Canon wrote a letter in Latin, dated October 15, 1851, in which, having first expressed his own faith as being in conformity with the Apostles' and the Nicene Creed and Jewel's *Apology for the Church of England*, he expressed his desire to see 'the true faith of Christ in Spain placed under the powerful shadow and protection of the Anglican Church.' The Spaniards, he said, having only Romanism before their eyes, were losing faith and morals, and sinking into atheism or irregular belief. 'Will you, then,' he wrote, 'associate yourselves together for the work of the Gospel in these regions? Will you in your charity lead this people to the true faith of Christ? Will you recall them from atheism or indifferentism to the Church of God? Establish Evangelical missions and support them with your pious alms. The Romanists labour night and day to propagate their errors; they send their fanatical missionaries round the world, and all sorts of sectaries run eagerly to the work. But ye, who profess the true faith of Christ, will ye leave a thirsty people to perish, and give them naught out of your abundance when they ask? Nay, my most beloved brethren; for if the Lord hath given you five talents, ye will gain five other talents to be good and faithful servants.' The letter ended with a salutation from 'your brethren in captivity' to 'the holy Anglican Church of God,' and begged for the transmission of some of the works of the English reformers for translation, 'that the light of the Gospel may be spread through these regions and prepare the soil for receiving the seed of Truth and Life.' It was not for seventeen years after this time that anyone was allowed by law to profess himself a Protestant in Spain.

On arriving at Seville, I found at the Hôtel la Reina my brother and sister, who had spent two winters in Spain, one winter in an hotel, the other in a *casa de pupilos* (boarding-house), where they met none but Spaniards.

'It is a pity,' I said, 'that I was not able to be here for the Holy Week ceremonies of Seville.'

'Yes,' was the answer — 'as a spectacle to be witnessed for once, but not as a religious ceremony. The week has been a most instructive lesson on the evil of making religion a spectacle of this kind, and we have been heartily disappointed. The cathedral has been crowded, but not with worshippers. The inns and private houses have been full to overflowing, and Holy Week has been the week of the greatest amusement to one class, and of the hardest work to another class, of the whole year. Worse behaviour in church we never saw. The processions are very splendidly arranged, much better than those in Malaga ; but they are mere shows, and the cloak of the Blessed Virgin and the dress of the Nazarenes are discussed just as a gentleman's or lady's dress at a ball. The Nazarene dress in which they walk in procession is a long cap about a yard high, like the old Sanbenito caps, a robe with a train about three yards in length, and a veil over the face.

'On Thursday we saw four processions with nine groups of figures. Good Friday presented the most festival appearance of all. There were processions all day long. The whole population was out in the streets to see them, boys clambering everywhere that they ought not, and being driven down by the police ; men and boys selling nuts and gingerbread and water. There was no ill-temper or quarrelling, and no drinking, except water ; the people seemed to have met to enjoy themselves, and they did it. There was one unfortunate occurrence. A procession bearing the image of Our Lady of Hope fell in with another bearing that of Our Lady of Montserrat, and they fought for precedence. The former gained it, but the fight occasioned a panic in the great square, where there were, it is supposed, 20,000 persons. The Brotherhood of Our Lady of Montserrat, wearing high caps with flaps over the face that blinded them, and long trains that entangled their feet, were quite helpless in the confusion, and went down, we were told by an American, "like ninepins." When order was restored, the Infanta and all the royal party took candles and walked with them to console them. Our Lady of Montserrat had a splendid new robe of blue velvet, and there was a great display of plate all round her.

'We had come down from the steps on which we were standing, intending to go home, when there rose up a clatter of voices round us, chiefly caused by the ecstatic delight of an old woman. "It is the best procession of all, and it has not been out these 118 years." "How many years did you say, señora?" "One hundred and eighteen years. My father lived to be seventy-six, and I am of a good age, and he could remember it when he was a boy; and it comes all the way from Santa Paula, and it won't be back till eleven o'clock at night. It's the best of all! it's the best of all!" When the image came near, she squeezed herself and the man next to her a step higher to make room for us. "Look! look! the Princess, the Princess! And that's the Duke, and that's the Major-domo, and that's the General and all the great people of Seville." When all had passed, our old friend shook hands affectionately, and the last words that we heard from her were, "There never was such a procession!" Really religious people probably keep away from these scenes, and go quietly to their own churches. The images of Our Lord in His sufferings seemed strangely out of place in such a merry, tumultuous company.'

'And what are your experiences as to the religious position St. Mary holds ?'

'On April 11, 1851, we heard a sermon preached in Seville Cathedral, from which the following are extracts:

'"The whole Book of the Lamentations refers to the sorrows of Mary, the Queen of Angels and of the Blessed Sprits ; Mary's sorrows were the greatest in the world. From the time that her Son was born all His sufferings were ever present to her mind, and yet, from her free love and charity for the human race, she willed to offer Him up. The sufferings of Mary were so great that, if they were divided among all the creatures in the world, they would suffice to destroy the existence of all. God, who sent an angel to comfort His Son in His agony, sustained her with His arm, that she might not perish through her sufferings. Her sufferings differed from those of the Martyrs, not only in being more intense, but because they suffered for the salvation of their own souls; she, who was without spot or stain, purely through charity, that she might be the redeemer of the human race. The Martyrs, in their torments, were often supported by consolation from God, which sometimes made their bodily pains appear light to them. She was utterly without it. . . . Under the Law there were two altars near together—that of burnt offering and that of incense. From the one were heard the groans of slaughtered victims, from the other the voice of praise. The first symbolized the cross whereon Jesus was offered, the second the heart of Mary. . . . I will say, with St. Bonaventure, that all that Jesus suffered in all the various parts of His body —all the sufferings were gathered together in one in the heart of Mary. . . ."'

'And the popular books of devotion are of the same character. The book of prayer given by the Archbishop of Santiago de Cuba when holding a mission at Malaga desires that the following prayer to the Most Holy Virgin be said the first thing every morning:

'"O Virgin and Mother of God, I give myself to Thee as Thy child; and for the honour and glory of Thy purity I offer Thee my soul, my body, my powers, and my senses; and I beseech Thee to obtain for me the grace of never committing any deadly sin. Amen, Jesus. *Ave Maria* (three times). My Mother, behold Thy child! My Mother, behold Thy child! My Mother, behold Thy child! In Thee, my sweetest Mother, I have put my trust; I shall never be confounded."'

The Cathedral of Seville was the grandest of any that I saw in Spain, indicating, when compared with the Alhambra (Granada) and the Alcazar (Seville), the superiority of the Gothic to the Moorish race. Opening out of it is the Sagrario to which Blanco White was attached, and connected with it is the beautiful Moorish campanile called the Giralda. On the Sunday that I was at Seville there was a bull-fight, deferred from Easter Day to the following Sunday, and the whole city was alive with excitement. After luncheon I went to the top of the Giralda, and from it had a distant view of the amphitheatre, only part of the arena of which was from thence visible. When I came back from Spain to Oxford, I was telling the story against myself, of having been tempted to the top of the Giralda for such a purpose, when Dean Stanley, who was present, clapped his hands together, and cried out: 'Oh, I am so glad you did that; for I did just the same when I was in Seville, and I have been half ashamed to acknowledge it! It is delightful to find a fellow-transgressor!' From the Giralda the bull-ring presented a singular appearance. Sometimes the bull came bounding into our vision in pursuit of a picador, or chasing an audacious chulo to the side. One bull I saw fall as if by magic under the sword of the matador, which was at that distance invisible, and then the gay team of mules appeared for a moment, and whisked his body from the arena. The usual complement of eight bulls was slain, and from twenty to twenty-five horses were gored to death. The next morning the local papers gave a detailed account of the deaths of the bulls and horses, but, as usual, omitted to mention that two men had been carried out—whether alive or dead none knew, and few cared. There was staying at the Reina, a German who was characterized rather by bluntness of sensibility than by fastidiousness and delicacy of nerves ; he, however, expressed himself quite sickened by the sight of the gored horses. The entrails of one he saw fall out in a mass, after many wounds, to the ground. Another was sinking with the weakness of approaching death, and the picador in consequence got off his back ; but he was at once assailed by the cries of the spectators, who made him remount and push on the poor animal to be gored once more. ' It is in truth a piteous sight to see the poor mangled horses treading out their entrails, and yet gallantly carrying off their riders unhurt ' (Ford). The Infanta and the Duke of Montpensier, as well as the chief people of Seville, were of course present. Indeed, no royal personages could be popular in Spain who discouraged bull-fighting. Mr. Ford states ' that a choice box in the shade, and to the right of the President, is allotted as the seat of honour to the Canons of the cathedral, who attend in clerical costume, and such days are fixed upon for the bull-fight as will not by a long Church service prevent their coming.' At the conclusion of the sport we walked to the amphitheatre to see the matadors, picadors, and chulos come out in their variegated dresses. There was a great crowd covering the space near the doors. Men were crying crayfish claws, water, and other eatables and drinkables, and the merits of the bulls were being eagerly discussed in loud and excited tones.   This was Sunday at Seville.   In the morning many of the shops had been open, and everyday work had been going on.   In the afternoon every thought and every feeling had been swallowed up in the interest of the bull-fight, and the evening appeared given up to cards, billiards, and dominoes in the casinos and cafés.

CHAPTER VII

Oxford—W. E. Gladstone.

ON my return to Oxford I printed the experiences of my brother and sister and myself in a book called *The Practical Working of the Church of Spain.* It was this book by which Bishop Whittingham was interested, as recorded above, and shortly afterwards I was thanked for it by Bishop Blomfield, whom I met at Cuddesdon; and it led to his appointing me one of the Preachers at the Chapel Royal, Whitehall.*

This was the only occasion on which I met Bishop

---

* The same book drew from Dr. v. Döllinger the following letter :

'When the most welcome gift of your book on Spain arrived, I could not write immediately to thank you, for it was on the eve of my leaving town. I have now found leisure to read it through, and the result is that I have rarely met with a book written with such a spirit of thorough fairness and justice, besides its being full of solid information, and such information as I was particularly anxious for. The present disorganized and anarchical state of Spain goes far to confirm your estimate of twenty years ago. I think it is one of the most interesting historical problems—a problem which occupies incessantly my thoughts—by what means and operating causes the moral and political collapse—and, as it were, bankruptcy—of a nation so gifted, and once so prosperous and powerful, has been brought about. Doubtless religious corruptions and a great perversion of moral principles have a great deal to do with this phenomenon.

'With my earnest wishes for your health and my hearty thanks for your kindness,

'Believe me to be, my dear Meyrick,
'Your sincere friend and obedient servant,
'I. DÖLLINGER.'

158

Blomfield, who, as Bishop of London, practically governed the Church of England during the archiepiscopate of Archbishop Howley. To him we owe the use of the surplice instead of the gown in preaching, and also of the stole or scarf. Being asked whether the scarf was not confined to chaplains and dignified clergy, he said, with a twinkle in his eye : 'All my clergy may for this purpose regard themselves as my chaplains.'*

The office of Preacher at Whitehall Chapel, to which Bishop Blomfield nominated me, was in the appointment of the Dean of the Chapels Royal, the deanery being annexed to the bishopric of London. There were at this time two Preachers—one belonging to the University of Oxford, and the other to Cambridge— who held the office of Preacher for two years, each taking a month in turn. My colleague during my first year (1856) was Dr. Atlay, afterwards Bishop of Hereford. Our sermons were delivered in the banqueting-hall of the old Whitehall Palace, which was then used as a royal chapel, and was much attended by members of Parliament and officials connected with it. It was from this hall that King Charles I. passed to the scaffold, which gave a real and personal interest to a sermon preached on the anniversary of his death. *There* he entered the hall ; *there* he was made to mount the stairs. Was that the window through which he passed ? What was the exact position of the scaffold ? We could almost hear his last conversation with Juxon. We could almost see him, as

> ' He nothing little did or mean
> Upon that memorable scene,
> But bowed his comely head
> Down as upon a bed.'

---

* The fact that the stole is unauthorized by law has led to the mistaken belief that the surplice is also unauthorized. The surplice was, in 1566 and 1604, appointed as the legal dress of the clergyman in his ministrations, and the law and canon have never been abrogated.

At Whitehall Chapel I preached a series of sermons on 'The Outcast and Poor of London; or, Our Present Duties towards the Poor,' the title being taken from Psalm lxxii. 4: 'Deliver the outcast and poor.' The subject had at that time hardly been treated either by preachers or philanthropists. Some of the details into which I went were, I believe, regarded as scarcely suitable to the dignity of the pulpit half a century ago. The course began with a statement of the evils to be combated in connection with—(1) the outcast, (2) the criminal, (3) the vicious, (4) the ungodly, (5) the stranger, (6) the poor. Then followed an enumeration of the remedial measures required, temporal and spiritual, the last of which were religion and education, true education being represented as consisting of—(a) intellectual development, (b) moral training, (c) religious teaching, (d) secular instruction. The question of denominational and undenominational education had to be argued then as it has now, and a considerable space was given to the subject.

In order to prepare these sermons, I attended a number of places on Sunday evenings in London where I might gain information about the evils that were to be combated. One of these was a secularist meeting held in the East of London by Mr. G. J. Holyoake. Mr. Holyoake declared himself to be an atheist, but he urged that the name 'secularist' was less unpopular in England than 'atheist,' and, further, that there might be secularists who had not adopted the tenet of atheism. To be a secularist, it was sufficient to ignore everything but this life and its interests. The professed purpose of the sect was, he said, 'to promote free inquiry,' by which was apparently meant infidelity; 'secular education,' which was identified with non-religious instruction; 'rational amusement and general culture,' by which was meant, in particular, the desecration of Sunday. Towards the end of his address Mr. Holyoake, looking towards me (I had gone there in my clerical dress), said it was a very difficult matter to know how to deal with the clergy; they were a learned body—acquainted with Greek, Latin, and Hebrew—and a powerful body. It was dangerous, therefore, to irritate them, and his advice was to conciliate them as far as possible. Already many were unwittingly doing the work of the secularist body by destroying or limiting the religious character of Sunday. As soon as he had sat down, an artisan who was next to me rose quickly to his feet, and said that he didn't see 'why Mr. 'Ollyoake should be so meek and mealy-mouthed towards those clergy. They hated the secularists, and he hated them, and the sooner we got rid of them the better. They were vagabonds.' Another man said that wherever he wanted to go he found the Bible like a dead-wall right ahead of him, and what they had to do was to knock it down. The whole scene was an interesting study of the practical infidelity prevailing among some of the artisan class in London, and it taught its lesson in regard to the light in which both Sunday amusements and the Bible were regarded. The various religious agencies then existing in London were enumerated in the lectures, which ended with sermons on the duty and happiness of doing good to others.

Oxford residents were much occupied during the fifties with the question of University reform. The situation was apparently created in the following manner—such, at least, was the belief in Oxford at the time: Mr. Goldwin Smith, demy of Magdalen, a good scholar, and a man of high ability, offered himself for a Fellowship at Queen's College. He passed the best examination, but he was in possession of a private income greater than that which the statutes of the college allowed its Fellows to hold, and on this

11

ground he was rejected. Being a man of singularly sensitive disposition, and prone to discover a personal injury or insult where none was meant, he was indignant at his rejection, and his feeling was shared by liberal reformers, who never allowed the claims of poverty to stand against those of ability. In a short time an address, signed by Stanley, Goldwin Smith, Jowett, and Lake, was forwarded to Lord John Russell (1850), which induced him to issue 'a Royal Commission to inquire into the state, discipline, studies, and revenues of the University and colleges of Oxford,' and almost every one of the Commissioners was selected from the school of Arnold and Stanley, the last of whom was appointed secretary, with Goldwin Smith as assistant-secretary. The Commission reported, and it at once appeared that the theories of the little knot of Oxford theological liberals, of which A. P. Stanley was interpreter, were to be forced on the University, if the Commissioners should have their way, by the heavy hand of the State. Oxford was to be declericalized and liberalized, and the means by which this was to be effected was mainly the substitution of a University and professorial system of teaching by laymen for tutorial and collegiate training under clergy. To meet the emergency, the Hebdomadal Board (the governing body constituted by Laud, consisting of the Heads of colleges and halls) appointed a committee to receive evidence and suggestions and offer recommendations, and the Masters established a Tutors' Association, which met twice a week to discuss the problems mooted by the University Commission. The report issued by the committee of the Hebdomadal Board, which was now doomed, was a feeble production; but it was supported by a paper of Dr. Pusey's of the utmost value, which deserves to be reprinted: for it was an able argument proving the infinite superiority of the collegiate system, as existing in Oxford and Cambridge, to the system of the German Universities, and it was based upon his own experience. Other Masters of Arts contributed evidence : Professor Hussey, Mr. Osborne Gordon of Christ Church, Professor Freeman, myself, and others. The object of my paper was to show the superiority of college life and discipline to the status of unattached students living separately in lodgings, and to deprecate the swamping of the tutorial by the professorial system.

At the meetings of the Tutors' Association some lively debates took place, in which Dean Mansel, to whom I attached myself, took the more conservative, and Dean Lake (one of those who had signed the petition to Lord John Russell)—who was ever striving to combine Arnold and Newman in himself*—and George Rawlinson of Exeter College, afterwards Canon of Canterbury, the more liberal side.

When the time came for an Act of Parliament to be based upon the report of the Royal Commission, Mr. Gladstone was a member of the Government as well as a member for the University. Mr. Gladstone loved Oxford, and his supporters loved and trusted him. He felt how tenderly the subject had to be treated, and the sympathetic attention that he paid to the suggestions and remonstrances of his constituents was astonishing and amazing. I wrote to him expressing a fear that the professorial and University element would be too predominant under the proposed scheme. At the same time I apologized for occupying his time, without having any claim upon him beyond

* For this reason Mr. Lake was regarded, rightly or wrongly, as a Mr. Facing-both-Ways in Oxford. When he was settled at Durham, he took up the rôle of patron of the Ritualist party in the Northern Province, while still keeping up a close friendship with Archbishop Tait.

that of being one of his constituents. His reply was as follows :

'DOWNING STREET,
'*April* 27, 1853.

'On the one hand, it is my sincere desire that my own opinions and conclusions, such as they are, in matters affecting the welfare of the University, should be completely at the command of every one of my constituents who may be anxious to know them ; while, on the other hand, I should feel the greatest reluctance to obtrude them upon anyone, or even to tender them to anybody acting in or for the University, inasmuch as such a tender must involve more or less of an apparent assumption of authority, which is the very last thing in my thoughts or wishes.

'There is a movement in the House of Commons, and in the public mind outside the University, which might take a direction adverse to its best interests ; and I have considered to the best of my power whether it is possible to give such a direction to that movement as not only to neutralize its dangers, but to make its force available for real good.

'It seems, I must confess, to me, that the recognition of the Professors as an integral part, so to speak, of the teaching and governing body is most important, probably even vital, to any such settlement of the Oxford question as shall secure the place of the University against formidable assaults from without.

'My own opinion is that the exclusively collegiate system which now rules in the University might be modified with great advantage to the vigour and efficiency of the colleges themselves, and that this modification cannot be brought about unless with the adoption of measures which shall give the Professors as such a substantive existence and a sensible weight in the academic sphere.

'I think that if as much as is necessary to fulfil these

terms be now withheld, in all probability the ground might he kept for a few years ; but the question would be found infinitely more difficult to deal with when the decisive time had arrived than it would if it is now opened and closed by a fair arrangement.

'What I have said is not only consistent with, but even flows from, a belief in the inestimable importance of the domestic system of the University, and an earnest desire to see the colleges not only maintain but strengthen their position in everything but the one point of an exclusive character in reference to a professorial system and an effective University organization.

'I write in great haste for to-morrow evening's post, but I know I may trust to your indulgence for all faults, whether of omission or of commission.

'I remain,
'Most sincerely yours,
'W. E. GLADSTONE.'

In a second letter relating to the government of the University, Mr. Gladstone specified five points on which he objected to the proposals of the Hebdomadal Board ; and turning again to the relations between the University and the colleges, he said that the legislative *settlement* of the question of University reform was most important, and that that could not be effected without some relaxation of what was invidiously but intelligibly termed 'the college monopoly,' and that the subjugation of the University to the colleges could not be mitigated while the Heads of the colleges had the exclusive power of initiation.

'I speak,' he said, 'of mitigating and relaxing, not of destroying, because I think the colleges ought to be, and will be, under any sound system the predominating power in the University. But I am convinced that an extra-collegiate competition will do many of them a great deal of good. I am sure you would say that the condition of several of them is not satisfactory, and the circulation of their blood wants quickening.'

At this time I published a letter to Sir William Heathcote, the other member for the University, on *The Clerical Tenure of Fellowships* (1854), deprecating their being laicized on the grounds both of equity and expediency. I sent a copy of it to Mr. Gladstone, and received the following reply:

'I have read the pamphlet you have been so good as to send me, and I confess I do not quite feel able to take the same view, or the same point of view, as yours with reference to the provision of the Oxford Bill respecting the Holy Orders of Fellows. Perhaps I have been hardened and my sight made dull by having received so many remonstrances, some of them from not inconsiderable persons, against the hyperclerical tendencies and effect of the clause in question.

'At the same time I have the utmost pleasure in acknowledging the fairness of spirit, and the absence of any disposition to find fault for the sake of fault-finding, as well as the ingenuity and ability with which you treat the question; and I even cling to the hope that, when the clause shall have been fully sifted by discussion, your fears respecting it may be at least partially mitigated.'

Up to this time the resident Masters of Arts had for the most part been acquiescent in the passing of the Bill, if not favourable to it. But just before it left the House of Commons a clause was introduced, not by Mr. Gladstone nor with his approval, going far to sever the connection between the University and the Church. The clause was proposed by Mr. Heywood, representing the Liberationists, and on the other side Lord Stanley significantly declared that his father, the late Prime Minister, was in favour of it. Under these circumstances the Government accepted the clause and hurried the Bill through the House of Commons. The change in the Bill thus effected came like a bolt from the blue on the Oxford residents. A few Masters of Arts met in my rooms at Trinity College, and determined on a petition against the admission of Dissenters, to be presented by the resident Masters. And a few days later another meeting resolved on a petition from the non-resident Masters of Arts to the same effect, both of them to be addressed to the House of Lords (1854). The manipulation of these petitions was left mainly in my hands.

At the same time I wrote a letter to Mr. Gladstone, from whom I received at once the following most courteous reply :

' DEAR MR. MEYRICK,

'There is not a word in the letter you have addressed to me that could call for the explanations with which you begin and end it. The only regret I have in connection with it, apart from such differences of opinion as it may open, is that its topics are so important that it is not possible for me to do justice either to you or to them in a reply.

'I am deliberately of opinion that Oxford has come off more cheaply with Mr. Heywood's clauses from a most embarrassed question than it could have done had the contest been prolonged. The point for which the Dissenters would have contended would have been, that, leaving theological office to the Church, they should have everything else. The point they have now gained is, that, leaving the whole teaching and governing power to the Church, they have everything else. I cannot think that those are terms inequitable in themselves to the Church in a country where five millions of people go to church on Sunday, and five millions to other places of worship. But the equity of the terms is one thing, and the Parliamentary title to them another. That title I think a serious evil; but I am confident it could hardly have been avoided after the majority of ninety-one—a fact the moment of which, as indicative of a certain state of general opinion, I do not think you sufficiently appreciate. You think the House of Lords would have thrown out the clauses; but let me assure you that what you saw and heard while present on the evening of the debate is a slight foundation to build upon.

'No one can be blind to the fact that Lord Derby conscientiously retains the opinions respecting sub-scription which he expressed long ago. You say truly that his son is not always the organ of his opinions; true, but neither does he always say or intimate that he is. You see Lord Derby did not oppose the admission of Dissenters to the University, such as it now is, but their admission in connection with the private halls, and, more strangely, in con-nection with the speeches of Lord Carlisle and Lord Lyttelton. Under these circumstances it is most doubtful whether the Lords could have been brought to wage war by rejecting the first clause, which had been sent up by a majority of ninety-one. But suppose they had; what would have followed? Simply the loss of the whole Bill; for the Commons would most certainly have refused to acquiesce in the amendment of the Lords, and the Parliamentary consequence of such a state of things is that the Bill drops. Now, with my conviction that the Bill gives a great accession of strength to Oxford, and therefore to the Church, and likewise with the experience we have had of the extreme difficulty of working such a measure through Parliament, I should have felt it a heavier responsibility to bring about the rejection of the Bill than to dismiss it with these clauses appended to it. Even, however, setting aside the evil of losing the Bill as a whole, I think that for the Dissenters' question you would have stood worse; that you would not have had a single year's peace; and that the longer the controversy was continued, the heavier the price to be paid for getting out of it would have been.   The first loss, if it be a loss, is the least.

'With respect to Parliamentary pledges, a Government may bind itself to resign or dissolve rather than allow a particular measure to pass, or, short of this, to oppose it through all stages, or, again, simply to oppose it.   You do not, I think, place our pledge in the first rank, but in the second.   I place it in the third.   I think it was our duty to oppose Mr. Heywood—which we did to the best of our power—and then to act for the best. But we were beaten; what next ?   Certainly, it would have been, not a breach of a particular pledge, but a most gross breach of duty on my part, if I for one had said, " I have now done with the pledge and with the interests of Oxford, and shall act independently of them."   But, on the contrary, my case is, that I did act for the real interests of Oxford, and the Church in Oxford, by adopting what I hope may prove, to say the least, a settlement of the question for no inconsiderable time.

'My own great hope is that Oxford will for her own future peace have a clear and decided opinion, when the time comes for expressing one, upon the Bill, and upon me as much connected with it.

'The Churchman founds, and I think rightly founds, his title to the University and college (I, at least, do not see my way to your distinction between them) endowments and privileges on his belief in the Church.   But suppose for argument's sake ninetenths of the people had left the Church, would the Churchman still be bound to demand exclusive possession for the other tenth ?   I will not attempt to explain; but I think you will see my meaning without more detail.

'On one other point only will I say a word. I think that when in political matters we come to examine what has been the system of concession, which you say (and I doubt not truly) causes so much apprehension, we find these two things: first, that it means in the main continuous adaptation of humanly devised laws and institutions to the varying needs of successive periods; secondly, that it is to such continuous adaptation that this country owes its freedom from revolutionary shocks and the stability of its institutions, as compared with those of countries where Governments have not "conceded." I might add a third, that, when we have been subject to anything like violent change, as in the case of the Reform Bill, it has been mainly due to the blind and uncompromising character of the previous opposition to alterations which reason demanded. I speak here of secular politics, of which I can contemplate the probable course for the future with tranquillity and cheerful hope. As to the politics of religion, the case is far darker; but, then, I must say the dangers and mischiefs which there confront us are not the creations of your kind or mine, but are the growth of periods when concessions were not in fashion, and might all have been avoided, had there been a disposition to do it betimes, at but a small fraction of the price which either you or I would now give, and perhaps vainly give, to escape them.

'I remain,

'Very truly yours,

'W. E. GLADSTONE.'

Mr. Gladstone continued the subject of Concession in a subsequent letter (September 4, 1854).

'There are but two words in your letter which call for an answer from me. The first is one which leads me to say in reply that I do not suppose there ever has been a principle or policy of concession, neither, I conceive, is there now. For the term implies that there is to be concession more or less irrespective of the rightfulness on the one hand, of the sacredness on the other, of the thing conceded. I have nothing to say for such a policy. It is sometimes right to concede a measure which one believes to be inexpedient ; but this must be limited to minor matters, and it would be monstrous in any man to make or keep politics as his profession who felt that proceedings of this kind constituted the staple of his work. But the adjustment of institutions to those measures of social right which vary from age to age with the shifting of the elements that compose society, though it may externally resemble a policy of concession, is, I conceive, a very different thing from it.

'There are many other topics which I pass by because too much would have to be said upon them ; but my second reason for writing was to give you the assurances, which I feared you still seemed to want, that the freedom and unreserve of your observations, so far from being in my eyes a liberty, will always be the more acceptable the further it is carried.

'I remain,

'Most truly yours,

'W. E. GLADSTONE.'

When the Bill was about to be discussed in the House of Lords (July 6 and 7, 1854), I went to London with the petition of the resident Masters, and took it to the house of Lord Derby, who was Chancellor of the University. Lord Derby was very gracious in explaining his views, and gave me an order of admission to the Strangers' Gallery in the House of Lords for the evening. There I found Edwin Palmer, J. G. Talbot, R. Michell, O. Gordon, P. Claughton, etc. The following evening I was introduced into the House, by the side of the Bar, by Arthur Gordon, son of Lord Aberdeen (now Lord Stanmore). The debate lasted till 2 a.m.

Lord Derby moved an amendment on the point of private halls, and, finding himself in a minority, desisted from further attempts. It was whispered that he did not desire an adjournment, because the Liverpool Races were being held the next day, and he was anxious to attend them.

The Bill was thus passed, and the victory of the Oxford Liberals was complete. Virtually or actually, the connection between the Church and the University, as such, was severed. Endowments were transferred from their object—the direct promotion of religion and education—to the maintenance of professional men in their struggle upwards in the world. Fellowships founded specially for the support of the clergy were secularized; the claims of poverty were disregarded; the most influential posts of instruction were transferred, potentially and actually, from clergy to laity; the University and professorial system of teaching was so strengthened and encouraged as almost necessarily to tend towards the degradation and absorption of colleges and college Tutors. The Church party was beaten all along the line. The University of Laud ceased to be, and a new University was started on its course, destined, unless some strong reaction should ensue, to lose more and more the old characteristics of an English University, and to be assimilated more and more to the German model.

The work of 1854 was completed by the University Test Act of 1871, and a final settlement was made in 1877. The results on the religious character of Oxford were bitterly lamented by Bishop Mackarness and Canon Liddon. One consequence has followed, the very opposite to that which was intended by those who assailed Oxford on account of the supposed overstrained religiousness of the clergy formed in its atmosphere. An Oxford in which the college Tutors need be neither clergy nor Churchmen could no longer be trusted as the nursery of the candidates for Holy Orders. It became necessary to establish theological colleges in almost every diocese, and these colleges have a tendency to create a priesthood much more narrow in its sympathies than the larger University, in which laymen and future clergymen associated together on an equality. The nation took away the Universities from the Church as a training sphere for the national clergy, and the Church was obliged to institute diocesan seminaries or colleges to perform the work which the Universities had done, a result which has been good neither for the Church nor for the nation.

The Oxford Architectural Society was at this time an object of considerable attraction to many of us, partly because Professor E. A. Freeman took so much interest in the subject of ecclesiastical architecture, as he showed afterwards by writing a history of architecture, and partly because it was attended by the learned antiquarian J. H. Parker, C.B., and by the eminent architect G. E. Street.

Some of us formed a small society for the purpose of discussing the relation between the Christian faith and the Christian styles of architecture in a manner more esoteric than would have been suitable for a public society. Having exhausted our subjects, or getting tired of them, we determined to bring the society to a close; but it occurred to some of us that the nucleus thus formed might be useful for another purpose. Many young men came up to the University from pious homes and well taught at their schools, who found themselves solitary and lonely in their various colleges, and ran the risk of being absorbed into the idle or noisy set to be found in each college.

It was thought that these men might be gathered up, and that they might find in a body of sympathizing elders a strength to resist the various temptations to which they were exposed. The members, therefore, of the society who were specially interested in architecture withdrew, and the others set out on their new quest. There was some difficulty in organizing the new plan, and I was requested to ask Dr. Pusey for his advice. Dr. Pusey was at this time engaged in the institution and establishment of sisterhoods, and he grasped at this application, which he thought might be utilized for the institution of brotherhoods also. But that was not our purpose. Full of the notion that he had taken up, Dr. Pusey first proposed that the members of the new body should make a rule of always walking with their eyes turned to the ground, to avoid temptations and as a mark of humility. I said that I thought that such a practice was not natural for young men, nor good for them. Instead, Dr. Pusey suggested that as a mark of membership we should all wear round our loins a girdle of flannel or other material as a token of self-restraint. 'And then,' said Basil Jones demurely, to whom I recounted the interview, 'you will no doubt call yourselves the Worshipful Society of Girdlers.' We did not adopt either of Dr. Pusey's proposals, but we accepted, on his recommendation, the name of the Brotherhood of the Holy Trinity and some simple suggestions which might help us towards a good life, such as that we should rise early, use prayer, public and private, be moderate in food and drink, and avoid speaking evil of others. Some of us used to meet once a week in one another's rooms and say the Penitential Psalms, partly as a religious exercise, partly to make better acquaintance with the young men who joined us. And some during Lent had their breakfast before the chapel service, which was at half-past seven. But these things were purely voluntary; there was no moral compulsion on any one to do them, nothing wrong if they were not done. Time passed, and some of the members were not contented with anything so vague; they wanted rules, not suggestions. If I recollect right, the chief mover in this direction was R. M. Benson, afterwards of Cowley, and he was supported by H. P. Liddon. I opposed, saying that principles were better guides to the conscience than rules. Reference was made to Dr. Pusey again. He proposed a compromise: there should not be rules, but only rules-to-be-aimed-at, and these should not be binding on any except such as definitely adopted them, the other members remaining as before. A year or two passed, and then the greater number of those that had adopted the rules acknowledged that they had made a mistake. Instead of engaging to rise early, they had bound themselves to a definite hour, such as half-past six; instead of prayer, they had to say specified prayers at specified hours; instead of moderation in food, they were to drink only one glass of wine and have so many helpings at meals, eating nothing at other times. Those who were observing these rules felt that they were dragging behind them through life a load which God had not bound round their necks, and those who failed to observe them felt that they were making sin where God had not made it. The brotherhood reunited on its old basis. But after this time I did not for long take an active part in it, and whether it exists still, and if so in what shape, I know not.

CHAPTER VIII

IN 1853 the experiences of myself and my brother
(Michel Fellow of Queen's College, Oxford) in 1850
and 1851, in France, Italy, Germany, Switzerland, and
Spain, bore fruit in the institution of the Anglo-Continental Society. We had found that throughout the
Continent of Europe, and specially in Spain, there
was a yearning for something better, something more
spiritual, than the modern Church of Rome could
supply; and a profound ignorance of the position
occupied in Christendom by the Anglican communion.
We had found the Church of England, sometimes
ignorantly, sometimes wilfully, misrepresented in all
the countries where the Papal Church had sway, as
consisting of an unorganized mob, a mob with no
definite faith, held together by the authority of the
English Sovereign, who was the Anglican Pope,
and legislated for by Parliament; and the belief
was general that it had been set up in England by
Henry VIII. in place of the Catholic Church, because
the latter would not allow him to put away one wife
and take another. Many Continental Churchmen,
especially in Spain, were dimly aware that they were
floundering in a bog of superstition and falsehood;
but how could they distinguish true from false? A
large proportion could not read at all; if they could

176

read, they had no Scriptures to serve as a standard of truth. Many of the clergy were men maintaining an institution from which they derived their bread; a few, more enlightened, and therefore discontented with their position, were seeking for better things. The example given by the English service at Gibraltar, where Archdeacon Burroughs was officiating as chaplain, served to inspire some of the clergy and the laity in Spain with a hope of reformation on the model, and with the help, of the Anglican Church.

I have already mentioned two pathetic letters of a Spanish Canon, exhibiting his desire for more light and truth. 'I believe,' he said, 'that there is no propaganda in the Anglican Church, and little anxiety to lead other Christian nations which groan under the errors of Popery, to abjure them and to breathe the pure air of evangelic truth and primitive Christianity. But I desire to make myself well acquainted with the doctrines of your Church in order to be one day useful to my country.' It was hard to resist such an appeal as his, and it seemed highly desirable both for the sake of foreign Christians, who, in the Canon's words, were 'losing their faith and morals and sinking into atheism,' and also for the sake of clearing away misrepresentations of the character of the English Church, to take measures to exhibit the faith of the latter, and to show to the former that there was a catholicity which was not Papal. No programme of the Anglo-Continental Society was at first published, but Bishop Cosin's Latin work on *The Religion, Discipline, and Rites of the English Church* was republished as a pamphlet and sent to a certain number of people in England, with a circular stating that it was intended to publish similar works, illustrative of the doctrines, discipline, and constitution of the Anglican Church, which might attract the attention of members of other branches of the Church, and have such effect upon

12

their minds as it was natural and right that they should produce. Among those who responded warmly to the proposal were : Bishop Samuel Wilberforce, Bishop Charles Wordsworth, the Rev. T. L. Claughton (afterwards Bishop of St. Albans), A. C. Coxe (afterwards Bishop of Western New York), G. Moberly (afterwards Bishop of Salisbury), Christopher Wordsworth (afterwards Bishop of Lincoln), Basil Jones (afterwards Bishop of St. David's), W. E. Gladstone, Lord Robert Cecil (Lord Salisbury), Lord Charles Hervey, A. J. Beresford-Hope, J. G. Hubbard (Lord Addington), Sir William Heathcote, William Gibbs, John Keble, F. C. Massingberd, Roundell Palmer (Lord Selborne). The first occupation of the society was the preparation of short treatises for use in various languages, and its objects were declared to be three :

1. To make the principles of the English Church known in the different countries of Europe and throughout the world by means of the publication and dissemination of books and tracts illustrative of the doctrines, discipline, status, and religious spirit of the English Church, and of the character of her Reformation.

2. To help forward the internal reformation of National Churches and other religious communities by spreading information within them rather than by proselytizing from them.

3. To save men whose religious convictions were already unsettled from drifting into infidelity, by exhibiting to them a purified Christianity which they might be able to embrace.

I was secretary of this society for forty-six years, my colleagues being successively Dr. Godfray, Lord Charles Hervey, Archdeacon Huxtable, and Mr. S. Oldham. My acquaintance with Dr. Godfray was made in a singular manner. I had travelled down from Scotland during the night in order to record that vote for Mr. Gladstone which gave offence to Lord Robert Cecil (p. 88).   During the same night Dr. Godfray had been travelling up from the Channel Islands for a like purpose.   We met in the early morning, about five o'clock, in a little inn near Paddington (there was then no station hotel), where we waited for the first train to Oxford.   Finding that we were both Oxford men and bent on the same course, we joined company at a breakfast or supper, whichever it might be, not knowing each other's names.   During the meal Dr. Godfray said to me : ' Have you seen a valuable book lately published by a Fellow of Trinity College, called *The Practical Working of the Church of Spain ?*   The writer's name is Meyrick.'   I acknowledged the authorship, and found that he was deeply interested in the state of religion on the Continent, specially in France, of which he knew most.   Here was just the man that I wanted for my brother secretary, the more as, being Jersey-born, he talked French as freely as English ; and not only that, but was also a good classical French scholar, who could translate from Latin or English into the best French. We worked heartily together till his death.

Another very valuable brother secretary was Lord Charles A. Hervey, Rector of Chesterford, a parish previously held by Bishop Blomfield,* in the neighbourhood of Cambridge, and brother of Lord Arthur Hervey, Bishop of Bath and Wells.

Lord Charles's health not being very good, he was obliged to spend a considerable part of his time in

---

* Bishop Blomfield passed from the rectory of Chesterford to that of Bishopsgate, and he then became Bishop of Chester.   Hence the lines :

'From Chesterford to Bishopsgate
  Did Charles James Blomfield wade ;
Then, leaving Ford and Gate behind,
  He's Chester's Bishop made.'

travelling. In the West Indies, in Egypt, in Honolulu, at the Cape, in North America, in South America, as well as in France, Italy, Malta, Switzerland, he exerted himself to spread a knowledge of the true principles of the Church of England. He was specially interested in the question of Catholic reform by his experiences in Malta, whence he returned in 1844, accompanied by Dr. Camilleri, a priest in Italian Orders, afterwards incumbent of Lyford, near Wantage, who died in 1903. Lord Charles Hervey was a typical representative of a small class of clergymen found in the English Church, which it is to be hoped that the English Church will never be without. Equal in secular rank to the highest in the land, and able thereby to gain a hearing for his Master's cause in houses not always accessible to clerical influence, he made himself the equal of the humblest of his brethren in the ministry of the Church without effort or anything approaching to ostentatious stooping. It has been said that a titled class is a good for the nation at large, earned at the expense of the titled class itself. He was one of the few that are utterly unharmed by the distinctions of the world or by that consciousness of belonging to a caste, sometimes cherished as a poison-root in the hearts of men and women too proud or too well-mannered to allow such a feeling ever to be exhibited. An earnest and hard-working parish clergyman, a genial companion, an unswervingly loyal friend, an accomplished linguist, a scholar and a theologian, a sound and devout Churchman of the old Anglican type, without a leaning either Romewards or towards Puritanism, he passed away in 1880, leaving a wide space vacant. He was succeeded in the secretaryship by Archdeacon Huxtable.

The society occupied itself during its first six or seven years in publishing tracts or pamphlets which might serve to show foreigners the character of the

Church of England, and incidentally to suggest the desirableness of internal reform, in the Unreformed communities, on the model of the primitive Church. During these years thirty such pamphlets were issued in Latin, French, Italian, Spanish, Portuguese, German, modern Greek, Armenian ; the total number published by the society was nearly 200.   At the same time correspondence was entered into with residents in France and Italy who were interested in the subject of reform.   There were still remains of Gallicanism to be found in France, though, in fact, there is no stand-ing-ground for Gallicans in the new French Church which was created by Napoleon in the first year of the last century.   The old traditions still lingered, and held together a small body of men who would not accept the Papal autocracy.   Montalembert had a small school of followers ; Laborde, Prompsault, and Wallon protested against the dogma of the Immaculate Con-ception ;   Garcin   de   Tassy, a learned Orientalist, represented the old Gallican School in its best form ; Père Hyacinthe and Père Gratry had not broken with the National Church, but were showing themselves powerful opponents of Ultramontanism.

Intercommunication soon arose between Anglican and Gallican Churchmen.   In 1856 l'Abbé Guettée instituted the *Observateur Catholique,* and a few years afterwards   the   *Union   Chrétienne.*   In   these   two periodicals he gladly welcomed letters and papers written by Anglican Churchmen, and, acting for the society, I took advantage of his goodwill to present the position and the doctrines of the Anglican Church to his readers.   Guettée commented on these con-tributions, and on the letters which were written in opposition to them, in a spirit of most perfect fairness. He also published a valuable history of the Church and a history of the Jesuits.   But how were these books to be sold ? and how were the periodicals to be maintained ? With few exceptions, French ecclesiastics were now Ultramontane ; Guettée had been condemned by Bishop after Bishop for his Gallicanism, which they denounced as something approaching to, and equally bad with, Protestantism. Guettée had no private income or fixed ecclesiastical provision, and the circulation of his writings was prohibited by authority. Any priest known to subscribe to or to receive copies of his periodicals became a marked man ; and for a priest to become a marked man in France, where, with comparatively few exceptions, the Bishop's power over him is despotic, is ruin. How was Guettée to live ? 'We could have his services,' said Dr. Godfray, 'for £100 a year.' But it is not a practice of the English Church or of English societies to subsidize writers in such a case. It is, I believe, the practice of the Russian Church. However that may be, Guettée found it necessary, or thought it right, to join the Russian Church, and, taking his plunge, he came up as M. Wladimir Guettée. From this time the character of the *Union Chrétienne* was entirely changed. M. Guettée showed himself irritated with Anglicans, and bitterly hostile to the Anglican Church, while everything in the Oriental Church was perfect. Nevertheless, the leavening of the French clerical mind had continued for many years, and was not without its effect. Bread cast upon the waters is not to be found till after many days.

For Italy I entered into communication with Count Ottavio Tasca. This patriotic nobleman, having his residence in the North of Italy, was driven from home and country by the Austrian Occupation, to which he would not submit. Twice he narrowly escaped with his life. Once his palazzo was attacked by the Austrian troops, and he was saved by a party of Garibaldian volunteers who arrived at the nick of time. Another time he was pursued by Austrian soldiers to the Lake

of Como, whence he fled on foot across the Swiss
border. He suffered exile for ten years while his
house and patrimony were wasted by the enemy. He
chose Hyères for his place of exile, and there he was
fortunate enough to meet, season after season, English
families, from whom he received sympathy which
ripened into friendship. He used in after-years to
tell how much he was impressed by the influence which
religion appeared to exercise over their lives ; they
seemed not only to accept dogmas, but to believe
truths. Then he inquired into the nature of their
religion, and found that their faith was simple and
reasonable, and such as he could embrace, especially
as that did not involve subjection to the Curia and
the Pope, whom he regarded as the enemies of his
Sovereign. One of the Englishmen with whom he
associated was Mr. R. F. Wilson, Mr. Keble's curate,
who was at Hyères for his wife's health. Mr. Wilson
wrote to me asking if I could not give the Count some
translation work to do, as he could derive nothing
from his estates. I at once sent him a pamphlet,
Papal Supremacy tested by Antiquity, to translate, which
he gladly undertook to do. He was at this time reduced to such straits that he could not find stamps for
his letters—a very great distress to a proud and free-
handed gentleman. This was the first of sixteen translations which the Count made for the society at my
request, two of which were a volume of hymns and
some extracts from Keble's *Christian Year*, for he was
a poet as well as a prose-writer. He also had the
Italian gift or art of improvising. On his return to
his ruined home, he was appointed by the Italian
Government superintendent of the hospitals in Lombardy during the war of 1859. Besides attending to
the bodily wants of the sick and wounded, he supplied
them freely with New Testaments or small portions
of Holy Scripture, and prepared a simple uncontrover-

sial manual of soldiers' prayers, taken partly from the English Prayer-Book. The Bishop of Bergamo, hearing of this, wrote to the Minister of War complaining of his proselytism. The Minister asked the Count for an explanation, and, on receiving it, assured him that there was nothing which any good Catholic or patriot could object to in his action, and encouraged him to persevere. The Count possessed many decorations, among which the most valued was the Commander's Cross of the Order of SS. Maurizio and Lazarus, as showing the favour of his Sovereign and being a record of his services to his country. In his last illness, Mr. W. C. Langdon, a presbyter of the American Church, administered the last rites to him, and for this reason, as well as his general character for heresy, the Bishop of Bergamo forbade his body being taken into the church ; but the whole population of the place and neighbourhood thronged to his house to do him honour, and accompanied his funeral procession to the cemetery.

In Spain the Rev. J. B. Cabrera, while still an exile at Gibraltar, translated into Spanish Bishop Cosin's work on the English Church, and at a later date Bishop Harold Browne's *Exposition of the Articles.* Preparation was thus made for active exertion in different countries when the due time should have come ; and this came—for Italy in 1861, for Spain in 1867, for Germany in 1871, and for France in 1878.

CHAPTER IX

Ireland—Irish Church missions—Inquiry classes—Maynooth.

DURING one of my vacations in 1854, I visited Ireland for the purpose of seeing with my own eyes what was the effect of the Irish Church missions, as conducted specially in Connemara. I first went to Dublin, and there I attended the discussion or inquiry classes, which were open to all that pleased to come, and those that came were allowed to ask any questions on religious matters or discuss subjects previously appointed. There were three such classes held weekly. The first that I went to was conducted by Mr. McGuigham; there were about fifty persons present, and the subject was, 'Is Confirmation a Sacrament?' After the exposition of a psalm, and a prayer, the chairman called on a Mr. Barrey to speak. But before he could begin, one of those present insisted on rediscussing last week's subject. 'Sit down,' said the chairman—'sit down, or go out.' Then, as the interruption continued, 'Take that man by the shoulder and put him out, or send for a policeman.' Someone went for a policeman, on which the disorderly speaker stalked out. Then Mr. Barrey began. He would prove his point on Roman Catholic testimony; then he read a passage from Dr. Doyle saying that there were three conditions necessary for a Sacrament—the outward part, the inward grace, the institution by Christ. But there was no such institution of Confirmation recorded. Further, the form used at present by the Church of Rome for the rite was novel. He spoke for a quarter of an hour, which was the limit for each speech. He was followed by an angry Roman Catholic, named Flood, who spent his quarter of an hour in abusing the previous speaker. What did he know about it ? At what University had he graduated ? By whom had he been ordained ? The speaker would defend the Catholic Church against him. Next came a fierce Protestant ; then another on the Protestant side ; then another on the Romanist side. After that came speeches of five minutes. The last Romanist speaker justified the present Roman usage on the principle of development. The Romanist who had spoken first did not approve of this, and exclaimed that the other did not know what he was talking about. At the conclusion the chairman said he wished to explain to his Roman Catholic friends that we held Baptism, Holy Communion, and Confirmation as much as they did, but we said that ours was the true, and theirs a corrupted, doctrine about them. He then proposed to end with a prayer. 'If ye would pray to the Blessed Virgin,' cried Mr. Flood, 'I would stay.' As he moved off, the chairman said good-humouredly : 'She is a great deal better employed than in listening to us.' He then said a simple prayer, and the meeting broke up in the most quiet and orderly manner possible.

On another occasion the question was, How to use Scripture so as to understand it. The first said, 'By reading it'; the second said, 'When I was a boy, the way in which I found out whether a potato was good or not was by asking my mother. If she told me 'twas good, I ate it ; and if she said it was bad, I threw it away ; and so I do now what my mother tells me.' 'And how do you know what Mother Church says ?' 'By asking the priest.' 'And what do you say ?' said the chairman to a third. 'I am an unlearned man, but

I can understand what you read me out of the Scriptures.' 'And you ?' This man read the verse from the Acts, 'How shall I understand without someone to teach me ?' This delighted the first speaker on the Roman Catholic side, and he winked at me, as much as to say that that was incontrovertible. 'And you ?' said the chairman to a young woman. 'By asking the help of God's Holy Spirit.' 'Well, boys,' said Mr. McGuigham, 'that's not a bad plan, neither; and do you recollect a text about that ?' '"How much more shall your Heavenly Father give the Holy Spirit to them that ask Him ?"' said two or three at once. Here the class abruptly came to an end, as it was nearly church time.

Similar inquiry classes were held in Galway. I attended one a week later. There were about seventy present. The first question asked was, 'How can you prove that the Bible is God's Word ?' Mr. Brownrigg, the chairman, answered: 'By external and internal testimony and the agreement of all Churches.' 'But I want you to prove it from the Bible.' 'If you mean that you want a text showing the value of the Holy Scriptures, you may take that addressed by St. Paul to Timothy, "From a child thou hast known the Holy Scriptures, which are able to make thee wise unto salvation. All Scripture is given by inspiration of God, and is profitable for doctrine, for reproof, for correction, for instruction in righteousness" (2 Tim. iii. 15). And our Lord recognised the Old Testament as the Word of God.' Then came the inquiry, 'When did the Protestant Church begin ?' To which Mr. Brownrigg answered: 'When Christianity was first preached in Ireland by St. Patrick.' 'But St. Patrick was not a Protestant.' 'No; because the false doctrines against which protest is made had not then come into existence. But he held the faith which Protestants now hold, and not that which Roman Catholics hold.

To be a Catholic is one thing, and to be a Roman Catholic is another. When Catholicism became corrupted into Roman Catholicism, it was necessary for right believers to be Protestant against Romanism.'

The boys were as quick-witted and forward as the men. In the mission-house at Galway I examined about sixty boys and girls in the Creed. When we got to the Resurrection of the Body, one of the boys asked where the soul was before it was reunited to the body. I replied that that had not been fully declared in Scripture. 'Sure, they are in Purgatory,' shouted the boys together. 'The penitent thief went to Paradise,' I said. They thought that he would have been excused, but that all others must go to Purgatory, 'because there was no other place for them to go to.' 'And how do you know that there is such a place as Purgatory?' 'Because the Church says so.' 'And how do you know that the Church says so?' 'Because the priest says so.' 'And who told the priest?' 'The Bishop told him.' 'And who told the Bishop?' 'I think,' said one voice, 'that the Pope told him.' 'And who told the Pope?' The Pope had not yet been made infallible by the Jesuits, and Dr. Manning and Mr. Odo Russell at the Vatican Council, so there was silence. Fifteen years afterwards they would not have been at a loss for an answer.

I heard another application of the text relating to the penitent thief in a controversial class held by Mr. McCarthy in Dublin, at which about 700 persons were present. Did not the thief on the cross, inquired a Roman Catholic, have to suffer punishment for his sins, though the guilt was forgiven him, and so must not everyone suffer for sin either by penance in this life or by Purgatory in the life to come? Mr. McCarthy replied that he suffered by the law of the land because he had transgressed its precepts, but that in the sight of God he was wholly forgiven on his penitence. At the same class another asked how the chairman knew that the Bible was God's Word at all.   As the inquirer was a Roman Catholic, Mr. McCarthy replied with an *argumentum ad hominem* by reading the anathema of the Council of Trent on all who denied it.

At Maynooth I had some conversation with the Dean of the college, Dr. Gaffney.   He said that Newman's book on development was written before he was a Catholic, and was disallowed by the Church.   The Immaculate Conception (which had in that year been adopted at Rome) was not to be proved by Newman's doctrine of development, but had always been held in the Church.

'By St. Bernard, for instance ?' I said.

'What St. Bernard objected to,' he replied, 'was the institution of a festival by the Church of Lyons; but that was only because it had not the sanction of Rome in doing so.'

'But,' I said, 'St. Bernard gives his reason for objecting, and it is not that.'

'Ah, well, it has always been held;' and he began turning over his Breviary to find some quotations on the subject.

'But is not the extract from St. Augustine, as well as many other passages in the Breviary, spurious ?'

'Ah, that is true,' he replied; 'but it is so difficult to get anything altered in the Breviary, because there are so many copies printed.'

'But have there not been several editions of the Breviary ?'

'Some, but not many.

He told me that there were at Maynooth twenty Professors and upwards of 500 students.   Their manual of dogmatic theology was Perrone's *Prælections*, and of moral theology Scavini's, Rome having condemned Bailly on account of his Gallicanism, and Scavini being based entirely on St. Alfonso de' Liguori.   Gallicanism

was, happily, now superseded in France by Ultramontane or Roman sentiments. He had himself been
at St. Sulpice for several years, and he believed Louis
Napoleon to have become deeply pious, and to be an
instrument in God's hands for the strengthening of the
Church in France. In Austria, too, the young Emperor
was much more friendly to Rome than his predecessor,
who would not allow the Austrian Bishops to go to
Rome for the canonization of Liguori. He walked
with me through the new, handsome quadrangle of
the college, and we parted at the gate on very friendly
terms.

A few days later I went to the Galway Queen's
College. There were fourteen Professors there, five
of whom were Roman Catholics. The students were
about seventy in number, of whom forty-five were
Roman Catholics. The Pope had condemned the
college, and therefore none but laymen could be now
Professors there. Two of the Roman Catholic Professors gave up their post by the command of Archbishop McHale when the Pope condemned the colleges.

I had witnessed the very irreverent manner in
which the poor are buried, after their bodies have left
the church, in Spain and in the South of Italy. In
Spain they are laid in a long shallow trench, passing
from one side of the cemetery to the other, without
coffin and without any words of prayer; and in
Naples they are put out of sight in a very perfunctory
manner in a vast receptacle for corpses.* Seeing a

---

* 'The Campo Santo here (Seville) is rather more untidy than that
at Malaga, but in all material respects much the same—a large square
space surrounded with four high walls, in the width of which are the
niches for the dead, rising in tiers one above another ; the centre
space all coarse broken ground, and overgrown with nettles. We
passed through the first court into a second, and there I expected to
see the coffin placed in one of the niches and walled in ; but no,
there was a wide, shallow trench running all across this interior
square, which seemed to be filled up about halfway. A couple of

funeral pass in Galway, I followed to witness the
Irish method of burial. It was not revolting like the
Spanish method, but it was more singular. The gate
of the cemetery is generally kept fastened, but when
a funeral takes place the entrance is open to anyone.
There were as many as fifty or sixty women following
the coffin on the present occasion in a somewhat disorderly manner. As soon as the gate was unlocked,
they spread themselves about the churchyard, throwing themselves down upon the tombs of their relatives.
Then they half lifted themselves, and, bending their
bodies backwards and forwards, raised the 'Irish howl.'
At first they exhibited no real grief, but soon the
physical exercise produced a corresponding feeling, and
they began to pour forth real and bitter tears, crying
all the time at the tops of their voices with a not
unmelodious cadence, sometimes beating the stone or
the ground with their hands and sometimes kissing
it, and again bursting out with an astonishing volume
of sound.

The churchyard was kept very negligently, so that
many of them seemed to be sitting in the nettles.
While I was looking at one party, an unusually loud

---

men were beckoned to the spot, who came with their hoes and hooked
out a little place about a foot deep in the loose ground ; the coffin
was then opened, and the body taken out and laid in the hole. The
sexton took the pillow that had laid under its head, and tore it into
rags and spread it over the face of the corpse, while his companion
threw a few basketfuls of earth, and then jumped down himself and
trod it in. I had stood close by, and watched the whole proceeding
up to this point with a kind of creeping horror ; but now I could bear
it no more—it was literally treading on the corpse's face. I turned
away and left, and the others followed me. I had been present the
whole time ; I heard no voice of prayer, and saw no sign of it, except
that for a moment, as the corpse was laid in the ground, the attendants
took off their hats. "And this," I said to myself, as I walked slowly
home and watched the evening shadows come over the meadow—"this
is the burial of Christ's poor in Catholic Spain" (*Practical Working
of the Church of Spain*, p. 241).

cry would call my attention to another spot, where
nothing could be seen but a red gown prostrate among
the nettles. Sometimes there was a chorus of yells
throughout the churchyard. The burial was performed in a very slovenly way. The grave was very
shallow, and I counted six skulls, which had been
thrown out and were lying by the side, besides
numberless bones. A friar came and sprinkled the
coffin with holy-water, and read the Latin prayers
over it as soon as the nearest woman had been
hushed a little, so that his voice could be heard; the
body was then laid in the grave, and the men standing
round kicked in the bones and the skulls, most of
which broke as they fell; two people with spades
tossed in the mould, and the old stone was put on
again, the only difference being that it stood a little
higher. Meantime the women continued their exercise, and I went round and watched them closely, at
which some cried the louder, though some were so
much engrossed with the grief into which they had
worked themselves as to notice no one. In about an
hour the cemetery was again silent.

As I came out from the churchyard, two men, of the
shopkeeper class, showed me the neighbouring Fran-
ciscan church, and entered into conversation. I put
to them a question which I have put to any Irishman
to whom I had the opportunity of speaking on the
subject, 'What is an indulgence?' Never once did I
find the slightest apprehension of the subtlety that
the temporal punishment of sin is forgiven by an indulgence as distinct from its guilt and eternal punishment. 'It is having our sins forgiven if we have right
dispositions and do what the Church orders us.' 'What
is the difference between a plenary indulgence and
an indulgence for forty days?' They had not the
least idea; one hazarded the answer that, if you did
what you should, the sins which you had committed

during the last forty days were forgiven in the latter
case, and during your whole life in the former.
Indulgences also got people out of Purgatory, and
the existence of Purgatory could be proved from
Scripture. 'Indeed! how?' 'Blasphemy against the
Holy Ghost should not be forgiven in this world or
in the world to come, but so as by fire.' I told him
that the first part of the text came from the Gospels,
and the last from the Epistles. 'Ah, but it was
understood in the Gospels.' I advised him to read
his Bible more carefully. The other then burst in:
'I would not give my old coat for the Bible and all
that's in it.' I pointed out to him gravely the pro-
fanity of the words he had used, and said that I was
sure that if he had a Bible he would never say such
a thing. Of course he had none.

Passing through the street on my return, I heard
a characteristically Irish conversation between two
old women. 'He tells me my house is dirty,' moaned
one to the other, 'and, sure, there is the little pig;
and will I turn him out into the street?' 'No, indeed,'
said the other.

At Clifden, which was the centre of the Connemara
movement, I made acquaintance with Mr. D'Arcy,
a kind, white-headed old man, to whom the Irish
missions owe much.

The D'Arcys once owned a large house called the
Castle, which has now passed from their hands. Close
by it was another house, which my guide told me was
called a 'rabbit-warren,' because there were so many
jumpers (converts) going in and out of it at all times.
The priest, he said, always curses it as he passes.

'And whom does he curse?'

'The housekeeper!'

'And does he curse him in the church, too?'

'Yes, almost every Sunday.'

'At what time?'

13

'After Mass.'

'What does he say ?'

'He curses the people in the house, and tells us not to speak to them.'

'What good does the curse do ?'

'Troth, and I don't think it does much good !'

'And do the people avoid speaking to them ?'

'In faith, they don't !'

This sort of social excommunication, however, became a very real thing, and was the foundation of the system of boycotting.

Shortly afterwards Mr. Goodisson, the clergyman of Ballynakill, gave me an illustration of the cursing system prevailing in Ireland : 'Last week the Roman priest had gone to an old woman's field and desired his man to take a tithe of the corn. The old woman went down upon her knees and cursed anyone who should take it. The priest had a stick in his hand, and struck her over the shoulders with it, making bruises, which she afterwards publicly exhibited. As she went on declaiming, he told her that if she was not quiet he would 'wipe off his feet against her.' This meant that he would wipe his feet along the ground against her, which was the same thing as shaking off the dust of his feet against her. She again went down on her knees, and prayed that any evil that might come of it might fall upon his head, and not hers. It happened that an accident befell the priest when he was returning, which caused much talk in the place.

At Clifden I witnessed for the first time a public recitation of the *Ave Maria*. There was a congregation of about twenty-four, and three priests were kneeling on the altar-step. They divided themselves into two sections, the first of which recited 'Hail, Mary, full of grace ; blessed art thou among women, and blessed is the fruit of thy womb, Jesus.' The other half continued the modern addition, 'Holy Mary, Mother of God, pray for us now and at the hour of death.' This was said ten times in succession. Then came the 'Our Father,' divided in half in the same way; then ten more 'Hail, Marys'; then the 'Glory be to the Father,' divided in half; after which again ten more 'Hail, Marys.' The rosary being concluded, there followed a litany, in which the name of some saint was read by one of the priests, and the whole congregation responded, 'Pray for us.'

The general charge against the Irish missions in Connemara was that they did not teach a positive Christianity, but only a negation of Romanism. I went to many churches in the neighbourhood of Clifden, and at Clifden itself, and I found that this charge was not justified by the character of the sermons preached and by the instruction given. Several orphan institutions had been established for the children of those who had died in the late famine. I examined the girls in the orphan house at Clifden, to see what the character of their positive teaching was.

'What religion were they of ?'
'The Christian religion.'
'Why are we called Christians ?'
'Because we trust in Christ.'
'Are we Catholics ?'
'Yes.'
'Do we hold the Catholic faith ?'
'Yes.'
'Where is that to be found ?'
'In the Bible.'
'And where its chief articles ?'
'In the Creed.'
'How many creeds are there ?'
'Three.'
'What are they ?'

'The Apostles' Creed, the Nicene Creed, and the Athanasian Creed.'

'Is it right to speak of Roman Catholics as the Catholics ?'

'No.'

'Why not ?'

'Because they are Roman Catholics.'

I then examined them in the books of the Bible and their chief contents, in which they showed themselves very well informed. At the end I said :

'Can you tell me what is the chief doctrine of Christianity ?'

There was a pause, and then one of them answered: 'Jesus Christ, and He crucified.'

They then sang an Irish hymn. It was a touching and interesting sight. Here were forty-five girls who would have been in the workhouse, or living like other children in Ireland, 'with the pigs' and half naked, who were clothed, gentle-mannered, well taught, behaving as Christians and almost as ladies. There was an orphan institution for boys also, of whom there were thirty-eight. The two orphan schools together cost £100 a year. When the children are grown up they go out to service.

I came away from Connemara with the conviction that a thoroughly good work had been done and was doing there. Before leaving Ireland I paid a visit to St. Columba's College, which owes its existence to Dr. Sewell, and was at the time conducted by my friend George Williams, of King's College, Cambridge. The tone of this school is somewhat different from that represented by the Irish Church Mission Society. My sympathies were with both the schools of Irish Churchmen represented by these two institutions. In Dublin I had preached in the highest and in the lowest church, and found myself at home in each.

CHAPTER X

DURING the years 1857-1859 I held several University offices at Oxford, being Public Examiner in Classics (Class and Pass), Select Preacher, Preacher at White-hall, Proctor, Examiner for the Johnson Theological Scholarship, Oxford Examiner at Rugby (where Arch-bishop Temple was Headmaster, and Archbishop Benson one of the other masters), University Ex-aminer at Winchester College (this last post I filled twice : on the first occasion I selected for the Goddard Scholarship Dr. Fearon, afterwards Headmaster of Winchester, and the second time Dr. Phillpotts, after-wards Headmaster of Bedford School). Owing, per-haps, to the strain caused by these occupations, as I also held the offices of Tutor and Dean in my college, my eyes began to give me trouble, and I went abroad to consult an oculist of great reputation at the time, named De Leuw. He was a Dutchman who lived in a little village named Gräfrath, near Düsseldorf. His name being very unpronounceable, he was generally spoken of by his title 'the Hofrath.' In the little village of Gräfrath there were collected a number of patients from all parts of Europe and America. There was but one hotel in the village, so that most of the patients had to lodge in cottages. The Hofrath's ways were primitive in character. He would make no appointments, but he came to the hotel every morning at 7 a.m., and went on seeing patients till 5 p.m. When he had finished with one, he desired his servant to introduce someone else, and if that person were not ready at the moment he lost his turn; in consequence, all the patients had to wait in the hall of the hotel, although many of them were not summoned. He was a kind and courteous old man. My trouble, he said, simply arose from wearing spectacles which heated and strained the eyes. He desired me instead to wear double glasses of a lower number than that which I was using, and gave me a prescription of two lotions, one for the eye, and the other for the forehead. He gave all his prescriptions in cipher, so that they could only be made up by one chemist.

At Berlin I paid a visit to Professor Hengstenberg, the foremost among the orthodox theologians of Germany. He was Doctor both of Philosophy and Theology, and leader of the Lutheran section of the Evangelical Church. The work by which he was best known in England was his *Christology of the Old Testament.* He received me in a very friendly manner, and showed me his library, which was the room of a hard-working student, containing a desk, a table, a few chairs, and an enormous number of books which lined the walls. He gave me an introduction to his son, who was pastor at Jüterboch, with whom I after-wards spent two days. Pastor Hengstenberg showed me the ritual books used by the Evangelical Church, and said that the Lutheran wing of the Evangelical Church desired to make them more full ; for the Evangelical Church of Germany is formed by a union of the Lutherans, properly called Protestants, and Calvinists, properly called Reformed. The chief authority in it is the Consistory, formed of clergy and laity nominated by the Crown, and a Superintendent for each province, who fulfils some of the functions of a Bishop. Pastor Hengstenberg lamented that so little sympathy was shown by the English Church. That they had not the Episcopal Succession was the result of circumstances which they regretted, and they believed that God would make up the deficiency. I told him the Anglo-Continental Society was meant to help towards union with Scandinavian and German Churches on such principles as the Church of England could accept, as well as to encourage reform in the Latin and Greek Churches. He said that he would gladly co-operate.

At Prague I saw little apparent effect remaining from the teaching and traditions of Huss and Jerome. Bohemia passed on the torch from Wickliffe to Luther, but her own light was quenched in blood by Maximilian of Bavaria. Had our too pacific James I. helped his son-in-law, and had the latter, victorious over his opponent, established a Church of Bohemia similar to the Church of England, which was clearly the idea with which Bishop Andrewes preached his remarkable sermon at the Prince's marriage, the religious state of Central Europe might have been very different. As it was, the Jesuits were introduced—their college, the Clementinum, is now used as a University—and they completed the work begun by the sword. The children of Protestants were taught to hate Protestantism as the children of Christians who formed the Janissaries were taught by their Mahometan masters to hate Christianity. A scene that I witnessed on the evening of my arrival indicated the present character of Bohemian religion. In the market-place there was a picture of St. Mary, with lights burning before it, in the pediment of a column. Before this picture a man of the people threw himself on his knees, and began singing hymns and chanting prayers to the Virgin. As he sang he was joined by more and more people, who knelt down, crossed themselves, sang, prayed, and bowed themselves before the picture.

In returning to England I paid a visit to the Archbishop of Utrecht, head of the Jansenist Church of Holland. I believe that no English Churchman had previously had any communication with the Dutch Jansenists, with the exception of J. M. Neale, who had twice visited Utrecht—in 1851 and 1854—for the purpose of writing a history of that Church. At that time Archbishop Van Santen occupied the See of Utrecht; he was now dead, and Archbishop Henry Van Loos had been elected. We held a long conversation together, and interchanged several books having reference to our respective Churches. Giving him one of the publications of the Anglo-Continental Society, I told him that he would find there the same principles as those on which the Church of Holland defended itself. In return he gave to me some Jansenist publications in Latin and in Dutch. At a later date the Archbishop gave valuable help to the German Old Catholics, holding Confirmations for them, and promising to transmit the episcopate to them, which promise was fulfilled by his successor in the see, who was at the time of my visit Bishop of Deventer.

The little Dutch Church, consisting now of three Bishops, twenty-eight clergy, and 6,000 laymen, is the heir and representative of the French Gallicans. Gallicanism was crushed in France by Louis XIV. at the instance of Madame de Maintenon and his confessor. But Archbishop Rovenius and the principal ecclesiastics in Holland had declared their approval in 1641 of the Gallican volume *Augustinus*, written by Jansen of Ypres, which had been condemned at Rome on the urgent demand of the Jesuits. From that time the Dutch Church was bitterly opposed by the Jesuits, though the Bishops still maintained their

subjection to the Pope. But in 1724 the Pope refused his consent to the consecration of Archbishop
Steenoven, and from that date has excommunicated
each Archbishop and Bishop upon his election and
consecration. There have been nine Archbishops of
Utrecht, seven of Haarlem, and six of Deventer, who
have been formally excommunicated by the Court of
Rome, and have maintained their position in spite of
their excommunication. At the time that I saw the
Archbishop there seemed little life in the Church, as
the reforms had not gone far enough to deny Roman
doctrine as well as Roman supremacy. Since their
formal union with the Old Catholics of Germany and
Switzerland, there is a better hope for their future.

CHAPTER XI

Cardinal Manning—Manning and Newman—Thackeray.

WHILE resident at Oxford in 1853 I was invited to a controversial dinner-party in London, at which four Roman Catholics and four members of the English Church (one of them Lord Robert Cecil) were present, the purpose of the party being to show to a young man present how superior Romanism was to Protestantism.

Dr. Manning and Mr. James Hope were present on the Roman side, and as soon as the servants had withdrawn Manning began to point out the superiority of the Church of Rome on the ground that she held a number of doctrines which were essential parts of the faith, and had been rejected by Protestants. When a pause came, I said that I thought it a very difficult thing to pass a judgment suddenly on matters of doctrine, but that we could judge on questions of morals. I ventured, therefore, to ask Dr. Manning how he accounted for the moral teaching of the Church of Rome, which seemed to be unaccordant with our ideas of truthfulness and honesty. He asked where I found the teaching of the Church of Rome on the subject, and I replied :

'In St. Alfonso de' Liguori's *Moral Theology*.'

'St. Alfonso,' he said, 'and his teaching are fully authorized by the Holy See, but you have misunderstood him. In allowing the use of equivocation or amphibology, and mental restriction, he does not authorize falsehood, because he says that they are not falsehoods.'

'But,' I said, 'is not the question whether they really are falsehoods, and not whether he acknowledges them to be so ?'

'He is right,' said Manning, 'in his justification of equivocation, and you will find much the same teaching in Jeremy Taylor.'

'I think not,' I replied, 'for Jeremy Taylor makes the essence of lying to be deceiving your neighbour, whatever form of words you use, while Liguori says that you may deceive your neighbour to any extent, provided that you use some form of words which, in your estimation, and to you, appears true. For example, you may deny that you have done something that you have done, provided that you prefix the words "I say" to your denial, because then what you mean is merely that you are making use of those words which follow the expression "I say." And, again,' I continued, 'I cannot understand how a man can be excused from the sin of theft if he steals a sum below a given amount, different amounts being fixed for different classes, from a King to a beggar, so that if you stole half a crown from one class it would be a mortal sin, causing death to the soul, and if from another class it would only be a venial sin, which would not diminish God's love towards you.'

'There is another work of St. Alfonso's named *Homo Apostolicus*, which will set his teaching in a clearer light,' replied Manning. 'I will bring this book to-morrow, and shall be happy to answer any questions on it which you like to ask.' With this the party broke up.

Manning brought the book next day, which led to a correspondence between him and myself, which was subsequently published, and was also the cause of my writing several articles in the *Christian Remembrancer*, which were afterwards put together under the title of *The Moral and Devotional Theology of the Church of Rome*. The correspondence consisted of nineteen letters, in which I assailed, and Manning defended, the two positions of the Roman Church: (1) That theft is venial unless a certain fixed quantity, differing according to the class of the person robbed, is stolen; (2) that, in making a solemn affirmation or oath, it is allowable to mislead another by using an equivocal word or an equivocal sentence or a mental restriction, the effect of which is not perceived by the other party to make the affirmation or oath of no avail in the judgment of the person making it. Two of the said articles illustrated my view on these points, and a third article exhibited the extravagance of the devotion to St. Mary that is now authorized. These articles restrained R. I. Wilberforce from joining the Church of Rome until he was overpersuaded by Manning.

Manning had at this time been a Roman Catholic for two or three years. On Newman's secession, Manning took up the rôle of the defender of the Church of England against Popery. But he was too much identified with the Tractarian party, now discredited by Newman's conduct, to be trusted by those in high places. In 1847 he learnt for certain that he would not be promoted in the Church of England. He was not prepared to live and die Archdeacon of Chichester. There were other worlds, and he would turn his eyes to 'pastures new.' In 1851 he submitted to Rome. His first journey to Rome after his submission was made with Monsignor Talbot, one of the Malahide family, who was himself a convert. The acquaintanceship of Monsignor Talbot, which soon ripened into friendship, was of the utmost moment to Manning; for Talbot was the Pope's Chamberlain, always ready to whisper into the ear of Pius IX.

suggestions which the old man, whose apprehension was not very keen, thought to emanate from himself or from heaven. In 1857 the Pope nominated Manning 'Provost of the Chapter of Westminster,' and in 1865 to the archbishopric of Westminster. In this position he ruled despotically over the Italian Mission in England, and kept his heel on Dr. Newman as long as Pius IX. lived. But on the death of Pius IX. (who had made him a Cardinal) he was lost. His *ipse dixit* could no longer make or mar men in England by his influence at Rome. Newman was made a Cardinal at the instance of the Duke of Norfolk and Lord Ripon, and Manning was left out in the cold. The effect on Manning was twofold : first, he became 'profoundly convinced of the incapacity of the Holy Office [at Rome], and the essential injustice of its procedures and its secrecy'; and, secondly, realizing that he had 'come from the broad stream of the English Commonwealth into the narrow community of the English Catholics,' he tried to regain some touch with a section, at least, of the English people by heading the party of social reformers.

'Mr. Henry George and Mr. Davitt found not only a ready access, but a warm welcome ; Mr. John Burns, Mr. Ben Tillett, Mr. Tom Mann, and others of a like kidney, preached their gospel at the Archbishop's house,' wrote his biographer. This, too, was a failure, and in his old age he looked sadly back ' with a strong yearning ' to the old days of his Anglican life. He was a high-minded man whose character was marred by a necessity of being first, and by a double-dealing justified by the Church of his adoption. In his earlier days he was an ecclesiastical politician, afterwards an actor in the petty intrigues of the Roman Catholic body in England, lamenting all the while that he was not working 'for the people of England,' but only 'for the Irish occupation in England.' The Archdeacon of Chichester was a nobler and, it would seem, a happier man than the 'Archbishop of Westminster.'

To one who knew Dr. Manning and Dr. Newman both in their Anglican and their Roman phases, it is a matter of singular interest to note the relations in which they stood to one another under each of these conditions.

In his undergraduate days Manning was not affected by Newman's influence. He had no intention of taking Holy Orders, and he held himself outside the religious movement of the day. In his last Long Vacation he began to go to St. Mary's, and heard Newman preach; and he was once asked to dinner by Newman. After his ordination, Manning, beginning as an Evangelical, grew by degrees into a High Churchman; but he was not one of the Tractarian leaders until 1838 at the soonest. On the publication of Tract XC., Manning, now Archdeacon of Chichester, began to draw off from the party, and with this view delivered a Charge containing an eloquent panegyric on the Church of England, and in 1843 he preached a sermon, on November 5, at Oxford, denouncing the Church of Rome. The day after this sermon had been preached, Manning walked over to Littlemore to call on Newman, but Newman, in whom a petty petulance was ever joined with his greater qualities, refused to see him. At this time, perhaps, first were sown the seeds of that mistrust which the two men entertained for each other to the very last. In 1845 Newman seceded, and again Manning stood forward as the defender of the Church of England, in an hour of peril, by his Charge of 1845. Up to this time Manning's course had been loyal and upright, incomparably superior to that of Newman. The relations of the two men as Anglicans here cease, to be taken up again under different circumstances and in a different spirit, when they were both members of the Church of Rome.

When Manning and Newman come into contact as members of the Church of Rome, their respective positions are changed. As Anglicans, Newman had been the leader, and Manning the follower, whom Newman could afford to treat with rudeness if he offended him. But this relation is now reversed. By a combination of energy and diplomatic skill, and by the employment of an extreme adulation of Pius IX., Manning raised himself to be at first the real, then— on Wiseman's death—the real and formal head, of the Roman Catholic body in England. He looked upon the 'old' Roman Catholic Bishops with a contempt which he hardly veiled. Newman was the only man who might be his rival, and either dwarf him in the public estimation or lead a party opposed to him. Against Newman, therefore, he was always on his guard, and throughout the life of Pius IX. he kept him in the background by whispering into the Papal ear, through Monsignor Talbot's lips, insinuations that Newman was not Papal enough to be trusted, being, as Ward put it, (1) disloyal to the Vicar of Christ, and (2) worldly.

The first sensible clash between the two men was on the subject of the education of Roman Catholics at the English Universities. In 1864 Newman bought a piece of ground in Oxford for building a hall over which he might himself preside. Bishop Ullathorne approved, but by Manning's influence, exerted through Wiseman on the Roman Propaganda, the scheme was forbidden. Two years later Bishop Ullathorne re- vived the question by a petition to the Propaganda. Leave was given for the establishment of a hall, but Newman's headship of it was prohibited, and later on the permission was altogether withdrawn for fear of that contingency. The whole affair was a duel between Newman and Manning, and Manning won.

The wounds received in the contest did not heal. In July, 1867, Newman wrote to Oakeley that the cause of the distance between himself and the Archbishop was his want of confidence in him, 'especially in matters concerning myself.' A fortnight later he wrote to Manning himself, acknowledging 'a distressing mistrust which now for some years past I have been unable in prudence to dismiss from my mind,' adding, 'your words, your bearing, and your implications . . . have not served to prepare me for your acts.' Manning at once wrote back that his feeling towards Newman was just what Newman's was towards him : ' I have felt you hard to understand, and that your words have not prepared me for your acts.' This mutual distrust 'was never cured,' says Manning's biographer. 'No attempt was ever hereafter made on either side to restore lost confidence. They never wrote or spoke again in terms of intimacy' (p. 306). Manning still kept up ' professions of friendship for Newman, whilst accusing Newman in private of being an unsound or disloyal Catholic' (p. 311). It must be borne in mind that Manning's 'in private' meant 'in the ear of the Pope,' through the channel of Monsignor Talbot, and in his conversations with Roman Catholics in London. The squabble (it cannot be dignified by a higher title) spread from the two parties chiefly interested to their followers, between whom bitter animosities sprang up and were cherished, under cover to the outside world of perfect unity of feeling and peace. And the pettiness of it all ! Father Coffin took Cardinal Reisach to see the site which Newman had destined for his hall at Oxford, and Newman petulantly burst out in a letter to Monsignor Patterson with complaints of 'the incomprehensible neglect' thus shown to him. Talbot

is sure that Newman is organizing the laity to govern
the Church. 'What is the province of the laity?' says
the Pope's Chamberlain, writing to Manning. 'To
hunt, to shoot, to entertain? These matters they
understand, but to meddle with ecclesiastical matters
they have no right at all. . . . Dr. Newman is the
most dangerous man in England, and you will see
that he will make use of the laity against your Grace.
You must not be afraid of him.' This, and a great
deal more about 'the detestable spirit growing up in
England,' which had been repressed by Wiseman,
'who knew how to keep the laity in order' (p. 318).
Poor laymen! To hunt, to shoot, to entertain, is all
that they are fit for, and they must leave the rest to
their priests!

Manning himself, as an ecclesiastical statesman,
rose above the bitterness of his followers, or, at any
rate, above expressing it. He saw that 'a conflict
between him [Newman] and me would be as great a
scandal to the Church in England and as great a
victory to the Anglicans as could be.' So he held his
hand, though Monsignor Talbot continued urging him
to 'stand firm' against the 'old school of Catholics,'
who would 'rally round Newman in opposition to
you and Rome.' Newman's 'spirit must be crushed,'
according to the Pope's Chamberlain. What he had
written was 'detestable,' 'un-Catholic,' 'un-Christian.'
So great was the harmony of soul among the Roman
Catholics in England, that Manning looked upon the
Irish as his allies in keeping down the English.
'Every Englishman,' says Talbot, 'is naturally anti-
Roman,' and 'Dr. Newman is more English than the
English.' 'The thing that will save us,' replies Man-
ning, 'from low views about the Mother of God and
the Vicar of the Lord is the million Irish in England
and the sympathy of the Catholics in Ireland' (p. 325).
So the English 'laymen' are not only to be kept down

14

by their prelates, but by a phalanx of Irishmen—not a happy prospect for men with any sense of an English-man's liberty and self-respect.

Newman felt, if he did not know, that Manning was intriguing against him, and he could not forgive him. 'The world accuses him [Manning] without provo-cation of thwarting me, and the *primâ facie* proof of this is that his entourage acts with violence against me.' At the end of a long correspondence, suave on Manning's side, tart on Newman's, Newman writes : 'I do not know whether I am on my head or my heels when I have active relations with you,' words 'which made a reply hardly fitting on my part'—wrote Man-ning. Manning accounts for the 'divergence' between them by the 'well-known morbid sensitiveness' of Newman, which made 'his relations with Faber, the late Cardinal [Wiseman], Father Coffin, and the London Oratory, undergo the same change as his re-lations to me.' So far from having hindered Newman's being prominent in the Church, he had, he professed, endeavoured to effect it by putting his name forward at Rome for a bishopric in 1859, an endeavour which was defeated by the Bishop of Newport denouncing Newman at the moment before the Propaganda for heresy. Newman's unforgiving mistrust is best accounted for on the hypothesis that he supposed Manning not to have dealt fairly by him when he pro-fessed to recommend him, and perhaps having brought about the denunciation for heresy to counteract his pretended purpose. Afterwards he refused to come to Manning's consecration unless 'he might take it as a pledge on my part that I would not again endeavour to have him consecrated as a Bishop'—a petulant reference to an old grievance. Newman's 'morbid sensitiveness' may have been a factor in this unseemly squabble, but a larger factor was Manning's resolution that a man who might lead a party in opposition to himself and in hostility to the extremest claim of the Papacy should never have the opportunity of doing so as long as he could prevent it.

But when Pius IX. died he could prevent it no longer. The Duke of Norfolk and the Marquis of Ripon insisted on Newman's being recommended to Leo XIII. as a Cardinal, and after a few moments' silence, with bent head, Manning undertook to convey their choice to the Cardinal Secretary at Rome. When Newman heard of the Pope's intention, he was overwhelmed by his 'condescending goodness.' But his letter of acceptance to the Cardinal Secretary was misunderstood by Manning, who took it as a refusal, and announced in the *Times* that the offer was refused, at a time when the offer itself was as yet an ecclesiastical secret. Newman was alarmed and indignant. 'As soon,' he writes to Manning, 'as the Holy Father condescends to make it known to me that he means to confer on me the high dignity of Cardinal, I shall write to Rome to signify my obedience and glad acceptance of the honour without delay.' Manning 'repaired his error' by informing the Pope of the mistake he had made, and the nomination was confirmed. Newman declared himself 'overcome by the Pope's goodness,' and said to his brothers of the Oratory, 'The cloud is lifted from me for ever.' During the remainder of their lives the two Cardinals met but twice—once in 1883, when Newman paid a formal visit to Manning in London; and once in 1884, when Manning returned the visit at Birmingham. In 1890 Newman died. The fear of being dwarfed by his superiority having passed away, Manning made a fervent address 'in which he drew a most touching and pathetic picture of his relations with John Henry Newman, which he described as a friendship of sixty years and more.' 'Cardinal Manning,' writes his biographer, 'perhaps not unnaturally forgot his prolonged opposition to

Newman in Rome and in England; forgot his avowed hostility and mistrust; forgot that for half a century —from 1840 to 1890—he had not met or spoken to Newman more than half a dozen times. It seems almost a pity to disturb the illusion indulged in by Cardinal Manning, and left as a legacy to future generations, that he and Newman were knit together in the bands of the closest friendship for sixty years and more. . . . Manning's mind and memory were taken possession of by an overmastering idea, so that in his illusion he saw only the what might have been, and not the things that were. . . . What, then, is the truth? Not more than three or four years before the illusive and fancy picture of 1890, Cardinal Manning avowed and put on record his condemnation of Newman in terms so clear and incisive as to leave no room or foothold for an after-fiction of friendship. . . . Instead of friendship, there was a life-long opposition' (p. 754).

It is a miserable picture—a petty personal squabble between the two leading English Roman Catholic ecclesiastics lasting for forty years. Who could have believed that the Newman and the Manning that we knew in the Anglican Church could have been kept in permanent hostility to each other by jealousy, spitefulness, and unforgiving tempers, which continued to operate until death closed the career of one of them? Had they both remained in the Anglican Church, and had Manning become Archbishop of Canterbury, can we imagine his whispering, intriguing, plotting to keep Newman shut up at Littlemore, lest he should rival him in influence? And had he done so, can we imagine Newman irritated beyond endurance by such treatment, and refusing all advances towards friendship or social intercourse with him? There is something more wholesome in the wider, larger, fresher atmosphere of the Church of England than in the confined air of the Roman Catholic body in England.

In the year of my proctorship at Oxford (1857) I resided for the greater part of the vacations, and consequently I was in residence when Thackeray offered himself as a candidate for the city of Oxford. As he was dining with me after his first day's canvassing, I said to him:

'You must be in a different position from most men who canvass a strange constituency, as you must be known by fame to most of those whom you visit.'

'Now,' he said, laying down his knife and fork and holding up a finger, 'there was one man among all that I went to see who had heard my name before; and he was a circulating librarian. Such is mortal fame!'

He was not elected; and it is probable that he would have been a failure in the House of Commons, like Mill and other literary men. He was not able to make an effective speech. At the end of one of his addresses at Oxford he told the meeting that they might moralize over the fact that a man who with a pen between his fingers could go on writing without a pause, could yet speak in public no better than he had just done. The speaking was chiefly done for him by Charles Neate, Fellow of Oriel. On the Sunday I was going by the morning train to London to preach at Whitehall Chapel, and Thackeray and Neate travelled up by the same train. After some conversation, in which Thackeray expressed his sense of the loss suffered by those who were married in registrars' offices, from not receiving the Church's blessing on their marriage, I took my sermon out of my pocket and began to read it. Thackeray leant forward. 'I never before saw a naked sermon. May I take it in my hand?' He glanced over a page or two, and handed it back, saying, with a smile, that he had had a new experience and got a new idea. I met Thackeray again at Ghent, as I was returning from Holland, and we walked up and down together during the half-hour that luggage was being registered and paid for. I found that he was quite aware of the existence of the Jansenist Church of Holland, and said what good Anglicans Pascal and the Port Royalists would have made if they had been born in England. He was shocked at the deification of St. Mary that he had witnessed. He asked me if I was going by Ostend. I replied, No ; I disliked the Ostend passage when the sea was rough, and was going by Calais. Each time after that, when we emerged from the station to the open platform in our walk, he looked up to the sky. ' Do you think there will be a wind ? Perhaps I had better go by Calais, too.' I told him that, at least, at present the weather seemed propitious. ' Yes,' he said, ' I will try Ostend. That sky '—pointing upward—' is indeed charming ; and were it not that one's work lies in London, and where one's work is one's happiness is, we should be loth to leave it for England's fogs.' No wind sprang up, and we each reached home over a calm sea.

I saw no trace of cynicism in Thackeray. His conversation was easy and natural ; he did not pose as a literary lion ; he did not seem politically ambitious, nor, in consequence, much disappointed when not returned to Parliament for the city of Oxford.

During the year of my proctorship I made one of a deputation which went from the University of Oxford to congratulate the Queen on the marriage of the Princess Royal to the future German Emperor. The deputation consisted of the Vice-Chancellor, the two Proctors, and nine Doctors of Divinity or Masters of Arts. We were met at Buckingham Palace by the Earl of Derby, who wore his robes as Chancellor of the University, and a number of Masters of Arts fell in behind the deputation, according to a privilege enjoyed by members of the Universities. So great was the pressure made by these Masters of Arts when the doors of the audience chamber were opened that we reached the royal presence almost, but not quite, at a run. The Queen was sitting on a low throne, with the Duchess of Sutherland standing on one side of her, and another tall lady on the other, who seemed almost to overshadow the Queen, placed as she was below them. Lord Derby read our address to the Queen, and she received it from his hands, after which the Vice-Chancellor and the senior Proctor kissed hands, and the Chancellor read the names of each of the other members of the deputation, who bowed to her and received a gracious salutation in return. We found it rather a difficult matter to back out from the royal presence, as the Chancellor's robes and our University gowns did not readily lend themselves to the process. Luncheon was provided for us at the palace, and we returned to Oxford the same day. Forty years afterwards I met at Blickling the gracious lady for whose welfare England was then praying— the Empress Frederick, mother of the present German Emperor. She came with her brother, the Prince of Wales, to see Blickling Hall, and still had much of her youthful energy.

CHAPTER XII

School inspectorship—Rev. R. Aitken—Bishop Harold Browne.

IN 1859 I married Marion S. Danvers and gave up residence in Oxford, accepting an inspectorship of schools offered me by Lord Salisbury (the father of the late Prime Minister), who was President of the Council. My first district was Cornwall, with part of Devonshire. I went first into Cornwall, and though I previously knew no one in the county, for the six months that preceded my marriage, I went only twice to an hotel ; on all other occasions I was received hospitably, mainly by the clergy. The house to which I went most frequently was Porthgwidden, the residence of the Rev. Thomas Phillpotts, nephew of Bishop Phillpotts, whom I helped in his Sunday services. No one is better qualified to judge of the work done by the clergy than an Inspector of Schools. The Bishop is an ' episcopus,' or ' *over*-looker '; the Inspector is an ' *in*-looker.' During the next ten years I visited about 3,000 parsonages and schools (often, of course, the same year after year), and was admitted to the confidence of the clergy. Almost everywhere the state of the school was an indication of the parson's zeal, and he, generally speaking, was the only person interested enough to give time and money for the education of the labourers' children. Judging by the specimens that I saw—perhaps favourable specimens, because I only went to parishes in which there were schools to be inspected—I came to the conclusion that the English clergy were a body that any Church might be proud of. There was no theatrical posing, no merit-earning by strange asceticisms according to the Romanist ideal of saintship, no emotionalism of the Wesleyan, but a quiet, sturdy English way of doing their duty to their Master and to the flock with which He had entrusted them, not looking for anything in return—promotion, success, wealth ; content to bear hardness without thinking that it was hardness, or that it was anything but part of the day's work ; and concealing a very real love for their Lord under a reserve of speech which refused to exhibit deep feelings to the public gaze. 'Clerus Anglicus stupor mundi' is, and always was, an extravagance, but certainly the English clergy may compare favourably with any national priesthood. One reason of this is the class from which they are drawn—namely, the gentry ; while the priesthood on the Continent is recruited almost wholly from the peasant class ; a consequence of which is that the latter are unable to affect the mind of the gentry, who perhaps for that reason have for the most part in France and Italy, and to a great extent in Germany and Spain, given up their hold on Christianity, while the English squire is content to be taught by his uncle or brother. There are eccentricities in every class, but I never found any in the clergy with whom I was brought into contact that were calculated to cause more than a good-humoured smile. These of course I found. For example, I rode to a school within riding distance from Truro with my wife. On arriving, the incumbent formally asked the reason of my coming.

'To inspect the school,' I said.

'No, sir ; the school is not to be inspected.'

'It makes no difference to me,' I replied ; 'but as a building grant was made for the schoolroom, it is open for inspection.'

' No, sir, no,' he repeated ; ' but it is beginning to rain : I hope the lady and you will come in.'

We dismounted, and for two hours, during which the rain lasted, we talked of everything except schools. Then came luncheon, after which my host walked up to me, and, with a bow, said :

' I shall be obliged, sir, if you will inspect the school buildings.'

Fortunately, I was able to say that the buildings were good, and then, with another bow, he said :

' Now, sir, I shall be further obliged if you will examine the children.'

The reason of my host's singular conduct was, I learnt, that a previous Inspector on his arrival at the door had called out to a person working in the garden, ' My man, is your master at home ?' when the ' man ' was really the ' master,' and had added injury to insult by reporting badly of the school.

The Cornish children were very intelligent, being the sons and daughters of the Cornish miners. The best schools were equal to any of the best schools of the present day, though this was before Mr. Lowe's new code, which has since been revised, re-revised, and superseded. I wrote the article in the *Quarterly Review* against many of the provisions of that code in January, 1860.

The most striking personage that I saw in Cornwall was Mr. Aitken, the father of Mr. Hay Aitken, Canon of Norwich. I spent a few days with him at Pendeen, of which he was incumbent, while I inspected some schools in the neighbourhood. We were caught in a storm as he drove me to one of the schools, and while I was conducting the inspection he went to a cottage to dry his coat. While this was being done, he converted the woman of the house, reducing her first to tears and then to exultation. His method with women was generally to look them straight in the eyes (he was a man of considerable presence), and demand of them sternly: 'Do you know God?' 'I hope so,' was usually the timid answer. 'Hope!' exclaimed Aitken; 'have you only hope? You had better know for certain that you do not. What you must have is not hope, but assurance.' In most cases women yielded and became his disciples—at least, for a time. Aitken was a common referee for clergy and laymen who were in distress of mind. They knew that they would be welcomed, and came in numbers to his house. His method with them was different. He put them, I was told, often several at a time, each in a separate room, and desired them to continue repeating, 'I know that I have been saved—I know that I have been saved,' again and again, and not to come out of the room until they were assured that they were saved, which occurred after the exercise had gone on long enough. Aitken's lieutenant in Cornwall was Rev. W. Haslam, and Aitken recounted to me the circumstance of his conversion. 'We were sitting,' he said, 'he and I, at this table, and the fly was about to come to take away Mr. and Mrs. Haslam after their visit, when Mrs. Aitken and Mrs. Haslam entered the room, and Mrs. Aitken walked up to me and said: "Mr. Aitken, if Mr. Haslam goes away from this house an unconverted man, the blood of his soul will be on your head for not having dealt faithfully with him." "Oh, you are right," cried Haslam; "God be merciful to me a sinner!"' And so he returned, after more prayer, to his home. On the following Sunday I was told that a Wesleyan exclaimed aloud, as Haslam was preaching, 'Hallelujah! the parson's converted.' After some years of diligent preaching of the dogma of sudden conversion, Haslam went to Mr. Hockin of Phillack, and said that he had been doing work, but not the Church's work. Mr. Hockin gave him a part of his parish in which to work on

Church lines, which he did for a time, and then he returned to his old views. After some years I met Mr. Haslam in Norfolk, and on my asking him if he had there a large sphere of work, he replied, with a smile : 'I have a small parish, but there is upon me the care of all the churches.' He died in 1905.

Mr. Aitken gave me an account of an interview that he had with Bishop Samuel Wilberforce and others at Cuddesdon. 'I began by explaining the way in which God deals with souls when He draws them to Himself. After I had proceeded some way, Bishop Wilberforce interrupted me : " I agree with very much that you say, Mr. Aitken. I do not doubt that God does of His gracious mercy call back many from a sinful life in the way that you describe. Your error, I think, is in holding that this is His universal method ; on the contrary, I regard it as the method which He occasionally and exceptionally uses."' 'That is the way, and none other, in which He deals with souls,' said Aitken. 'Then, continued the Bishop, 'I have another strong objection to your system ; it makes men so self-satisfied and uncharitable towards others whom they choose to set down as unconverted.' 'Yes,' said Bishop Selwyn, who was one of those present, 'I had an example of such self-assurance as I was leaving my diocese [he was then Bishop of New Zealand] for England. Just as I was stepping into the boat, a man came to me and asked to say something to me. I turned aside with him, but I found that he had nothing to say except, " Bishop, do you know God ?"' 'And, my lord, what answer did you give to that man ?' 'I thought him not inquiring in a right spirit, and I passed by his question with a general expression of faith and hope.' 'Well, my lord,' said Aitken, 'you have the character of a great missionary Bishop to the heathen ; but I tell you that I would rather that my soul were as one of those heathen than as you showed yours to be by giving him that answer.' 'Well,' said the Bishop, smiling, 'you speak plainly, at any rate.' Archdeacon Clerke then took up the discussion, and, in his slow and grave voice, said: 'I think I understand you, Mr. Aitken; you say that we require to be assured of the time when we became God's forgiven children.' 'Yes, yes; that is it.' 'I have a perfect assurance on that point,' continued the Archdeacon. 'Indeed, indeed! pray give us your experiences.' 'My father was a thoroughly truthful man, and he assured me that on a certain day I was baptized.' 'Very dark—very dark,' said Aitken, recounting the interview to me. 'There was not one of those present who was a converted man except dear Bishop Wilberforce, and he was much misled.'

At Launceston I made acquaintance with three Miss Meyricks, who had purchased a house, which they had named Bôd Meyrick. They were all three elderly ladies. I sat next the youngest of them, Miss Harriet Meyrick, at luncheon after the examination of the school. As soon as an opportunity occurred, she turned to me and anxiously asked what my arms were. I replied: 'Three burning brands.'

'And your motto?'

I replied that I was so degenerate a Welshman that I might not pronounce it properly in Welsh, but that its English meaning was 'Have God, have everything: God and enough.'

'And have you got the Cornish chough on your crest?'

'Yes,' I replied, 'on the top of a castle.'

I told her that I had a seal with the arms in my portmanteau.

'Would you bring it to me,' she said, 'to-morrow? for I find that we are cousins.'

The next morning I found her so much delighted with the seal that I gave it to her, after having had another engraved for myself. In acknowledgment of my cousinhood she showed me some of the family records which she had by her.

'Do you know the story,' she said, 'of my grandfather and his marriage with Lady Lucy Pitt ?'

She told it to me as follows: Meyrick and another, being among the head-boys of Westminster School, contrived to scrape acquaintance with two girls in the neighbourhood who were treated at home with severity. After a time it occurred to them that it would be a happy adventure to be married. The preliminaries of marriage were not at that time so difficult to get over as at present, and on an appointed day the two boys and girls met at a church in the Fleet ; but up to this time they had not quite determined which boy should marry which girl. Both the boys preferred Lady Lucy Pitt, who was a daughter of Lord Londonderry, and there was almost a fight in the porch on the subject. Meyrick being the stronger of the two, the other boy yielded, and satisfied himself with the cousin of Lady Lucy. Meyrick was married to Lady Lucy Pitt, and they went across the Channel to France, whence Meyrick wrote to his father a letter then in Miss Harriet Meyrick's possession, asking his pardon, and saying that until he heard he was forgiven they would stay abroad. A painting of the two runaways exists, I believe, at Boconnoc in Cornwall, with other Pitt portraits, though I do not recollect seeing it. Miss Harriet Meyrick claimed me as her cousin as long as she lived.

At the end of about a year I passed from Cornwall and Devonshire to the East of England, having as a district, first, Essex, Suffolk, and Norfolk, conjointly with Mr. Mitchell, afterwards Norfolk and part of Suffolk by myself. The first six months I spent in Cambridge in the house of Professor Harold Browne, non-resident at the time, to whom I had brought an introduction from Mr. T. Phillpotts. This was the beginning of a friendship greatly valued by me, which lasted as long as Bishop Harold Browne lived. At this time he was Norrisian Professor at Cambridge. In 1864 he was appointed Bishop of Ely, and in 1874 he passed from that diocese to the larger sphere of Winchester, where he succeeded Bishop Wilberforce. In 1868 he had been nominated by Disraeli as Archbishop of Canterbury, but the Queen was resolved on the appointment of Tait, and the Prime Minister gave way. On Tait's death, in 1882, expectation again pointed him out for the primacy, but now he was too old. The Queen and Mr. Gladstone both wrote to him, declaring his age to be the one impediment to his succeeding to the great See of Canterbury. In 1890 he found it necessary to resign his bishopric, and in December, 1891, he passed away. Harold Browne cannot be regarded as the ablest among his contemporary Bishops—Bishop Wilberforce was that—nor perhaps the most learned—Bishop Christopher Wordsworth may have been that. But he was a singularly wise man, his mind being so well balanced that he leaned too far in no direction, but gave each principle and each fact its due weight, without allowing it to exclude from view other principles and other facts as true as itself. He was also widely and deeply loved, because he had himself an unfailing fount of sympathy and affection ever springing up within him, which called out a response from all about him and from any that had communication with him. No truer representative of the Church of England's best self could be found. He had in their perfection her faith and clinging to the truth, her moderation in limiting one truth by its equally true counterpart, her simple piety, her learning, her reverence for all that is holy, her respect for primitive Christianity, her shrinking from the inventions of men which boasted to be revelations of

God, and from innovations on the once-delivered truth, her firm confidence in the overruling providence of God, however dark might be His ways; and he illustrated in himself no less the calm and equitable temper of the Church of England than her theology. He once said, with a smile, that Oxford was a hill-top where streams of thought rose, which flowed down with foam and clatter, but that, having reached the level ground, they took their course through Cambridge, and came out calmer, and he ventured to think more wholesome, than when they entered it. If that were true, Harold Browne was a Cambridge man in the whole tone and temper of his mind. His chief literary work is his *Exposition of the Thirty-nine Articles*, which was based on lectures delivered by him at Lampeter College. When one of our American Episcopal guests was introduced to the Bishop, he stepped back, and said, ' So that is Harold Browne on the Articles ! My brother, I don't know how the Church of Christ got along at all without that book,' to the confusion of the Bishop's modesty. It has been said that Hooker's *Ecclesiastical Polity*, Pearson on the Creed, and Harold Browne on the Articles, contain a résumé of the Anglican theology.

CHAPTER XIII

Reform in Italy and Spain—Baron Ricasoli—Signor Minghetti—
Cardinal Andrea—Bishop Cabrera.

IN 1861 the Anglo-Continental Society completed its constitution by electing Bishop Harold Browne its President, and this brought me much in contact with him.

The Bishop attended the committee and presided over the annual meetings of the society, except on one occasion, when he ceded the chair to Archbishop Longley. The state of Italy was at this time such as to invite the attention of Churchmen. Pius IX., being supposed to have betrayed the popular party, had become a byword of reproach among his countrymen. In Turin, Passaglia, a short time before the champion of the Immaculate Conception, was excommunicated with 900 priests. In Milan a Società Ecclesiastica was formed, consisting of four Canons and eighty-nine clergy, which the Jesuit organ, the *Civiltà Cattolica*, denounced as 'scandalous, schismatical, revolutionary, guilty of rebellion against the Pope and the holy Roman See' (April, 1862). At Brescia Canon Tiboni preached and published in favour of the restoration of the Bible to the people; the vulgar tongue; both kinds; abolition of compulsory confession and celibacy; election of Bishops; restraint of Papal domination. In Florence Bianciardi edited an influential reforming newspaper, the *Esaminatore*. In Naples a Società

Emancipatrice, with an organ, the *Emancipatore Cattolico*, was instituted, consisting of several thousand clergy and laymen ; and there, too, lived Cardinal Andrea, who seemed pointed out as the leader of the reformation.   In Sicily a similar society was established, with an organ, *Luce ed Amore*.

To see what was the real spirit of the nation underlying these phenomena, the Anglo-Continental Society sent Dr. Camilleri, a priest formerly officiating in Italy, and then curate to Lord Charles Hervey at Chesterford, to make a report of the state of the country from a religious point of view.   He was also instructed to 'encourage internal reformation' (*a*) 'by a distribution of the society's works'; (*b*) 'by explaining by word of mouth the limits of the legitimate jurisdiction and authority of the Bishop of Rome, especially with reference to the liberties of the Churches of North Italy and Sicily'; (*c*) 'by convincing men, both by argument and by the example of the English Church, of the possibility of a National Church reforming itself, and being at once Catholic and Protestant—Catholic, as maintaining the faith and discipline of the Holy Catholic Church ; Protestant, in rejecting Papal usurpation and dogma.'   Dr. Camilleri visited Turin, Milan, Genoa, Pisa, Leghorn, Florence, and Bologna ; and the result of his mission being to show that there was a strong reforming tendency in Italy, the society appointed five agents to act for it in that country, one of whom was Count Ottavio Tasca. The American Church co-operated by sending Dr. Langdon to represent it, and to work in accord with the society, of which he was a member.   Bookshops were opened where the publications of the society and other like works might be obtained, and short tracts were prepared and issued specially adapted to the circumstances.   One of these publications had a somewhat singular history.   Bishop Christopher Wordsworth wrote 'Three Letters on the Relations of the State and the Church in Italy,' urging the establishment of an independent National Italian Church. To these were added seven letters written by Prebendary Ford, Rev. W. E. Scudamore, Rev. G. R. Portal, and myself. The pamphlet thus formed, having been translated into Italian under the name of *Dieci Lettere*, was sent to every member of the Italian Parliament, and the thanks of the President of the Chamber were formally returned for it. Wordsworth's letters had been translated by Signor Pifferi, and the Cardinal Archbishop of Fermo, believing Signor Pifferi to have been not only the translator, but the author, offered him valuable preferment on the sole condition of his writing nothing more.

So keen was the antagonism between the young kingdom of Italy and the Papacy, that no less than thirty-four sees became vacant, the Pope refusing to consecrate the nominees of the Crown. All seemed progressing towards the establishment of a National Church, under its own Archbishops and Bishops, independent of the Papacy. By 1866 it had become necessary for the King's Government to decide whether to defy the Papacy or to make terms with it. Baron Ricasoli had now succeeded Cavour as Prime Minister, and he was in heart a Protestant; but he did not dare, as a politician, to break with the Papacy. He chose a policy of reconciliation, and by it the reformation movement in Italy was crushed—at least, for that generation. The nomination to the vacant sees was given up to the Pope; the oaths of vassalage which bind Roman Catholic Bishops to the Pope, and the bonds which attach the lower clergy to the Bishops, were drawn tighter. Loyal and patriotic priests were given up to the vengeance of their superiors, who made it their first work to stifle the spirit of reform which had been venturesome enough

15—2

to make the Vatican tremble. In every corner of Italy the Church reformers were hunted down and silenced. Finding themselves helpless, they returned to the old system, according to which they might believe what they liked and live as they liked, provided they said and did nothing to the detriment of the authority of the Curia. Priests became more than ever the slaves of the Bishops, and the Bishops were more than ever the slaves of the Pope. Six years after this time Minghetti, the Italian Prime Minister, said to me that the great obstacle to the welfare of Italy was the hostility of the Bishops.

'Is not that hostility,' I said, 'to be expected, when the Bishops are nominated by the person who ostentatiously declares himself the enemy of Italy? and cannot it be remedied by a law forbidding the oaths taken by the Bishops to the Pope, and by giving to the clergy the right of electing their Bishops?'

'Certainly,' said Minghetti; 'but, unhappily, there is no public opinion which would back up statesmen in taking such a course. Laymen are, for the most part, content with disregarding and despising religion in general because presented to them in the Papal form.'

In 1866 Papalism won the day in its struggle with Nationalism, and it appeared that the time was not come for Italy's ecclesiastical emancipation.

At this time I was brought into communication with Cardinal Andrea. On June 12, 1866, he was suspended by the Pope from his bishopric of Sabina on the alleged ground of his living at Naples in disobedience to the Papal summons to Rome, and for arrogance in writing letters to justify himself; but the real reason was that in political matters he had espoused the national cause in a firm though quiet manner. On July 6 the Cardinal wrote and published a letter of appeal to the Pope, better informed, in

which he declared that the brief of June 12 was an act
'radically unjust and uncanonical'; and he demanded
a formal trial, reminding His Holiness that 'all other
Bishops were his equals so far as order by Divine
institution went, and inferior only in jurisdiction
according to the limits laid down by the Œcumenical
Councils'; that 'a Bishop was placed to rule the
Church, not by man, but by the Holy Spirit'; and that
'there was no ecclesiastical dignity more sublime or
independent than that of a Bishop.' The next month
he wrote to Cardinal Patrizi in like terms, and engaged
Professor Passaglia to write a defence of the liberty
and independence of Bishops. Passaglia's volume was
published in 1867, and the Cardinal courteously presented a copy of it to me, in return for which I wrote
a letter, framed on the model of one of Archbishop
Wake's letters to Dupin, expressive of a longing to
see the Cardinal place himself at the head of an
Italian Synod and revindicate the ancient liberties of
the Italian National Church. The Cardinal returned
his thanks, and requested me to send him books
bearing on the subject of the letter. In the autumn
of 1867 His Eminence determined to obey the Papal
summons, and to go to Rome. Before doing so he
wrote his will, in which, speaking of his struggle
with the Pope, he distinguished between the man and
the Pontiff. Giovanni Mastai had erred, being deceived
by Antonelli, who was 'an Ahitophel'; by Patrizi,
who was 'an ignorant flatterer'; and by Caterini, who
was 'a rogue.' Before setting off for Rome, he sent
me a message requesting me to put no faith in any
recantation that might be attributed to him. If he
signed any, it would be by compulsion. On his
arrival at Rome he was put under strict surveillance,
and was no longer able to write freely. In February,
1868, he sent me a book in which was contained a
paper with the words 'L' ultimo atto libero, fatto in

Napoli' (This was my last free act done in Naples), in
the Cardinal's handwriting. On April 11 he demanded
leave to return to Naples, which was refused by
Antonelli. He replied that he would not remain later
than May 21. On Wednesday, May 13, he had a
personal interview with the Pope, and received permission to go. The next day, May 14, after his usual
drive, he was taken suddenly ill at six o'clock, and died
at eleven o'clock the same evening. The body was
opened by three medical men in the presence of three
ecclesiastics, and they declared that there was nothing
in the state of the body to explain his sudden death.
His papers were, according to custom, sealed up and
carried to Antonelli's house. The Pope officiated at
his funeral. Eusebio Reali, Professor in the University
of Siena, expressed the general belief in Italy in a
letter written to the *Unità Cristiana* of May 24, in
which he said : ' I, and many others, have received the
sad news with sorrow, but without surprise. I thought
that on the day on which the unhappy Cardinal went
to Rome he ran wilfully into the arms of death. He
who had gone out thence, three years ago, as an
adversary, could not return except as a victim.' The
natural head of the reforming party, which was
especially strong at Naples, was thus removed out of
the way of Antonelli and the Curia.

Fifteen years after Ricasoli's submission, a movement towards reform was begun in Italy on a much
smaller scale, and with fewer anticipations of a great
result, to which the society gave a helping hand ; but
it now turned its attention especially to Spain, where
liberty of conscience was declared in 1868. Since the
time that Protestantism had been burnt out of Spain
by Philip II. and the Inquisition, the profession of any
faith except that of the dominant Church had been
contrary to law, and punishable with death or im-
prisonment. A Spaniard from Catalonia, desirous of

a Protestant education, had been sent to England by the Rev. M. Powley, Chaplain at Gibraltar, and, after training at St. Aidan's, was ordained by the Bishop of Gibraltar and sent by the Anglo-Continental Society to Gibraltar, where he conducted a service in the Spanish language, translated from the English Prayer-Book. But he was not allowed to open his mouth outside the British lines. Gibraltar was also the refuge of the Rev. J. B. Cabrera, who occupied some part of his time in translating Bishop Harold Browne's *Exposition of the Thirty-nine Articles* for the society. When, in 1868, Queen Isabella, who had long scandalized Europe by the combined profligacy and bigotry of her Court, was deposed by a revolution conducted by General Prim, the refugees in Gibraltar found Spain opened to them, and Protestant congregations were established in all the chief towns in the Peninsula. Most of these congregations were Presbyterian in character, but some 2,000 out of 10,000 souls declared themselves Episcopalians under the direction of the Rev. J. B. Cabrera. The latter body, to which the Anglo-Continental Society gave such help and support as it could, organized itself so definitely during the next ten years that, in conjunction with the Portuguese reformers, it petitioned the Lambeth Conference of 1878 to extend to it a brotherly recognition; and it requested the Archbishop of Canterbury or the Archbishop of Armagh to nominate a Bishop to superintend its work. Lord Plunket, who was present as Bishop of Meath, was much interested by this appeal of Spanish brethren, and from hence originated his work for Spain which culminated in the consecration of Bishop Cabrera. For the present, Archbishop Tait, speaking in behalf of the Lambeth Conference, advised the petitioners to be content with the assistance which Bishop Riley, lately appointed Bishop for Mexico by the American Church, was willing to offer them.

Lord Plunket wrote to me to ask if the Anglo-Continental Society would come to the assistance of the Spanish reformers in respect to material help. On consideration, it appeared best that a separate organization should be instituted for Spain and Portugal, the proceedings of which were annually reported to the committee of the Anglo-Continental Society by Lord Plunket.

CHAPTER XIV

Norwich—Bishop Pelham—Dean Goulburn—Canon Heaviside—
W. E. Gladstone.

DURING my residence in Norwich (1861-1869), the Bishop of the diocese was Dr. Pelham, the last of the Bishops said to have been appointed by Lord Palmerston at the instance of Lord Shaftesbury. He was a man of great personal piety, and devoted to the work of his diocese; deeply loved by those who knew him well, and respected by all. In his episcopate a difficulty occurred in respect to the Church Congress. At the previous Congress it had been stated by Hugh Stowell that he was sure that the Bishop would welcome the next year's Congress at Norwich. Accordingly, Norwich was fixed upon, and the previous Congress was dissolved. When the time came for making preparations for the new Congress, Hugh Stowell was dead, and the Bishop had received no invitation; and without an invitation he did not see his way to act. The difficulty arose from there being at that time no permanent Congress committee, and therefore nobody connected with the Congress from whom an invitation could emanate, so that there appeared a danger of the lapse of the year's Congress. The Bishop felt that his scruple would be removed if he received an invitation from the diocese; a public meeting was therefore held in Norwich, which appointed a committee to canvass the clergy and leading laity of Norfolk. The great majority being in favour of the proposal, a resolution was passed that the diocese, as shown by the canvass, desired and invited the Bishop to preside at the meeting. The Congress was held, and turned out to be one of the most important in the series, being attended by Dr. Pusey, Bishop Wilberforce, Bishop Harvey Goodwin, and others. The Bishop, as usual, showed himself an excellent chairman.

Dr. Goulburn, who succeeded Dr. Pellew as Dean of Norwich on the latter's death, united in himself the better qualities both of the Evangelical and the Oxford Movement. His sermons and books were, and are, of great influence. He had a devoted following in Norfolk.

The Dean had Meyrick for one of his Christian names, and on my inquiring what was the cause of it, I was told the following tale: The Dean's father, when a young man, engaged himself to be married to a lady, whose name, if I recollect right, was Chetwynd. They had not sufficient means on which to marry. After the engagement had continued for some time, Miss Meyrick, an aunt of Miss Chetwynd, an elderly lady stiff with ceremony and brocade, said that she should 'desire to see that young man.' On his arrival, she received him with a ceremonious curtsey in return for his bow. Having asked him some questions, and conversed with him for a short time, she dismissed him with the same formal curtsey with which she had received him. But as he went away she said: 'I think, sir, that this marriage must proceed.' As she was the means of enabling the wedding 'to proceed,' Mr. Goulburn's eldest son was named Meyrick after her. I did not trace the lineage of Miss Meyrick, but she was no doubt connected more or less closely with the Meyricks of Bodorgan, as she spelt her name with a y representing the u in the

Welsh *Meuric*, from whom the Meyricks of Bodorgan, and all who spell their name in the same way, are believed to be derived.

The only resident Canon was Canon Heaviside, an able and active-minded man, who took part in the work of most of the philanthropical and religious societies of the city. His motto seemed to be ' Live, and let live '; he was never known to say an unkind word of anyone, and his house and table were open to all his friends and acquaintances. He had taken high mathematical honours at Cambridge, and had been examiner at Haileybury under the old system.

There is in Norwich a clerical society called by the singular name of the Boat Club, because the first five members of it had been in the habit of rowing in a four-oar on the river for exercise. Acting in behalf of this society, I exerted myself to establish a ' Churchman's Club,' where young men employed in the shops might find a resting-place when unemployed, and read books or newspapers, and be supplied with coffee. A committee of management was appointed, partly consisting of the clergy and partly of the young men, and arrangements were made for weekly classes and annual public meetings. The subjects of instruction for the classes were the Bible, Church history, ecclesiastical music, shorthand, and some others. I undertook the class of Church history, beginning with the Acts of the Apostles, and going on to sketch the story of the primitive ages. I continued it each week during one winter and spring. The numbers attending the class were not great, but those who came were much interested. One of them was a man employed in a factory, and nearly sixty years of age. The club was afterwards amalgamated with the Church of England Young Men's Institution.

A considerable part of the external business of the diocese was done by Canon Hinds Howell. After his ordination he was curate to Bishop Phillpotts of Exeter, but when his half-brother, Dr. Hinds, was appointed Bishop of Norwich, he migrated from the West to the East of England, becoming Rector of Drayton and Honorary Canon of Norwich in 1855. In 1868 he was elected Proctor to represent the clergy of the Norwich Diocese in Convocation. He was a type of the well-to-do, high Tory, despotic parsons, who ruled their parishes with a rod, apparently of iron, but which every parishioner knew to be wrapped round with so soft a material, made of love and kindliness, as never to hurt. When he was past eighty, I was walking with him to the village school, which he or his daughter (and sometimes both) visited every day, when he saw, on the bank above us, a boy who ought to have been at school. 'Where are you going, sir?' cried Howell. The boy grinned and did not answer. Howell leaped up the bank as if he had been twenty, and, seizing the boy by the collar of his coat, demanded ferociously where he was going. The boy, still grinning, said that the governess had sent him home. 'What for?' said Howell. 'Mother was taken bad last night,' said the boy. 'Eh?' said Howell; 'tell her I'll call in the course of a few hours. And if she wants any soup, go to the Rectory for it.' Then, resuming his ferocious tone, 'And, you young rascal, another time, answer when you are spoken to.' The boy grinned again, and went on his way, having known all along that parson meant no harm to him. Men of Howell's stamp loved their Church and loved the poor, and England owes much to them.

In the autumn of 1868 was held the Church Congress at Dublin, which I attended in company with Bishop Harvey Goodwin, then Dean of Ely.

On my way to Ireland, I stopped for two nights with Dean Howson at Chester. He was the joint author, with Conybeare, of the *Life of St. Paul—*

a man of ability, piety, and geniality. Some years later he did good service at the Conferences of Bonn by showing that the Old Catholics had the sympathies of some, at least, belonging to every section of the English Church. He there co-operated with Canon Liddon, and they showed an agreement in all essentials. On his proposal, a clause was added to Dr. v. Döllinger's statement of the doctrine of the Holy Communion, as he feared that its aspect as a sacred feast was not indicated with sufficient prominence.

From Chester I went to Bangor, and thence to Bodorgan. The house is beautifully situated, with a distant view of Snowdon, and approached by a long drive bordered on each side, first by turf, and then by shrubs. I was welcomed cordially by Mr. Fuller Meyrick, the owner, and he exhibited to me some of the treasures of the library. I found there a book containing an account of families connected with the house of Bodorgan, together with the arms to which they were entitled in addition to the general Meyrick arms. Among them was a shield representing three cocks, and a statement that it belonged to 'Meuric, King of Dyned, from whom they of Kidwelly do descend.' These were arms which my grandfather brought with him when he came into England from Kidwelly. At a later date, when paying a visit to the Bishop of Bangor, I was driven to Bodorgan, together with my daughter Mabel, by Archdeacon Pryce, but at that time, unfortunately, the owners were absent.

In Dublin I was interested to meet a Mr. Samuel Meyrick, whose family had been settled for 200 years in Ireland, having emigrated there from Wales. He belonged to the Meyricks of Bush, descended, like the Caemarthenshire branch, from Rowland Meyrick, Bishop of Bangor.

Archbishop Trench, who presided at the Congress in Dublin, was at the time in great distress owing to the Irish Disestablishment, which was then impending. I asked him whether he thought it desirable to hold a meeting of the English Churchmen then in Dublin to strengthen his hands in resisting the measure; but he judged that things were gone too far, and that such a step would be useless, and Bishop Wilberforce, whom he consulted, was of the same opinion. It was at this Congress that Dean Magee, soon after appointed Bishop of Peterborough, and subsequently Archbishop of York, preached his famous sermon on the text 'Come over and help us.' The three most eloquent ecclesiastics of the Anglican Church took part in the discussions of the Congress — Bishop Wilberforce, Bishop Magee, and Bishop Alexander of Derry, afterwards Archbishop of Armagh.

On my way to Dublin I paid a visit, together with Dr. John Ogle, to Mr. Gladstone at Hawarden. We were most courteously and kindly received, and after luncheon Mr. Gladstone took us into his library, the rule of which was that visitors might talk as they would on their first visit, but afterwards must keep a severe silence. After some conversation, the subject of evolution and Darwinism came up, and Mr. Gladstone said very emphatically: 'Is there any proved instance of one class passing into another? I know none.'

My first acquaintance with Mr. Gladstone was made in the year 1849 in Dalkeith Palace, where he made a passing visit. The Duchess of Buccleuch asked me to show to him a part of the park called, if I recollect, the Oak Walk, and this gave me an opportunity of a good deal of conversation, in which I was much struck by the frankness with which Mr. Gladstone spoke on Church subjects with a young man not yet a Master of Arts. At a later time, when Mr. Gladstone was candidate for the University of Oxford, I voted for him each time that he stood, and I had a general invitation from him to breakfast with him any Wednesday that I was in London. Sometimes these breakfasts were attended by few, sometimes by a large number, frequent guests being Sir Robert Inglis, the elder member for Oxford, Bishop Wilberforce, and Lord Lyttelton. When he became Prime Minister many leading politicians were present. On one occasion the Marquis of Cavour and a French notability sat on each side of Mr. Gladstone, and it was interesting to note the ease with which Mr. Gladstone passed from Italian to French and from French to English in addressing one or other of his guests.

There were three things which brought me into communication with Mr. Gladstone, in addition to University reform, of which I have already spoken : they were the interest that he took in the Old Catholic Movement, his love for Italy, and his antagonism to the modern Roman system, which he termed Vaticanism, to which was afterwards added his antagonism to the rationalist Biblical criticism. On the first he wrote to Madame Novikoff: ' My interest in the Old Catholics is cordial. A sister of mine died in virtual union with them after having been Roman over thirty years. They may do great good, and prevent the Latin Church by moral force from further extravagancies.' To the editor of the *Labaro* he said : ' I heartily wish prosperity to the Reform Movement begun within the Italian Church. I think it most important that it should become fully known in England, and the more frequently and largely it is brought before us, the better. But I need not add that the vitality of the movement must depend, with God's help, on its really Italian character and on its having its roots in Italian soil. For my part, I am not animated by the spirit of controversy on such a question ; but when members of the Latin Church feel with Döllinger that it is impossible to lay a safe foundation on an historical falsehood, and that truth, faith, and liberty will stand or fall together, I cannot, as a Christian, deny them my sympathy. However, I am not disposed to act individually, and my desire on this, as on other questions, is to act in accordance with the authorities of the Anglican Church, and especially with the Archbishop of Canterbury, whom we regard as our spiritual head.'

To the *Libero Edificare* he wrote : 'My humble hope for Italy lies in a reformation of its Church from within its own bosom on the basis of the ancient Christian Creed.'

When Dr. v. Döllinger called the first Conference of Bonn, Mr. Gladstone's interest in Old Catholicism was redoubled. Mr. Gladstone, Bishop Harold Browne, and Bishop Christopher Wordsworth were the three Englishmen of leading position who saw what Döllinger's movement might become, and what great results might follow to the Church at large from the attempt made by him to combine all non-Vaticanized episcopal Churches in an anti-Roman alliance. Mr. Gladstone heartily embraced the conclusions of the first Conference, and before the second Conference he wrote a warm letter of approval to Dr. v. Döllinger, explaining that he did so ' from my firm confidence in your wisdom, and my profound sympathy with what I believe to be your general purpose.' Immediately after the second Conference at Bonn, held in August, 1875, the committee of the Anglo-Continental Society determined to raise funds for the education of Old Catholic students at Bonn, and I preached a sermon in Lincoln Cathedral on the subject.

Mr. Gladstone wrote : 'I thank you very much for your able, clear, and very interesting address. I

should be most happy to join in the proposed sub-
scription, if, as I have no doubt, it has the approval
of Dr. Döllinger. What I would advise is a small
meeting of friendly persons in London next February
to consider how the matter should be put forward and
generally how to help.' Accordingly, Mr. Gladstone
met some of the members of the committee of the
Anglo-Continental Society in Delahay Street, and he
gave £40 towards the fund for scholarships for the
Old Catholic students at Bonn in 1875, and £20 in
1876. In respect to showing English sympathy with
the cause, he wrote: 'I do not at present see any
better method of proceeding than that proposed by
Mr. [Beresford] Hope.' This was an address to
Döllinger, which was signed by 3,800 clergy and
4,250 laymen.

In the following year Mr. Gladstone wrote to me:
'As respects Bonn, I was much pleased with the
recent address of Bishop Herzog, and with the letter
of Abbé Deramey in your *Correspondence of the
Anglo-Continental Society* just received; but I do
not know enough of the position and of the relation
of the Swiss to the German Old Catholics to be prepared to take any active part about it. Your *Foreign
Church Chronicle* seems to me to fill a great gap, and,
if well supported, to have great promise of utility. I
propose to subscribe to it, wishing it all manner of
good.' On my asking Mr. Gladstone to join the committee of the Anglo-Continental Society, he replied:
'Neither political considerations nor want of confidence in the least degree obstruct my agreeing to
your kind request, but I have a dislike to the
ostensible assumption of duties which I know I
cannot fulfil, and *therefore*, unless you strongly wish
it otherwise, I would rather remain on your lists as
a simple contributor. I would on no account send
you such an answer, were I not under the impression

16

that a sign of approval is, in truth, as completely given in this way as it can be in any. I am very glad to hear that the society grows. It was to be expected at its early stages its progress should be slow, and I have no doubt you find much difficulty in finding vents for your publications on the Continent.'

Mr. Gladstone's love for Italy commenced when, in his letters to Lord Aberdeen, he made his noble appeal to the public opinion of Europe against the treatment by the King of Naples of Baron Poerio and his companions, who were thrown into prison on no other ground than that they had the reputation of being Liberals; and from that time forward Italy cast over him that fascination which she alone of all countries seems capable of exercising. This has been indicated by some of the passages already quoted respecting the growth of the Old Catholic Movement in Italy.

In 1862 I forwarded to him some letters written by Italians, and in sending them back he wrote: ' I return these interesting letters, which before to-day I had not found time to read. If Garibaldi would come to England, he would have a great reception. In the matter of Rattazzi as against Ricasoli, I cannot but think Italy has lost much by the last change of her Ministry; but I trust, notwithstanding, that all who wish her well will rally round the Italian Government as such, and cause the country to present one face to friend and foe. It is impossible not to regard with profound interest the possible, or indeed probable, course of religious affairs in Italy, nor I think can any individual blame himself—at least, I hope not—if, in intercourse with his friends there, he speaks according to his convictions and his hopes, within the bounds of truth and reason.' At the same time he was afraid of any interference from without which might give offence to Italian susceptibilities. When I asked him to speak on the subject of Italian reform, he replied : 'I am afraid there is more than one conclusive reason against my complying with your request, that I would attend and speak at the proposed meeting of the Continental Society ; but that which at once and principally operates with me is, that I think the relative prominence which my name, through accidental circumstances, has acquired in Italy with respect to several great public questions, renders it highly inexpedient for me to interfere in any design which aims directly and publicly at influencing the course of religious questions. The effect of my doing this would, I think, be to damage both.'

Mr. Gladstone's hostility to the existing tendencies in the Church of Rome was exhibited by his powerful denunciation of 'Vaticanism' and the less well-known proposal that he made to the British Cabinet to adopt the course recommended, at Döllinger's instigation, by the Bavarian Government, to prohibit the admission of the dogma of the Pope's Infallibility into European States as incompatible with civil allegiance. This proposal was made at the time that the Vatican Council was sitting, and I have already stated why it was not adopted.* Mr. Gladstone's attitude towards Vaticanism was not merely the result of an antagonism to the Vatican Council, but was a permanent trait in his character. As late as the year 1891, he wrote, in a letter which was published, that he 'did not in the least degree withdraw his profound opposition to the Vatican as the mortal enemy of human liberty.'

There was another theological point which brought me into contact and sympathy with Mr. Gladstone. This was the question of modern criticism, designated by Mr. Gladstone as 'negative criticism,' which was showing itself in its chief advocates to be rationalistic in its character. The three leading men who first

* See p. 59.

16—2

gave warning of an approaching danger were Bishop Ellicott, Bishop Charles Wordsworth, and Mr. Gladstone, and their warning was followed by a Declaration, chiefly inspired by Dean Goulburn, signed by thirty-eight Churchmen, of whom I was one, in the last month of 1891. Mr. Gladstone's contribution to the subject was a book entitled *The Impregnable Rock of Holy Scripture*, in which he offered the most convincing proof of the antiquity and sanctity of many of the Psalms to which that character had been denied, and of the genuine character of the Mosaic legislation.

In 1891 I had written an article remonstrating with the late Bishop of Manchester for throwing his shield over rationalistic impugners of Holy Scripture, and for arguing in favour of the theory of the ignorance of the Lord Jesus Christ on the hypothesis that He had voluntarily laid aside His knowledge. I sent a reprint of the article to Mr. Gladstone, and received the following reply :

' DEAR MR. MEYRICK,

'On the morning when I received your very interesting letter I was laid down with influenza.

'I think you entirely dispose of the Bishop's argument. The subject [of our Lord's knowledge] is so lofty and mysterious in itself that I do not venture to enter upon it, but I apprehend that in *nothing* was He Himself deceived, and in *nothing* did He deceive others.'

Mr. Gladstone was a great statesman : whether in that capacity he did or did not make serious mistakes in South Africa and the Soudan, in Oxford and in Ireland, I am not now inquiring. He was also a great Churchman, superior to most of his contemporaries, whether lay or ecclesiastical. That so true and faithful a Christian (one of his last sayings was, ' All I write, and all I think, and all I hope, is based upon the Divinity of our Lord—the one central hope of our poor wayward race '), so outspoken a defender of the Christian revelation (witness his *Impregnable Rock of Holy Scripture*), so firm an opponent of the whole system of Popery (witness his *Vaticanism* and his sympathy with Old Catholic reform), so righteous an enemy of tyranny (witness his early letters to Lord Aberdeen and his efforts in behalf of Bulgaria and Armenia), should have been Prime Minister of England, and *because of* those qualities and of that character should have been honoured in his death, without regard to his political views, as no other man within our memory has been honoured, is a thing of which Englishmen may be proud.

CHAPTER XV

Incumbency of Blickling—Bishop Christopher Wordsworth—Archbishop Benson—Bishop Lightfoot—Bishop Cleveland Coxe.

IN the autumn of 1868 I was instituted to the living of Blickling and Erpingham, which led to my resignation of the office of H.M. Inspector of Schools, after holding it for ten years, and to my leaving Norwich. In the same year Dr. Christopher Wordsworth was nominated Bishop of Lincoln, and he appointed E. W. Benson, then Head of Wellington College, and myself, as his examining chaplains, and we accordingly attended him on his consecration in Westminster Abbey, February 24, 1869. It was my usual practice to go to Riseholme twice in the year for the examination of candidates, and on the Bishop's resignation in 1884 he gave me a copy of the Benedictine edition of the works of St. Chrysostom, with the following inscription : 'This copy of the works of St. John Chrysostom is affectionately offered to his very dear friend, brother, and chaplain, the Rev. Canon Meyrick, in grateful remembrance of his faithful and loving service, wise and learned counsel, and tender sympathy and help, by his thankful fellow-labourer, C. Lincoln. Christmas Day, 1884.'

Bishop Christopher Wordsworth was one of the truest successors and representatives of the Anglican divines of the seventeenth century that we have seen in our own days. He had their learning, their literary

246

diligence, their firm grasp of Catholic truth, their un-compromising hostility to Popery, their resistance to Puritanism, their distrust of latitudinarianism, their wholesome way of knowing what they meant and saying it, their courage, their manliness. Throughout the time of the Tractarian Movement there were thoughtful and learned men who did not identify them-selves with the Tractarian party, though co-operating with it on many points and on many occasions. Such were Archbishop Trench, Bishop S. Wilberforce, Dean Hook, and Wordsworth. Archbishop Trench was removed from the scene by his Irish archbishopric. The other three men did much towards closing the breach which Newman's secession had made in the walls of the Church of England, and by their learning and personal firmness confirming perplexed souls in the faith of their forefathers. Wordsworth, like his father, brothers, and son, was a fine scholar, and it was delightful to see in him the scholar underlying the theologian, and giving him a sympathy with all belonging to the republic of letters. The Church of England has been, and is, singularly happy in having prelates who, while they are Bishops first and above all things, are also scholars and men of general cultiva-tion and learning ; that gives her a hold on the educated classes, which in every other European country have, to a large degree, fallen away from the Christian faith.

Wordsworth was made for a Bishop, and the absolute agreement of his own personal views with the doctrine, tenets, traditions, and sentiments of the Church of England, in their extension and in their limitation, made his position as an English Bishop a singularly happy and fortunate one. He was loyal, to the inner-most core of his heart, to the Church of which he was a chief officer, both in her Catholic and in her Pro-testant aspect ; and he had no difficulty in reconciling these characteristics, but always felt and maintained that the one necessarily involved the other under the conditions of modern Christendom. His diocese claimed and received his first care, but it did not make him forget the claims of the province and of the National Church. Nor, again, did the affairs of the National Church so absorb his attention as to make him careless of the fortunes of the Church Catholic. He shares with Bishop Harold Browne and Mr. Gladstone the distinction of having realized how great a thing the Old Catholic Movement might be in respect to the whole of Christendom, by making foreign Christians recognise the difference between true Catholicism and mediævalism. Realizing the evils of the system culminating in Popery, he threw himself into the thick of the battle against Roman claims and doctrines. His *Letters to M. Gondon*, together with the sequel, *On the Destructive Character of the Church of Rome both in Religion and Polity*, are not only a brilliant specimen of controversial polemics, but serve as a repertory, from which antipapal weapons may be drawn for all time. The great literary work of his life was not, however, controversial, being a commentary on the whole of Holy Scripture. His literary and public acts exhibited only one side of his character. His affectionateness was shown, like that of Bishop Harold Browne, in private and family life ; the combination of simplicity and elevation of tone exemplified at Riseholme and Farnham gave to those who witnessed it a lesson on the superiority of the system which permits married life to its clergy to that which forbids it, even when the results of the latter are not conspicuous for their evil. Bishop Wordsworth determined on his resignation at the end of 1884, and carried it out early in 1885. Two months later he died, and was buried at Riseholme near Lincoln.

My brother examining chaplain was, as I said, E. W. Benson, a most pleasant colleague to work with.

We met twice a year at Riseholme to conduct the examinations, and after he had become Chancellor of Lincoln I occasionally stayed with him and Mrs. Benson, when I preached at the cathedral in virtue of my non-residentiary canonry. When leaving Lincoln for Truro, of which he was appointed Bishop in 1876, he wrote to me as follows:

'*December* 20, 1876.

' MY DEAR BROTHER,

'I do trust that this is a call, even because it is unwelcome to leave the Bishop and the students and the happy, happy work, for work to which I do not feel equal. Our brotherly work together, your constant genial and loving interest in all that I had in hand—though my deep interest in your work never could culminate in any real activity simply because hours and hands were quite full—is, I assure you, a sweetness not ever to be forgotten. I hope we shall many a time welcome you at Truro. . . . We all are praying for Cornwall, and we hope we may trust you for the like prayers.

'Your ever affectionate

' E. W. BENSON.'

He announced his appointment to the primacy to me in the following characteristic postcard in Greek: Εὔχου ὑπὲρ ἐμοῦ · ἔξωθεν μάχαι, ἔσωθεν φόβοι (Pray for me. Without are fightings, within are fears), indicating the modesty and humility with which he began his great archiepiscopate—an archiepiscopate made great not only by his talents, his zeal, his energy, his enthusiasm, his perseverance, but by his modesty, his humility, his courtesy, his quiet good sense, and, above all, his personal piety.

Archbishop Benson was one of a trio, each of whom did good service to the Church—Westcott, Lightfoot, Benson. The ablest and most learned of these was

Bishop Lightfoot, who was a worthy successor of the great Bishop Butler in the See of Durham; but Benson had qualities which made him more suited for the office of Archbishop of Canterbury than either Lightfoot or Westcott. Benson had sympathy with all parties within the Church, and though, no doubt, he gave encouragement to the Ritualist section of the clergy by the judgment that he passed in the Archbishop's Court in the case of Bishop King of Lincoln, yet, as time passed and the views of the Ritualistic party developed themselves, he grew more and more alienated from them, and he more and more discouraged them. He took a warm interest in the Old Catholic Movement on the Continent, signing the address of thanks to Döllinger in 1874, and in 1885 presiding over a public meeting, held in the house of the Marquis of Bristol in behalf of the Anglo-Continental Society, at which he argued that it was our wisdom and duty to keep alive such sparks of reformation as were to be found in the Continental Churches, and so to fan them into a flame that a national movement might take place in them, as had been the case in England. Acting, like Archbishop Tait, for the Lambeth Conference, he gave to the Bishop of Salisbury (John Wordsworth) the charge of caring for the Italian Reformed Communion. The Archbishop's interest in the welfare of foreign Christendom was also shown by his Mission to the Assyrian Christians, and by the appointment of an Anglican Bishop at Jerusalem. His last efforts were given to drawing closer the bands which unite the English and the Irish Churches. He held earnest communications with Archbishop Plunket on the subject, but before the Lambeth Conference, for which they were preparing, was held, both the Archbishops had passed away.

Bishop Lightfoot first made his mark as a scholar and teacher in the University of Cambridge. His

reputation grew from the sermons that he preached
as Canon of St. Paul's, and when he had become
Bishop the Church woke up to the glad fact that
she had in him a prelate, already one of the first
theologians of his generation, and promising soon
to be known as a pre-eminently good administrator.
Whether in the sphere of criticism, or of ecclesiastical
history, or of apologetics, it is a pleasure to study any
work which emanated from his pen.   His works are
written with a perfect mastery of his subject, and we
see, as we read, that he would never have published
the book until he knew all that was to be known of
the matter with which he dealt.   Hard as he worked
in preparing his books and in study, he was the
reverse of a bookworm, being sympathetically alive
to all the interests of his friends, his Church, and his
country.   A good deal of unasked compassion has
been wasted on him for giving up his professorship
and accepting a bishopric.   I asked him once if he
regretted the loss of the greater opportunities that he
had had of writing books of theology, and he said,
No ; the years that he had been a Bishop had been
the happiest years of his life.   Occupation that was
merely literary would not have satisfied him.   As it
was, he was brought more closely into contact with
the hearts and souls of living men.   His ecclesiastical
interest was not confined to his diocese or to the
Church of England, but was conterminous with the
Church Catholic ; and while entirely without harsh-
ness, he was free from the unwholesome tenderness
towards the Church of Rome which ignores her
corruptions and refuses to condemn her encroach-
ments.   In a sermon preached at the Wolverhampton
Congress, he showed that he regarded the Anglican
communion as the hope of Christendom.   Having
pointed out that she retains the form of Church
government which had been handed down from

Apostolic times, and had cast off the accretions which had gathered about the Apostolic doctrine and practice, he declares that the central position which she thus holds is a vantage-ground which fits her to be a mediator when and wheresoever an occasion for mediation may arise.

'The Anglican communion,' he continues, 'now comprises within her embrace Churches established, unestablished, and disestablished. She has flourishing branches in every continent of the globe . . . . Nor is this all. With the ancient Churches of the East our relations are becoming every day more intimate. . . . What, then, shall we say? That catholicity has been restored to the English Church in a surprising way. Catholic indeed she was potentially before in her doctrine and polity; but now she is Catholic in fact, Catholic in her interests and sympathies, Catholic in her responsibilities and duties.' This position he pronounces to be 'a true inspiration to ourselves, and an untold blessing to mankind.'

His commentaries on some of St. Paul's Epistles and his edition of the Apostolic Fathers are possessions of permanent value to the Church.

A little before his death in 1890 Bishop Lightfoot came to Bournemouth, where I was staying at the time. I was glad to be able to pay him a last visit; I found him feebler, but otherwise quite unchanged.

In 1869 I received a visit at Erpingham from Bishop Cleveland Coxe, of Western New York. We had corresponded with each other as brethren beloved in the Lord for some twenty years, but now we first met in the flesh, and henceforth we were more drawn to each other with an increased affection; for his loving disposition and transparent truthfulness, added to his great abilities, could not fail to win the hearts of those with whom he associated and sympathized. He knew

England as scarcely one Englishman knows it, and, while an American patriot to his heart's core, he loved England as few Englishmen love it.   He felt in his inmost consciousness that England was his own country, whence he and his compatriots derived their origin, and he would not yield to any Englishman his claim to a share in the glories of our poets, our sovereigns, our warriors, and our statesmen.   Above all, he prized the Anglican Church as his own, divided indeed into the English and American communions for the last hundred years, but as much American as English till that division, and after that division still essentially and organically one.

His *Impressions of England* show his knowledge and his love of the old country.   Indeed, it was a pleasure to take a drive with him through the streets of London or the roads of rural England, and hear him tell what historical event each spot was connected with.   And if the event bore on the fortunes of the Church, his eye would light up, and it might be seen that he was living past times over again, as though he himself were acting or suffering as the Churchmen of the day acted or suffered.

He lived for Christ and Christ's cause.   All that he said (and he was an eloquent orator), all that he wrote (and he was a prolific writer), all that he did (and he was a man of incessant action), was inspired by an overmastering desire of advancing Christ's kingdom on earth.   His first striking poetical production, *Christian Ballads* (a copy of which he gave to my daughter Dorothy, his godchild), showed the deepest devotion to Christ's Church and to the Anglican Prayer-Book.   While he was still Rector of Grace Church, Baltimore, he brought out *Thoughts on the Services: designed as an Introduction to the Liturgy and an Aid to its Devout Use*, which passed through several editions.   Both these books popularized the

Church and her services at home and here. As he grew older he recognised two great opponents to Catholic truth—Popery and Neologianism—and against both he strove manfully and faithfully to the day of his death, as speaker, writer, pastor, prelate, his standing-ground being the same as that of Christopher Wordsworth or Dean Hook or Harold Browne among ourselves. One of his publications in opposition to Popery was a reprint in America, with an introduction by himself, of three articles contributed by me to the *Christian Remembrancer*, on Roman Moral and Devotional Theology, showing the teaching of St. Alfonso de' Liguori, authorized teacher of the Church of Rome, on truthfulness, theft, and Mariolatry.

The book of his issuing which had most influence upon me and upon many others was his *Sympathies of the Continent*, which contained the proposals of Dean Hirscher for the reform of the doctrines and discipline of the Roman Catholic Church as at present existing on the Continent. This book the young American presbyter introduced to the English-speaking reader, not only by a translation, but by a warm commendation, in which he pointed out how the highest minds abroad were yearning for an ecclesiastical system similar to that enjoyed through God's mercy by the Anglican Church, while they were still ignorant of its actual existence in England and America. This discovery which the young clergyman made in his first journey on the Continent sank deep into his heart, and affected the whole of his after-life and work. When the Anglo-Continental Society was established, founded by a brother clergyman of English Orders who had a similar experience in Spain and Italy as the American presbyter had in Germany, he held out both hands to me, and, with Harold Browne, Christopher Wordsworth, and Bishop Whittingham of Maryland, was one of the mainstays of the society until his death.

In 1895 he preached a great sermon at the Convention of the American Church, held in Minneapolis, called 'The Catholic Religion for the American People,' which ended with these words: 'Thank God, we look for the Resurrection of the dead and the life of the world to come.' In the next year he had departed this life.

CHAPTER XVI

Old Catholicism—The Vatican Council—The Bonn Conference—
Dr. v. Döllinger—Bishop Reinkens—Bishop Herzog—Archbishop
Lycurgus—Arch-Priest Janyscheff—General Kiréeff—A. J. B.
Beresford Hope.

IN 1870 the Vatican Council was held, at which a
Jesuit intrigue brought about, by a vote of 370 prelates, of whom 276 were Italian out of a total of 601,
the declaration of the Infallibility of the Pope, when
speaking *ex cathedrâ*, or officially, on a matter of faith
or morals, and a further declaration that the Pope was
the Universal Bishop of the Church. The opposition
to the new dogma had been led by the German
Bishops, supported by Darboy of Paris, Dupanloup
of Orleans, Strossmayer of Diakovar. After their
defeat in the Council, men asked what these Bishops
would do. Bound by oaths of vassalage to the Roman
Pontiff, and unable to exercise their functions without
his permission constantly renewed—fearing, too, for
the unity of the Church, which they valued more than
adherence to the truth—they one and all gave way.
The German Bishops met at Fulda and counselled
submission ; but among the presbyters of the German
Church there were men of too great learning to believe
the new dogma, and of too great honesty to accept and
promulgate what they did not believe. Dr. v. Döllinger
and thirteen associates met at Nuremberg in August,
1870, and refused submission to the novel doctrine.

The Archbishop of Munich demanded Döllinger's adhesion. Döllinger replied by an absolute refusal, publicly made, which brought upon him an excommunication in April, 1871. At this time I paid a visit to Munich, and spent the greater part of two days with Dr. v. Döllinger. It was a most interesting visit to make at such a moment. Döllinger was firm and decided without the shadow of a disposition to yield to the Archbishop's pressure. 'When they tell me to believe that the Bishop of Rome has been regarded by the Church as infallible, they might as well tell me to believe that two and two make five.' He was still in hopes that Bishop Hefele and Bishop Strossmayer might refuse to accept the Vatican dogmas. Dupanloup had not yet submitted, and Hungary had not given the *Regium Placitum* to the publication of the Bull, nor had Bavaria, although it had been published there. He gave me a copy of the *Declaration to the Archbishop of Munich*, which he had published, and I left with him some tracts relating to the Anglican Church. As we parted, he said, with a bright smile: 'We are walking in parallel paths with scarcely a barrier between us.' By the action of Döllinger and his thirteen associates at Nuremberg, the Old Catholic community was formed as a body separate from Rome, and by Conferences held at Munich in the autumn of 1871 and at Cologne in 1872 a beginning was made of its organization.

Immediately after the close of the Cologne Conference a meeting was held of Old Catholics, Orientals and Anglicans, presided over by Professor von Schulte, to consider the question of the union of the non-Vaticanized Churches. It was determined, on the President's proposal, that such union was desirable and attainable, and that measures should be taken to realize it. As a starting-point, Professor Michelis moved a resolution affirming the Divinity of Jesus

17

Christ, and the institution by Him of a Church on earth, which was unanimously adopted.

The Russian delegates proposed the acceptance of seven Œcumenical Councils ; Bishop Harold Browne and Bishop Whittingham declined to acknowledge more than six, and the subject was for the present waived. All accepted the rule 'Quod semper, quod ubique, quod ab omnibus.' The outcome of this meeting was the appointment of two Old Catholic committees, one to communicate with the Russian ' Friends of Spiritual Enlightenment,' the other, consisting of Dr. v. Döllinger, Dr. Friedrich, and Dr. Messmer, to communicate with Anglicans. Bishop Harold Browne, as President of the Anglo-Continental Society, nominated a committee in like manner, consisting of himself, Bishop Christopher Wordsworth, Professor John Mayor, and myself, requesting me to carry on the correspondence with Döllinger. Accordingly, I addressed to him a series of ten letters, stating the doctrine and position of the Church of England, and comparing the teaching of the Churches of Rome, Greece, and England on certain points. At the conclusion of the correspondence I sent copies of the letters to Bishop Harold Browne, who gave his approbation as follows :

'WINCHESTER HOUSE,
'*May* 15, 1874.

' MY DEAR FRIEND,

'I have read the correspondence, and I find nothing to object to. I think you have truly represented the doctrine, etc., of the Church.'

'*June* 30, 1874.

' MY DEAR MEYRICK,

'I return your paper of contrasts, or comparisons. I think it is very good.

'Most affectionately yours,
'E. H. WINTON.'

Döllinger resolved to reply to the Anglican and Russian communications by a *viva-voce* Conference, and accordingly he summoned the first Conference of Bonn to be held in September, 1874. In announcing to me the Conference, Döllinger wrote :

'I firmly believe that we, who claim to be true Catholics and professors of genuine, unadulterated Christianity, are obliged in conscience to make great concessions, and to introduce gradually considerable modifications wherever the departure of the embryo Vatican Church, as you call it, from the Ancient Church and its principles is evident. You have pointed out with perfect justice some of the indispensable corrections, and I trust that by personal discussion we may come to an agreement, or at least mutual toleration, respecting several other difficult questions.

'Believe me, my dear Meyrick,

'Always to be yours affectionately
and respectfully,

'I. DÖLLINGER.'

In reply, after apologies, I wrote :

'What I should desire to see would be something of this sort :

'1. That the attention of the Conference be concentrated on the teaching of the first five (or six) centuries, and that no documents of later date be taken into consideration.*

'2. That every question on which Old Catholics, Orientals, or Anglicans, or any two of them, disagree be referred to a committee of three—each question to a different committee—one member of the committee to be nominated by yourself, one by the Bishop of

---

* This and the next paragraph contain a prophetic anticipation of Dean Wace's 'Appeal' of 1904.

Winchester, one by the Arch-Priest Janyscheff; and that it be the duty of each committee *solely* to examine what was the teaching of the first five (or six) centuries on the subject submitted to it, without entering at all into the question of its being right or wrong, true or false.

'3. That each one of these committees report to a second Conference to be held this time next year.

'4. That the following subjects be, if necessary, committed each to such committee, for them to report on :

'(1) The Canon of Holy Scripture.

'(2) The Eternal Procession of the Holy Ghost.

'(3) Human Merit, including therein the question of Works of Supererogation and the Treasury of Merits applied by Indulgences.

'(4) The Septenary Number of the Sacraments.

'(5) Transubstantiation.

'(6) Denial of the Cup.

'(7) Form of Baptism.

'(8) Clerical Marriage.

'(9) Authority of the Bishop of Rome.

'(10) Dead Language.

'(11) Purgatory.

'(12) Any other question that may arise.

'If something of this sort be done, the effect of the Conference will not end in this one meeting, but will be permanent. You will forgive my boldness in writing ? May God bless you and your work !

'Yours most respectfully and affectionately,

'F. MEYRICK.'

The Conference was held, and the first six of the subjects designated above, and the tenth, were brought under discussion, together with the questions of Justification, Tradition, the Immaculate Conception, Confession, and Commemoration of the faithful departed ; and on all these points an agreement was come to by those present, the Old Catholics being represented by Döllinger, Reinkens, etc. ; Anglicans by Bishop Harold Browne, Bishop Kerfoot of Pittsburg, etc. ; Russians by the Arch-Priest Janyscheff, General Kiréeff, etc. ; Greece by Professor Rhossis ; Denmark by Provost Bloch. At the same Conference two important declarations were made by Döllinger—that he and his colleagues did not hold themselves bound by the decrees of the Council of Trent, and that they acknowledged that Communion ought to be given under both kinds. To prepare the way for a second Conference, a council of five was appointed, consisting of Dr. v. Döllinger (Germany), Arch-Priest Janyscheff (Russia), Professor Rhossis (Greece), Dr. Nevin (America), and myself (England).

In the following year the second Conference was held, when there were present eighteen German Old Catholics, seven German Evangelicals, twenty-four Orientals (from Russia, Greece, and Constantinople), fifty English and fifteen American Churchmen. The chief subject under discussion was the Eternal Procession of the Holy Ghost, while the Validity of Anglican Orders, Purgatory, Infallibility, and the Papacy were also brought under discussion. The subject of the Procession being too intricate to be dealt with at the public meetings, a committee was appointed consisting of Archbishop Lycurgus of Syros, Arch-Priest Janyscheff, Professor Ossinin, Archimandrite Anastasiades, Archimandrite (afterwards Archbishop) Bryennios, Dr. v. Döllinger, Bishop Reinkens, Professor Langen, Canon Liddon, Dr. Nevin, and myself ; Professor Reusch and the Rev. G. E. Broade acted as secretaries. This committee made me realize in a way that I had never done before the manner in which business had been conducted at the Œcumenical Councils of the Church. Nothing could exceed the gravity, the earnestness, the suavity, the good-temper, with which each point was contested by the representatives of East and West. After many schemes had been proposed and abandoned, a unanimous agreement was at length come to on seven propositions extracted by Döllinger from the writings of St. John Damascene. The authority of St. John Damascene was sufficient to make these propositions acceptable to, and accepted by, the members of the Oriental Church. They were accepted by the Old Catholics, and they were declared by a committee of the Convocation of Canterbury, to which they were referred for examination, to be orthodox.

Thus then an agreement was arrived at on this grave doctrine by Eastern and Western theologians for the first time since the Eastern Church, in the time of Photius, charged the Westerns with heresy for introducing the Filioque into the Creed.

At the first meeting of the above committee, an occurrence took place, light enough in itself, but perhaps not without significance. While the members were assembling, I was sitting near the window on a small chair, when Döllinger came to talk to me. As he insisted on my continuing to sit, I made room for him on my chair, and, that we might not fall, we passed our arms round each other's waists. While we were in this position, with our heads very close together, the door opened and Bishop Reinkens entered. The Bishop, who had a great deal of quiet humour, drew himself up (he was a man of considerable presence), and exclaimed: 'See a symbol of the unity of the Churches. Oh that we had a photographer to show to Christendom the type of our accomplished work!' 'Accipio omen' were the words which naturally suggested themselves as we rose and greeted him in return.

The members of the committee and of the Conference carried back with them the resolutions that had been come to, with the view of obtaining for them the sanction of the Churches to which they belonged, and all hoped to meet again the following year for further counsel. Approval of the resolutions was expressed in the House of Bishops of the Convocation of Canterbury, and a Committee of the Lower House of Convocation reported that they found in them 'nothing contradictory to the formularies of the Church of England, or contrariant to sound doctrine, or that may not be held with a safe conscience.'

But Dr. Pusey, who had been occupying himself for ten years in an attempt, predestined to failure, to bring about a union by inducing the Roman Church to withdraw its more extravagant tenets and practices, could not bear the proposal, which had been made at Bonn, for the omission of the Filioque interpolated in the creed of Constantinople, because that would be likely to widen the chasm between the Anglican and Roman Churches, and the Roman Church contained Dr. Newman. He therefore set himself in violent opposition to the proposals of the Bonn Conferences, and in consequence of his strongly expressed views the report of the Committee of Convocation was not presented to the House. I ventured in vain to oppose his arguments in a series of letters published, with his own, in the *Times*. But it was impossible for Döllinger to continue his work of reconciliation without the authorized approval both of the Church of England and of the Oriental Church. And in the East, too, hesitation was shown. The Orientals could hardly believe that any way of agreement on the question of the Procession between themselves and the Western Churches could be found except by the Westerns entirely abandoning the Western formula for the Eastern. And, further, there was a natural hesitation on the part of the Orientals to touch a doctrine which had long served as a safeguard to themselves against the aggressions of Rome. Consequently, Döllinger did not receive the support which was necessary for his success either from England, or St. Petersburg, or Constantinople. In spite of his great age he must wait. And then followed political misunderstandings between England and Russia which would make the joint consideration of delicate subjects by the members of each country, it was thought, for the time difficult.

When once the Conference was broken off, its time for reassembling did not arrive during Döllinger's lifetime. His removal from the scene, and the closer relations entered into by the Old Catholics with the Dutch Jansenist Church, and a consequent alienation from the Anglican Churches, made the advantage of the reassembling less evident. Nothing was done till the year 1892, when an International Congress of Old Catholics was held at Lucerne, which seemed to be in some respects a ghost of the Bonn Conferences, where Old Catholics, Orientals, and Anglicans once more interchanged their views and sympathies. No practical results followed from it except the establishment of an *International Theological Review* (German, French, and English), conducted by Dr. Michaud, an able and learned editor, once curate of the Madeleine, Paris, now Old Catholic Professor at Berne.

The great man who presided over the Bonn Conference was born in 1799, and till 1863 was counted as a supporter of the Papal constitution of the Church. In that year a conference was held in which Ultramontanism succeeded in determining that German learning was to be subjected to the authority of the Italian Curia. Döllinger held his peace; he was silent, too, when the dogma of the Immaculate Conception was declared, and when the Syllabus of 1864 was promulgated. But these things led to his being less unwilling to take up the position forced upon him by the Vatican Council of 1870. At that Council Döllinger acted in the capacity of theologian for one of the German Bishops, but when the majority of the Council—a majority mainly made up of unlettered Italian Bishops—pronounced in favour of the Papal Infallibility, the minority submitted through fear of creating a schism. The Archbishop of Munich called the German theological Professors to him and proposed that they should give way as he had done himself. 'Whatever our personal belief may be, we must,' he said, 'submit, for Rome has spoken. Ought we not to begin to labour afresh for the Holy Church ?' 'Yes,' replied Döllinger, 'for the old Church.' 'There can be no new Church,' said the Archbishop. 'But they have made one,' replied Döllinger dryly.

After six months' delay the Archbishop demanded the submission of Döllinger and Friedrich. Döllinger replied by his 'Declaration to the Archbishop of Munich,' in which he uncompromisingly refused to accept the new dogma as a Christian, as a theologian, as an historian, and as a citizen. The following month (April, 1871) the Archbishop excommunicated him and Friedrich. Döllinger desisted from the exercise of his priestly functions, but maintained his theological position with the greatest firmness. In the autumn of the same year the first Old Catholic Congress was held, at Munich ; in the following year the second was held, at Cologne. After this Döllinger threw himself especially into the work of organizing non-Vaticanized Episcopal Churchmen in opposition to the Papacy, and with this end held the two Conferences of Bonn. At these Conferences Döllinger showed extraordinary powers both of body and mind. At the first of them the correspondent of the *Times*, though not in sympathy with the objects of the meeting, was moved to say :

'When the noble, benignant-looking old man stood

listening to the long, hesitating objections of many present with admirable patience and temper, he perfectly realized what I imagine to have been the appearance of those who, in the old times of the Church, were ready to suffer death and ·persecution in defence of what they believed to be the truth.'

At the second Conference, for four days he stood almost continuously in front of the assembled body of divines, taking up and replying to every speech as soon as it was made, in German or in English, and sometimes addressing the Conference continuously for hours ; in the committee he proposed, refuted, argued, receiving on his shield weapons from all sides, and returning them with irresistible force, allowing himself no break or interval except such as was sufficient for a plunge each day in the Rhine. And at the end of those four days he stood up as if he had been a man of thirty-eight instead of seventy-six, and delivered a speech of five hours' length on the disastrous effects that had been wrought on Western Christendom by the Papacy, passing in review, one after another, Germany, France, Spain, Italy, South America, Austria, and handling the affairs of each country with a fulness and exactness which would have been remarkable if he had confined himself to the history of a single nation ; and throughout the five hours he riveted by his voice and action the attention of everyone present, and retained their interest hour after hour, though addressing them in a language which to many was so unfamiliar that his meaning was only doubtfully guessed. Archbishop Plunket, recalling the scene, spoke at the Plymouth Church Congress with enthusiasm of ' " that old man eloquent," with keen and playful smile and busy brain, still all aglow with the quenchless fire of youth.'

According to a common practice of Roman Catholic controversialists, it was reported that Döllinger desired in his lifetime, and accomplished just before his death, a reconciliation with the Church of Rome. The report in both its forms was absolutely false. First it was said that he showed his submission by ceasing to say Mass on his excommunication. But Döllinger was always rather a Professor than a priest, and it was no pain to him to abstain from saying Mass himself, which he could and did attend when said by one of his Old Catholic colleagues. Again, it was said that he objected to the abolition of celibacy, and therefore separated himself from the Old Catholics. He may have thought it better policy to wait for a time, in order not to give occasion for the slander with which Vaticanists pursue reformers. But after the decision had been come to, he associated himself with Bishop Reinkens, in the most intimate way possible, as his colleague in holding the two Bonn Conferences, and at those Conferences he publicly declared that he spoke for his Old Catholic associates.

The report still continuing, he wrote a letter to Dr. Nevin, Rector of St. Paul's Church, Rome, in which he said that he desired Dr. Nevin to make known his contradiction to the lies that had been spread over Europe respecting his contemplated or consummated submission, as he had neither written nor done anything which could have given occasion to such rumours, which were nothing else but gratuitous inventions. In another letter, addressed to an Old Catholic clergyman, he declared definitely : 'As far as I am concerned, I consider myself to belong by conviction to the Old Catholic Communion.' As soon as he died, Mr. H. N. Oxenham boldly declared that he was reconciled on his death-bed to the Roman communion. To refute this statement, I wrote to Professor Friedrich, who had attended him during his last sickness. He replied, denying the charge *in toto*, in a letter which I sent to the *Guardian* newspaper :

'For a long time,' said the Professor, 'they played Döllinger off against the Old Catholics as though he had separated himself from them. The truth is exactly the reverse. Döllinger, as I pointed out in my notice on him in the *Allgemeine Zeitung*, was, and continued till his death, an Old Catholic; and, above all things, he would have nothing to do with the Church of Rome. His successor in the provostship said to me and a colleague of mine in his study on the day of his death, " So long as Döllinger was conscious, he thrust back every Roman Catholic priest."' When he had become unconscious, Extreme Unction was administered to him, and Professor Friedrich did not prohibit it. The Professor ends his letter: 'Roman Catholics will never allow themselves to be convinced, and will always repeat their false statements as soon as they are refuted.—Yours sincerely, J. FRIEDRICH (April 24, 1890).'

The conversions of Dr. Newman and Dr. v. Döllinger to and from the Church of Rome have been made a subject of comparison. If Newman slew his hundreds, Döllinger slew his thousands; the Old Catholics, whom he organized, number now from 180,000 to 200,000.

When it became certain that the protest against the Vatican innovations on the faith would not be joined in by Dupanloup, or Hefele, or Strossmayer, or any of the Bishops who formed the minority in the Council, the Old Catholic body determined to organize itself under its own Bishops. The first Bishop elected was Professor Joseph Hubert Reinkens. His *Nolo episcopari* was very hard to overcome, but at length he was persuaded, and his election took place on June 11, 1873, at Cologne. It was agreed on all hands that the best selection that was possible was made, for Dr. Reinkens united spiritual gifts with intellectual power—the Barnabas of the band, as some called him

—and under his guidance the movement escaped the danger, to which German movements are liable, of becoming a speculation rather than a faith.

It was important that his consecration should be performed by a Bishop whose authority the Roman Curia could not question on the score of the Succession. There was at hand a means of fulfilling this condition. When Madame de Maintenon and Louis XIV. persecuted the Port Royalists out of France, Jansenism made its home in the Church of Holland, which became so permeated with its spirit that a schism ensued between the Dutch and the Roman Churches. The Dutch retained all the Papal doctrines with the exception of the Supremacy, and continued to use the Roman liturgical books. Incurring excommunication by the Pope, the Dutch Church, with its three Bishops, found itself in a state of isolation, and welcomed, though with some hesitation, the anti-Papal Old Catholic Movement. Archbishop Van Loos of Utrecht made a Confirmation tour for the German Old Catholics, and readily promised to consecrate a Bishop for them. But the Archbishop died before the consecration could be effected, and Professor Reinkens was therefore consecrated by Dr. Heykamp, Bishop of Deventer, at Rotterdam on August 11, 1873. Thus the validity of the Old Catholic Episcopate, as transmitted by the Church of Holland, could not be disputed by Roman adversaries.

Bishop Reinkens presided at the annual Synods of the German Old Catholics, and took a leading part in their Congresses, until he died in the year 1896. In the year 1881 he came to England with Bishop Herzog for a meeting and religious services, organized by the Anglo-Continental Society. The meeting, which took place at Cambridge, was addressed by the two Bishops, and also by Bishop Harold Browne, Bishop Maclagan, and Bishop Woodford, as well as by Dr. Perowne, Vice-

Chancellor of the University, Mr. Beresford Hope, M.P. for Cambridge, and Mr. J. G. Talbot, M.P. for Oxford. On the following Sunday the two Bishops received the Holy Communion, together with their Anglican brethren, in one of the churches in Cambridge, and sermons were preached by Bishop Harold Browne, Chancellor Lias, and myself. From Cambridge they went on a visit to Archbishop Tait at Addington, to Bishop Christopher Wordsworth at Riseholme, and to Bishop Harold Browne at Farnham, where they received the Holy Communion in the Bishop's chapel. After this they attended a meeting of the committee of the Anglo-Continental Society, and a conversazione organized by it in London, and were shown over Lambeth Palace by the present Archbishop, Dr. Davidson. Bishop Reinkens was succeeded by Bishop Weber.

At the second Bonn Conference the representatives of America who were present invited the chief members of the Conference to a final banquet before separating for their several countries. At this banquet I was sitting between Archbishop Lycurgus and Dr. Herzog. Dr. Herzog was not at that time Bishop of the Swiss Old Catholics, but it was known that he was likely to be elected. In 1871 he had refused to accept the Vatican decrees, being then Professor of Exegesis in the Theological Seminary of Lucerne. In 1872 he attended the Old Catholic Congress at Cologne, and resigned his professorship, being shortly afterwards elected Pfarrer of Olten. In 1875, at a Synod representing 66 priests and 73,000 laymen, Bishop Herzog was elected first Bishop of the Christian Catholic Church of Switzerland, and he was consecrated by Bishop Reinkens on September 28 of the same year, on which he was excommunicated by the Romish Bishops of Switzerland and by the Pope. Having made a vigorous reply to his excommunications, he

took up his residence at Berne, where I shortly afterwards spent a Sunday with hin, attending his church.

Personally, Bishop Herzog was disposed to cultivate the most friendly relations with the Anglican
Churches. Twice he attended the Conferences called
by Bishop Harold Browne at Farnham Castle for the
purpose of considering the relation of the Anglican
to foreign Churches, besides accompanying Bishop
Reinkens when the two Bishops visited Cambridge.
He also paid an official visit to the American Church,
which led to an important declaration on intercommunion by the American Bishops. At a Synod held
at Soleure by Bishop Herzog, a resolution was passed
stating that in essential things the Old Catholics of
Switzerland stood on the same Christian and Catholic
ground as the Anglo-American Church, and in a
Pastoral on Communion with the Anglo-American
Church the Bishop recounted the acts of Communion
that had taken place between the two Churches, and
defended the position of the Anglican Church both
in her Catholic and Anglican aspects.

But after the coalition with the Dutch Jansenist
Bishops, the Old Catholic prelates became much
hampered. In 1889 a joint declaration of doctrine
was made by the five Bishops, and this was accompanied by an understanding that neither the Dutch
nor the German and Swiss Bishops should enter
into any relations or negotiations with other Churches
except by joint consent. This necessarily alienated
the German and Swiss Old Catholics from the Anglican
communion ; for the Dutch were still Roman Catholics
in all but one point, and they denied the validity of
Anglican Orders on the same ground as that taken
by Romanists. Accordingly, when Bishop Herzog
was invited by the committee of the Norwich Church
Congress to read a paper at the meeting, he accepted
the invitation, and spent the day with me in Norwich,

and made a valuable address on the subject of National Churches; but he could not take part in any ecclesiastical functions, owing to the agreement of 1889, and he left England without further intercourse with English Churchmen. After their union with the Dutch Jansenists, the Old Catholics looked rather to the Orientals than to the Anglicans as allies. Bishop Herzog outlived Bishop Reinkens, and continues to reside at Berne, highly respected by all his countrymen.

The chief ecclesiastic of the Oriental Church present at Bonn was Alexander Lycurgus, Archbishop of Syros and Tenos. With him I had contracted a previous friendship when he came to England in 1870 for the purpose of consecrating a church at Liverpool. After paying a visit to Mr. Gladstone at Hawarden, and to Archbishop Thomson at York, he proceeded to Lincoln, where he was welcomed by Bishop Christopher Wordsworth, who was able to discourse with him in modern Greek. During his visit, the first Suffragan Bishop of the present generation (Mackenzie) was consecrated at Nottingham by Bishop Wordsworth, Bishop Jackson, and Bishop Selwyn. Archbishop Lycurgus, accompanied by an Archimandrite and a deacon, attended the consecration, and stood throughout the service, including the administration of the Holy Communion, within the rails of the chancel, Chancellor (Archbishop) Benson and myself, as Bishop Wordsworth's chaplains, standing next to him. Archbishop Lycurgus was much impressed by the service, and at its conclusion threw his arms round the neck of the newly-consecrated Bishop and gave him the kiss of peace, exclaiming: 'I trust that thou wilt be able to give a good account of thy stewardship this day entrusted to thee.' From Nottingham and Lincoln the Archbishop and his suite, accompanied by Rev. George Williams and myself, proceeded to Peterborough, where they had an interview with Bishop Magee, and attended the cathedral service, during which the verger asked the Dean whether he was to order the strange gentlemen to take off their hats, the tall Oriental hat being part of the dress of the higher ecclesiastic in the East, without which they never appear. From Peterborough the party went on to Ely, and there a Conference took place between the Archbishop, attended by two members of the Oriental Church, and Bishop Harold Browne, attended by Mr. George Williams and myself. A report of this Conference was afterwards published by the Anglo-Continental Society in English and in modern Greek.

A little later the Archbishop paid a visit to the two Universities, to the Queen at Windsor, to the Marquis of Salisbury, the Earl of Glasgow, Mr. Beresford Hope, the Bishop of London, and (for a few hours) the Archbishop of Canterbury (Tait), who was at the time suffering from illness, after which the Greek Prelate left England for Constantinople.

Writing to his sister, Archbishop Lycurgus said : 'On sailing from England, I raised my arms to heaven and blessed the land, praying from my heart that it may ever be covered by the all-powerful right hand of the Lord.' And a long letter to me ended as follows : 'I remember with the liveliest love and heartfelt affection your great and happy country, and I keep in my mind and in my heart the places through which I passed, and the friends by whom I was received with a magnificent hospitality. I assure you from that time there has grown up on our side, too, a lively affection for your Christ-loving nation, and the greatest desire for an increase of brotherly relationship towards your Church, which is so attached to orthodoxy and antiquity. May the Lord fulfil the prayers offered up by you and by us in the way which He knows to be best !'

18

On the Archbishop's arrival at Bonn, I accompanied the Bishop of Gibraltar on the visit of ceremony which is always paid in such cases in the East. He received me with warm tokens of welcome, but I grieved to see how much his powerful and upright form had been bowed by illness ; he had suffered for many months from an attack of pneumonia, and this was his last effort for the peace of the Church Catholic. He returned home to die, his last word being Τετέλεσται (It is finished). He died on October 17, 1875, and was buried in the island of Syros. The following is part of a letter written to me by the Archbishop from Syros on January 25, 1874 :

Αἰδεσιμώτατε φίλε !

Χαίρων ἐκομισάμην τὸ ἀπὸ 25 Νοεμβρίου ἀγαπητὸν γράμμα τῆς Ὑμετέρας Αἰδεσιμότητος, καὶ δόξαν ἀνέπεμψα τῷ Σώτηρι τῶν ὅλων θεῷ τὰ τῆς περιποθήτου μοι ὑγιείας Αὐτῆς πολύευκτα αἴσια πληροφορηθείς. Πολὺς γὰρ ἤδη χρόνος ἐστὶν, ἐξ ὅτου φίλος τις, αὐτόθεν ἐλθὼν, ἀπήγγειλέ μοι ὅτι οὐ πάνυ ὑγιῶς εἶχεν ἡ φίλη μοι Αὐτῆς κορυφή. Καὶ ἤλγησα (μάρτυς ὁ Κύριος !) μέσην καρδίαν, καὶ αἰσιώτερόν τι ἔκτοτε περὶ Αὐτῆς ἐπεπόθουν μαθεῖν ὡς δὴ περὶ φίλου λίαν ἀγαπητοῦ, ὃν ἔγνων σοφίᾳ τε καὶ ἀρετῇ καὶ θεοσεβείᾳ κεκοσμημένον, καὶ οὗτινος ἡ μνήμη ζωηρά ἐστιν ἀείποτε ἐν ἐμοὶ, ὡς δὴ κἀκείνη περὶ ἧς ἐν τῇ ἐπιστολῇ ἀναφέρει, ἡ ἐν ἀγάπῃ ἀδελφικῇ συνδιάλεξις μετὰ τοῦ σεβασμιωτάτου ἐπισκόπου τοῦ Ely, τοῦ λίαν μοι ἀγαπητοῦ καὶ περιποθήτου ἐν Χριστῷ ἀδελφοῦ, ἧς οὐ μόνον ἁπλοῦς τις ἀκροατὴς, ἀλλὰ δὴ καὶ συγκοινωνὸς ἡ ὑμετέρα ἀγάπη ἐγένετο. Ἐπειδὴ δὲ διὰ τοῦ γράμματος καὶ τὰς μαρτυρίας ἀξιοῦτέ με καταγράψαι ὧν ἐξ ἄλλων τε ἐμνημόνευσα τότε τῶν θείων πατέρων καὶ ἐκ τοῦ ἱεροῦ Χρυσοστόμου περὶ τῆς ἐπικλήσεως τῶν ἁγίων, προθύμως τὴν ἀξίωσιν ὑμῶν ἐκπληρῶ. Ἐξαιτοῦμαι δὲ παρὰ τῆς ὑμετέρας ἀγάπης συγγνώμην ὅτι ἕνεκα τῶν ἑορτῶν καὶ ἄλλων φροντίδων εἰς δεῦρο ἀνέβαλον τὴν ἀπάντησιν.

The Russian Society of the Friends of Spiritual Enlightenment was represented at Bonn by the Arch-Priest Janyscheff, Professor Ossinin (who died shortly afterwards), and General Kiréeff. What struck one most about them at first was the astonishing power that they displayed of speaking, both in public and private, in German, French, English, and Russian, all which languages they spoke as natives. They also showed a surprising acquaintance with theology and ecclesiastical history, proving themselves capable of arguing even with Döllinger. Arch-Priest Janyscheff was, and is, the head of the Theological College of St. Petersburg, and Confessor to the Tzar and the Imperial Family. He showed the utmost tolerance and sympathy both for the Old Catholics, with whom he has always striven to bring about intercommunion, and also for the Anglicans, whom he met at the Conference. Indeed, when I met him again at Lucerne, at an International Congress in 1892, he threw his arms round my neck and kissed me on both cheeks as a brother in Christ. I believe that the fact—if it be a fact—of the present Tzaritza not being required, when joining the Oriental Church, to condemn and denounce the Church which she left, was owing to the broad-minded tolerance of Arch-Priest Janyscheff, whose office it was to admit her. That tolerance was probably strengthened by the relations entered into by the Arch-Priest with the old Catholics and Anglicans at the Conferences and Congresses which he has attended.

General Kiréeff, Secretary to the Society of the Friends of Spiritual Enlightenment at St. Petersburg, and Aide-de-Camp to the Grand-Duke Constantine, is a singular instance of a layman and a soldier equally well instructed in theology with any ecclesiastic. He has shown himself deeply interested in the cause of the Old Catholics, with whom he has desired to see the Eastern Church enter into communion. At the same time he was much attracted by the Anglican Church. For many years a correspondence was kept up between him and myself, as representing the Anglo-Continental Society, on matters of issue between the two Churches ; and being in London at the time of the last Lambeth Conference, he was much struck by that gathering of Anglican Bishops from various parts of the world. General Kiréeff has been a constant contributor to the *International Theological Review*, in the pages of which he and I discussed together the subject of the Infallibility of the Church.

The two Professors at the University of Athens, Damalas and Rhossis, did not take a very active part in the debates at the Bonn Conference ; nor did the two Archimandrites, Bryennios (soon afterwards appointed Archbishop) and Anastasiades. But the latter addressed to me several earnest letters on the subject of intercommunion, which were published by the Anglo-Continental Society.

The chief English ecclesiastic was Bishop Sandford of Gibraltar, in whose rooms the English and Americans met every day for prayer and consultation. At this time Bishop Sandford had not long held his office, and he felt keenly the responsibility incurred by taking part in the Conference. He had been appointed to the bishopric by Archbishop Tait in the year 1874, and he kept up the tradition of courtesy and friendship which had been begun by his predecessor with the heads of the Oriental Church, carefully paying the ceremonial visits which are thought so much of in the East, whenever he made his visitations of the Anglican congregations within the jurisdiction of the Church of Constantinople. He did not see his way to give open encouragement to the Old Catholics in the western part of his diocese, because he considered that he was bound by international comity not to interfere with the Churches of those countries in which he himself held the position, more or less, of a stranger. Shortly before his death, which occurred before the day fixed for his resignation, he wrote to me :

'My dear Meyrick,
    'On next December 13 thirty years will have passed away since I had a walk with you at Torquay, and lunched with you, Mrs. Meyrick, and your daughter, Bishop Harris joining the party. We conferred together about my future work, which might have fallen upon you if your health had been stronger. I am very thankful that strength has been given me to bear the fatigue which the work involves, for nearly thirty years. But my doctor tells me that, if I attempted another long journey, I should break down again, and so, with his approval, I have told the King and the Archbishop that on February 1, when the thirty years will be complete, I shall resign the charge into younger hands. I wish that I could think of someone specially fitted for the peculiar work. He ought to have sympathy with the Eastern Churches and to take an interest in British seamen. He ought to be a large-hearted, liberal-minded Churchman. . . .
    'I am glad that we agree on the Macedonian Question. The attitude taken by the Greek Patriarch and by the Greeks generally towards their Bulgarian brothers is deplorable. The Patriarch has never forgiven the Bulgarians for seceding from the Orthodox Church. In an interview which I had with him in November, 1879, I expressed a wish that the schism might be healed, and no new division be added to those which already troubled the peace of Christendom. The Patriarch replied that he was ready to receive the Bulgarians back if they should show signs of penitence. The question, he said, was political, not religious. As I learnt from the Bulgarian Exarch and others, it was a question of patronage and a desire for independence that drove the Bulgarians to separate.

They saw all the high posts, bishoprics, and other preferments, appropriated by Greeks.

'. . . You were good to me and my brother John in his Oxford days. With kindest remembrances and best wishes,

'I remain, dear Meyrick,

'Yours ever sincerely,

'C. W. GIBRALTAR.'

There were two embryo Bishops of the American Church present at the Bonn Conference. One was Dr. Perry, who had travelled to Bonn from London with me and T. W. Bullock, Secretary of the S.P.G.; and the other was Dr. Henry Potter. Dr. Perry, on his return to London, preached a sermon on the Bonn Conference at Westminster Abbey, and on his return to America was elected Bishop of Iowa. He was a learned man, and held the office of Historiographer of the American Church. His interest in foreign reform movements continued throughout his life.

Dr. Henry Potter has for many years earned the respect of all Americans as Bishop of New York. At Bonn a question arose as to the members of the committee on the Procession of the Holy Ghost. The English present desired to appoint Dean Howson, Canon Liddon, and myself; but, as the Old Catholics were to be represented by only two members, it was ruled that there could only be two appointed by the English. To meet the difficulty, Dr. Potter proposed that the American Churchmen present should elect me and Dr. Nevin as the representatives, nominally of the American Church, but really of the Anglican communion, whether in America or England. I rose to withdraw my name, while expressing my gratitude for the confidence placed in me by my American brethren; but I was anticipated by Dean Howson, who declared himself unwilling to act upon the committee, the result being that Canon Liddon, Dr. Nevin, and myself were appointed.   Dr. Potter gave the impression of being a very strong man, and his after-life has proved that this impression was right.

At the hotel at which I was staying there were many members of the Conference, and among them General Kiréeff and his sister, Madame Novikoff. Madame Novikoff took the deepest interest in the results of the Conference, and had apparently come for the special purpose of gauging the effects of the Old Catholic Movement on the Russian Church. Afterwards she went to London, and there for season after season she has held a sort of salon, where the relations between Russia and England have been informally talked over.   By her own powers of conversation she has attracted men and women of various schools to her house.   On one occasion I met Mr. Kinglake there.   Mr. Gladstone was more than once present.   When questions arose between England and Russia, she took care to have the Russian side presented both in society and in the press.   Her influence in smoothing anti-Russian prejudices and feelings has been appreciable.   Like her brother, she has learnt to understand the character of the English Church better than most foreigners.   She went to Oxford to hear a sermon that I preached before the University on the schism between the Eastern and Western Churches, but she was not content with my representation of the Second Council of Nicæa and the Eastern use of icons.

The English layman who took most interest in the Bonn propositions when they were brought back to England was A. J. Beresford Hope, who drew up and circulated an address to Dr. v. Döllinger, thanking him for the Bonn Conferences.   This address was signed by 3,800 clergy, of whom thirty-eight were Bishops, and by 4,250 laymen, making in all 8,050.   A letter

from Bishop Harold Browne was enclosed with the
address, and the following inscription was added :

'Viro
Reverendissimo doctissimo
Pientissimo
IGNATIO J. VON DÖLLINGER, S.T.P.
Bonnensis
de fide catholica
Consessus
An. MDCCCLXXV habiti
Præsidi
Summa cum reverentia
Offerunt
Anglicanæ ecclesiæ
Episcopi clerici laici.'

At Cambridge Mr. Beresford Hope had been an
active member of the Ecclesiological Society, and in
that way he had come to take an interest, not only in
the architecture of churches, but in the fortunes of the
Church. He spent large sums in the restoration of
All Saints' Church in Margaret Street, London ; and
the establishment of St. Augustine's College, Canterbury is due to his liberality and Mr. Edward Coleridge's energy. To support the views which he held
in Church politics, he purchased the *Morning Chronicle*,
a London daily paper, and wrote in it a series of
letters signed 'D.C.L.,' which were very effective
at the time ; and the establishment of the *Saturday
Review* was due to him. He was married to Lord
Salisbury's sister, and I once saw Lady Mildred in
a Court dress resplendent with the famous Hope
diamonds. The Queen had given her a diamond ring,
which she therefore wore in going to Court ; but it
was by no means equal to many of the other diamonds
that she was wearing. No one set a nobler example
of liberality in connection with the Church than Mr.
Beresford Hope.

CHAPTER XVII

Spain—Italy—Signor Minghetti—Lord Acton—Père Hyacinthe
Loyson.

My health having broken down in the year 1870, I went abroad to Malaga, Algiers, Sicily, Italy, and the South of France. In Malaga it fell to my lot, in the absence of the Chaplain, to bury one of the English visitors who had died there. On the day of the funeral there were present in the beautiful English cemetery of Malaga from twelve to twenty of the chief young merchants of the city, who followed the service with bared heads and reverent demeanour, and some of them expressed themselves as touched by the ceremony which they had attended. When permission to build this cemetery was first extorted from Ferdinand VII. (for till that time our English dead were sunk in the sands by the seaside, a prey to the dogs or the waves, as too profane for the soil of Spain), one of the conditions was that it should be surrounded by a high wall, in order that no sign of a religious ceremony should be visible at the time of a funeral. The space surrounded by the wall has been outgrown, and, as shown by the instance given above, some progress in religious tolerance has been effected. It was not, however, till after Prim's revolution in 1868 that an English clergyman could venture to utter a word of consolation or prayer to English sailors taken to the Malaga hospital to die. The English Chaplain had been roughly treated for reading a letter to a sick man in the hospital a year or two before my visit.

The Roman Church has lost its hold over the middle class in Spain, but it is still powerful with the peasantry, who are for the most part illiterate and bigoted, but kindly disposed. During my stay at Malaga, a week of prayer for the Pope of Rome was appointed. I went to hear the chief sermon of the week, and very well worth hearing it was. The preacher commenced by saying that his objects were to prove that the Papacy was to be preserved as the mainstay of civilization, and that the present Pope was more excellent than all the Popes that had gone before him. With regard to the first point, he said he could prove it at once, for the history of civilization was nothing else than the history of the Papacy. For was not the history of Europe the history of the civilized world? and was not the history of the Church the history of Europe? and was not the history of the Papacy the history of the Church? Therefore the history of the Papacy was the history of civilization. At present the Catholic nations were at the head of civilization, and even England, in sending out to Spain scientific men to note the eclipse, had been obliged to put a Catholic priest at their head. Further, he had to prove that the Papacy was the mainstay of liberty, fraternity, and equality. Historically this had always been so. The Popes had always been on the side of the people, and this was why they were so obnoxious to Emperors and Kings. Had not the Popes supported the people of Italy against the German Empire? Had not Hildebrand resisted the imperial power, and why did he do this except from his love for the people? If they wanted freedom, justice, equality, they must insist on the temporal power being given back to the Pope. At the present moment this was wanted more than ever; for the

.

Teutonic and Slavonic nations were forming themselves into leagues under despots, and it was necessary that all the Latin nations should form themselves into a league, too, under the temporal presidency and headship of the Pope. The preacher then depicted Pius IX. as the most excellent and the most suffering of living men. Being a man of eloquence, he had so far worked on his audience at the end of his sermon—there were present about 500 men and 1,000 women—that, standing up, they joined him aloud in a declaration recited from his lips : that they protested before God, before angels, and before men, that they would not permit the Holy Father to be kept a prisoner, and that they would not allow the Vatican to be turned into a Calvary. In countries outside of Italy it was a general belief that Pope Pius IX. was kept in a dungeon, and slept upon straw. Straw, it is said, was sold in Ireland as that on which the Holy Father had lain.

During my visit to Palermo, I was fortunate in having opportunities of conversing with the Italian Prime Minister, Minghetti, who spoke to me with great frankness as to the political and ecclesiastical state of Italy. I asked him if it were possible that the Bishops could be loyal and patriotic citizens of the Italian kingdom while they were nominated by the Pope of Rome. He allowed that there was every probability that they would be disloyal, but thought that after a time they would not have so much power, owing to the growth of non-Romanist sects and other causes.

'But,' I asked, 'is it necessary to accept as an inevitable fact the disloyalty of the Bishops of the national Church ? In England there are none more loyal than the English Bishops.'

'That,' he said, 'is owing to the difference between Catholicism and Protestantism.'

'Should you not rather say the difference between the Papal and other systems ?' I asked.

For a moment he did not seem to grasp the distinction, but presently he said :

'It may be so.'

'But is Italy really to acquiesce for ever,' I continued, 'in an unpatriotic Episcopate ?'

'What would you do ?' he replied.

'Could not the Bishops be otherwise nominated, and could not a law be passed making the oath of feudal allegiance and submission taken by every Bishop to the Pope illegal ?'

'How could they be nominated ?'

'Our Bishops in England are nominated by the Crown, which is found in practice to work well.'

'That would be impossible in Italy. We believe that all interference on the part of the State with spiritual or ecclesiastical matters should be done away with.'

'Interference, yes ; but may there not be circumstances in which intervention is justifiable and just ?'

'Bishops nominated by the King would not be acknowledged by the mass of Church-people.'

'Then, cannot you fall back on the primitive practice, and let the Bishops be elected by the clergy and laity of the diocese, and consecrated by the Metropolitan ?'

'There is no sufficient public opinion to enable us to act thus.'

'And how is such a public opinion to be formed ?'

'That,' he said, 'I cannot tell. It is enough for us that it does not exist.'

Subsequently I asked him if it were impossible to have an Italian Metropolitan distinct from the Pope if the Pope continued irreconcilable. He said that it was impossible, for the same reason as before, that there was not sufficient public opinion in its favour. He gave me his speech on the liberty of the Church, and I gave him the *Report of Convocation on the Election of Bishops.*

The question, How is public opinion to be formed? returned upon me with renewed force at Naples.

' If,' said an Italian friend with whom I was discussing it, ' if the Government would take it up——'

' The Government,' I replied, ' cannot form public opinion, but must follow it. Men of the people must form it from below.'

After discussion with five or six Italian gentlemen, I proposed the following address, which was translated by one of them into Italian : ' Is it possible that the Bishops of Italy can be patriotic men while they are nominated by the Pope, who declares himself an enemy of the kingdom of Italy ? Is it possible that the Bishops can be loyal to the King and to the Italian Constitution while they bind themselves by oath "to defend the royalties of St. Peter," and "to attack and oppose with all their might all rebels against our Lord the Pope"? What remedy for so great an evil ? Let every Italian earnestly consider this question, and do his best to give help to his suffering country.'

Permission was asked by my Neapolitan friends to set up the above as a placard on the walls. But it was forbidden by the police, lest it should give offence to the Pope. The same thing occurred in Rome and Florence, but the address was published in two or three Italian newspapers, and copies of it were circulated through the post.

In Rome I had several conversations with Professor Tommasi, of the Roman University. Like most Italian Liberals, he thought that no help could be given to the national and reforming party within the Church by the State, though he allowed that the scepticism of the educated and the Ultramontanism of the Jesuitical party formed the chief danger of Italy as a nation.

' Does the liberty of the Church,' I asked, ' mean no

more than the liberty of the Pope to nominate Bishops hostile to the nation, and liberty of the Bishops to suspend patriotic priests at their will ?'

'Parliament cannot interfere,' he said. 'We have granted general liberty, and leave the Church to settle its own affairs.'

'With what results ?' I inquired.

'The results,' he said, 'are evil, as shown by the suspension of a priest by his Bishop for officiating to some of the King's soldiers [a case which was occurring at the moment]. But how are we to obviate them, and yet preserve our principle of washing our hands of all religion ?'

'Is not,' I said, 'the Papal system different from that of all other Churches and religions ? Is it not practically, in one of its aspects, a temporal power under an absolute despot ? and does not this temporal power require to be confronted by the more legitimate temporal authority of the civil power ?'

'Liberal politicians are not prepared again to entangle themselves in religious matters,' he returned ; 'but there are at least two great encouragements,' he continued. 'Free principles are undoubtedly rooting themselves in Italy, and the kingdom of Italy has won the prestige belonging to the occupation of Rome. What is now wanting is a movement by a leading ecclesiastic.'

'And what protection would he and his followers have from the State if they were deprived of their benefices and salaries by the Pope ?'

'None.'

'Then, they would be starved ?'

'Unless they could find support for themselves.'

'Under these circumstances it is not wonderful that there is no Döllinger and no Hyacinthe in Italy.'

Père Hyacinthe was at this time in Rome, where I had the pleasure of making his acquaintance and that of Mrs. Merriman, who afterwards became his wife.

Spending the winter of 1875 at Torquay, I saw a great deal of Lord Acton, and had much conversation with him on the state of religion on the Continent. He had resided in Rome during the session of the Vatican Council, where he used his influence with the Bishops to prevent the declaration of Infallibility, and kept Mr. Gladstone acquainted with the course of the Council's proceedings, as Mr. Odo Russell, instructed by Manning, informed Lord Clarendon of them. Since the publication of the dogma, Lord Acton had followed Döllinger's action with the greatest sympathy, having himself been at one time a pupil of Döllinger, and holding the same sentiments with him. There is no doubt that had he lived on the Continent he would have cast in his lot with the Old Catholics ; but in England he felt himself hampered. He was not prepared to join the Church of England, chiefly owing to a repulsion that he felt to the school represented by Dean Stanley ; and at the same time there seemed to be hardly room for an Old Catholic body between the Church of England and the Papal communion in England. About a fortnight before Christmas Day, he came to me and said that the Roman priest at Torquay had written to him asking for an interview. 'I think,' he said, 'the reason of his doing so is to forbid my Communion at Christmas, and that will be a serious indication to me of what should be my duty in the future.' But the priest in question was too wise to alienate so influential a personage. The purpose of the interview was not to forbid, but to invite, his presence. Lord Acton told me that he did not believe, and could not believe, the infallibility of the Pope, as defined, any more than Döllinger, who declared that he could as soon believe that two and two made five. He said that he should appoint a private chaplain with the same sentiments as himself, and proceed just as if the Vatican Council had not been held. Soon after this Lord Acton left Torquay, and I had no more communication with him, except by the interchange of a few letters. Professor Friedrich stated in a letter written just after Döllinger's death that Lord Acton had urged him to stand by Döllinger in his last sickness and prevent the intrusion of any Roman priest.

In July, 1878, the second Lambeth Conference was held, and M. Loyson, or Père Hyacinthe, came to England to watch its proceedings. He had been ordained in the year 1851, and became next year a barefooted Carmelite. In 1864-1868 he was, by Archbishop Darboy's appointment, preacher at Nôtre Dame, and was found to be a greater orator than any since Lacordaire. But Hyacinthe was anti-Vaticanist, on which account the General of the Carmelites forbade him to touch on controversy. Hyacinthe returned answer that he could not be a 'dumb dog unable to bark,' and that if this were required of him he must leave the convent, to which the General replied that he would thereby incur the greater excommunication. Hyacinthe left the convent and sailed for America. Returning to France the next spring, he published a protest against the dogma of Infallibility, and declared his adhesion to the Old Catholics. But till the year 1878 French law did not permit him to speak publicly on religion in France, and when he gave a lecture on morals a Commissioner of Police was present to see that he did not touch on doctrine.

At the second Lambeth Conference, held July, 1878, a Commission was appointed consisting of the Archbishops of Canterbury, York, Armagh, and Dublin, the Primus of the Scottish Church, the presiding Bishop of the American Church, the Bishops of London, Long Island, and Gibraltar, to enter into communication with any Old Catholics who might desire the help of the Church of England. In the following week Bishop Harold Browne held a Conference at Farnham to consider the relations of the Anglican Church with members of other communions. At this Conference M. Loyson besought the Church of England to help him in building up a Reformed Gallican Church, and a resolution was moved by the Bishop of Western New York (Bishop Coxe), seconded by the Bishop of Lichfield (now Archbishop Maclagan), and supported by the Bishop of Moray and Ross (Bishop Eden), and passed, 'that this meeting, having heard a statement from M. Hyacinthe Loyson, resolves that it is desirable to extend to him sympathy and support for his work in France, and that the secretary of the Anglo-Continental Society be requested to institute a special French fund for that purpose.'

From Farnham M. Loyson came with his wife on a visit to me at Blickling, and while in my house wrote to the Archbishop of Canterbury, praying for the help offered by the Lambeth Conference, and asking to be placed provisionally under the superintendence of the Anglican Episcopate. The Archbishop (Tait), as President of the Commission, referred him to the Primus of the Scottish Church for guidance and direction, and the Primus associated with himself, in the task imposed upon him, his colleague, Bishop Cotterill of Edinburgh. In February, 1879, M. Loyson, with his hands thus strengthened, opened a church in the Rue Rochechouart. In this church Bishop Herzog, acting for the Scottish Primus, held a Confirmation in the summer of 1879; and in August of the same year the Bishop of Edinburgh, Bishop Reinkens, Bishop Herzog, and M. Loyson, received the Holy Communion together at Berne, as Bishop J. Wordsworth, Bishop Herzog, and Herr Cech did at Salisbury afterwards. At the same time M. Loyson issued a programme of the reform that he desired, which contained five propositions :

1. The rejection of Papal Infallibility.
2. The election of Bishops by the clergy and faithful people.
3. The celebration of the Liturgy and reading of the Bible in the vulgar tongue.
4. The liberty of marriage to the clergy.
5. The liberty and moralization of Confession.

With all his splendid qualities, M. Loyson had not the power of organization, and consequently his one congregation did not grow into many.   What was the reason ?   Probably it was that Frenchmen, unable to accept modern Romanism, had become indifferent to all questions of religion ; and possibly they were not inclined to attach themselves to a movement which had its chief centre in Germany.   M. Loyson thought that a more constant episcopal superintendence than could be supplied by the Bishop of Edinburgh (to whom the Bishop of Moray had delegated that function) was required.   Upon this the Bishop of Edinburgh resigned his office, to the great loss of the French Old Catholics.   M. Lartigau, Old Catholic curate in Paris, consulted Bishop Herzog as to the advisableness of consecrating M. Loyson as Bishop. Bishop Herzog wrote to inquire whether such was the wish of the English Episcopate, for which he had already acted.   Learning that this was not the case, Bishop Herzog declined to act.   M. Loyson then invited Bishop Jenner to his assistance, who gave him his co-operation to the year 1888.   But Bishop Jenner did not carry with him the authority of the English Church.   In 1888 Bishop Coxe of Western New York, as the head of a committee appointed by the American Bishops to look into the question of reform in France, held a Confirmation in M. Loyson's church in Paris, having first stated to the Archbishop of Paris the grounds on which he did so. Having come to England, Bishop Coxe spoke at a second Conference held at Farnham, in favour of helping M. Loyson in carrying out a reform on the basis of the Gallican principles of 1682, and his counsel was that the French congregation should place itself under the authority of the Archbishop of Utrecht, representing the Jansenist Church of Holland, which was so closely connected in its principles with Port Royal. This was done, and that is the position of the congregation in Paris at the present time, Père Hyacinthe having resigned the charge of it to a successor. Except for a visit that he paid me at Pau, I did not meet M. Loyson again until I went with Archbishop Plunket to Madrid. Stopping on our way at Paris, we dined with the British Chaplain, meeting our Ambassador, Lord Dufferin, and M. Loyson was one of the guests. We afterwards continued our journey to Madrid, and there M. Loyson laid hands, together with Dr. Noyes and myself, Count Campello and Dr. Cabrera, representing the English, French, Italian, and Spanish Churches, on a candidate for Holy Orders, whom the Archbishop of Dublin ordained. Père Hyacinthe still resides in Paris (1905); and though he is no longer connected with the congregation which he originally established, his voice still occasionally rings through France as the pioneer of a coming reform.

19—2

CHAPTER XVIII

WHILE I was at Torquay, where I spent several winters, I saw a good deal of the Baroness Burdett-Coutts. Her father, Sir Francis Burdett, had been squire in my father's parish, and the Baroness was the same age as one of my sisters. One of the first things that I remember was being dressed up in blue ribbons (Sir Francis Burdett's colours being 'true blue'), and seeing Sir Francis coming to confer with some of the voters of the neighbourhood on the lawn between the Vicarage and the church, while the bells rang to welcome him. My father, who was a Whig, voted for him, mainly on account of what he had been ; my uncle, who was a Tory, chiefly for what he was at the time. He himself said that he had made no change in his political tenets, but that the world had advanced so rapidly, that while in his youth he was regarded as a Radical, in his mature age he was counted as a Tory. I do not remember his face, but his figure made an impression on my boyish mind, as he was tall and thin and upright, and he was dressed in white corduroys which were much wrinkled. He gave a number of franks for letters to my father and my uncle, one of which, not having been used, I gave back to the Baroness, after the use of franks had long ceased, as a memento of past days. There was something singularly sweet and unpretentious in the Baroness's manner—a manner plainly resulting from her own character. At one of the Prince of Wales's parties at Sandringham, where she was making one of the house-party, which naturally kept itself apart from the county guests who were unknown to it, she took the trouble to come from her end of the room to sit with my young daughters, whom she had noticed to be there, to make them the more enjoy the evening.

She took a house in the neighbourhood of Blickling, where on one occasion I had the pleasure of meeting Albani, who, after making herself very agreeable at dinner, good-naturedly played dance music for the rest of the party, while I turned over the pages for her. The Baroness celebrated her ninetieth birthday in April, 1904. Few have used great wealth so nobly.

One of my most intimate friends and companions at Torquay was Sir William Martin, late Chief Justice in New Zealand, the friend of Bishop Selwyn and Patteson. Never was the advantage of the co-operation of State and Church better manifested than in New Zealand when Bishop Selwyn and Chief Justice Martin worked together for the good of the country. Every Sunday Sir William held a class of Maori lads, whom he taught, and he was always ready to give kindly advice to the natives who came to him in their difficulties. He was an excellent scholar in Oriental, classical, and modern languages, and it was his custom to give lectures in the Greek Testament to the students at St. John's College whenever the Bishop was absent on his episcopal voyages among the islands. All legal questions, secular or ecclesiastical, which arose in the new country were settled by him in a manner generally satisfactory to the applicants. In 1856 he had to come to England from ill-health, which caused him to resign his office, and he took occasion to go over with Sir John Patteson and Sir John Coleridge the Church Constitution for New Zealand, which had been drawn up by himself and Bishop Selwyn. As soon as his health allowed, he returned to New Zealand for the purpose of again working with Bishop Selwyn. But in 1868 Bishop Selwyn was translated to Lichfield, Bishop Abraham returned to England, and Bishop Patteson was killed in 1871. These changes, and his own still failing health, led him to come back to England, where he kept up his studies, philological and ecclesiastical. He told me once that he had read the whole of Bingham's *Antiquities* through from beginning to end—a book of immense value, which most persons are contented to refer to on special points for their elucidation.

His interest in the Old Catholics was very warm, and whenever a question involving the application of old principles to new circumstances arose, he was ready to give it his most patient and thoughtful consideration. On these occasions he became the judge once more ; his countenance assumed its judicial gravity, the case was brought forward, the arguments on either side marshalled and balanced, and the decision given. What distressed him most in England was the less loyal feeling which he found in the younger clergy than that which had existed in the more robust genera- tion represented by Bishops Selwyn and Patteson ; and he more than once expressed a sorrowful con- viction that the Eucharistic doctrine contained in many popular manuals was derogatory to the honour of God the Father, inasmuch as it represented Him as still unreconciled, and only restrained from inflicting punishment by the constant action of the Son in heaven pointing to His sacred wounds, and in a mystic sense continuing there the Sacrifice of the Cross. The Holy Communion, which he loved to attend, was to him a feast of God's children at God's board, a peace-offering exhibiting a joyous sense of communion already existing between the partakers and the reconciled Father, not a sin-offering to effect a reconciliation as yet unmade. On the last occasion that I was conversing with him, two subjects were mentioned which appeared to us to need restating under the present circumstances of the Church. 'Well,' said Sir William, with a smile, 'I am an old man, but I will undertake one, and you must undertake the other.' I shook my head, for the task that he laid upon me was the restatement of the doctrine of the Church of England on the subject of the Holy Communion. I did not undertake it then, but I was led afterwards to do so by some strange doctrines which I heard preached in churches at Hastings, which were not the doctrines of the Church in England.

Sir William Martin was an example of a devout layman, formed by the Anglican Church. Such men are not prodigies of asceticism to make the world go wondering after them, and they are marked by a simplicity and common-sense which makes those who seek after a sign think lightly of them. Why is this, but that their minds are evenly balanced, each quality being duly developed in proper proportion with the rest, the result of which is to produce a *man* in the highest perfection of man's nature ? Out of the best *men* are formed the best Christians—the truest saints of God. Such were, in the generation that has passed away, Sir John Patteson, Sir John Coleridge, Sir William Martin, Mr. J. H. Markland, Mr. W. Gibbs, Mr. J. G. Hubbard, and Roundell, Lord Selborne. May such laymen be never wanting to the Church of England !

Mr. Gibbs, named above, at the time that I knew him, was the eldest member of a well-known mercantile house. He built himself a beautiful residence at Tyntesfield near Bristol, where more than once I visited him.　His great desire was to make use of his wealth for the benefit and happiness of others.　To him Keble College owes its chapel, and, I believe, part of its endowment.　His house having derived some of its wealth from South America, he was anxious to give South Americans an opportunity of embracing a purer faith than that which prevails in that country.　He therefore joined the Anglo-Continental Society, and he was always ready with his purse to meet any expenses for living agency or for translations into Spanish (a language with which he was himself well acquainted), such as might be useful for Spanish Americans.　His interest extended to Spain, and he made himself answerable for the stipend of Antonio Vallespinosa, a young Catalan, who, desiring to embrace Protestantism, had come to England, and, after some years' instruction, had been ordained a deacon in England by the Bishop of Gibraltar, and appointed by him to hold in Gibraltar a service in accordance with the Anglican Prayer-Book translated into Spanish.　This was before General Prim's Revolution of 1868, and he continued to hold the service till that revolution occurred, when, like Cabrera and others, he passed from Gibraltar into Spain.　During this time Mr. W. Gibbs supplied me with funds for the stipend and necessary expenses of the young deacon.

Mr. Gibbs looked out for opportunities for doing kindnesses to all about him.　His daughter, unhappily, suffered from an affection of the lungs, and for her benefit he called in a medical man who professed to employ improved methods, and required his patient to visit him every day, for which visit he charged two guineas.　My own health had broken down, and I had come to London to see my physician.　Mr. Gibbs asked me to take a drive with him, and as we were coming back he laid his hand on my arm, saying: 'My dear friend, I want you to do a kindness for me.

I am going into the country to-morrow with most of my household, but I shall leave some of my servants, and I want you and Mrs. Meyrick to be kind enough to live in my house as my guests, excusing my absence, and then the visits to the doctor can go on just as usual, you taking the place of my daughter, and the doctor sending in his usual account to me at the end.' Then, without waiting for me to speak, he went on hurriedly to say how much he wished me to recover my health, and that this doctor might be so useful to me, etc. When I got in a word, and showed that I understood the kindness of the offer, he threw off the idea as one not to be considered. ' My dear friend, God has given me so much money that sometimes I don't know how best to use it so as to please Him. This will be a kindness to me, and I hope a benefit to the Church.' His kind old face put on such a pleading and deprecatory look as he urged his offer that I found it hard to say no. But I was not able to accept his proposal. At the time that I was Preacher at White-hall Chapel, I generally, during the London season, had luncheon with Lord and Lady Salisbury (father and stepmother to the Prime Minister) in Arlington Street, and dined with Mr. and Mrs. Gibbs in Hyde Park Gardens, returning to Oxford by the evening train.

In 1880 I went abroad to Pau, Biarritz, and Hyères. At Hyères, in the spring of 1882, a tame sparrow flew into the room in which my daughters were being given a drawing lesson, and on their bringing him to me he took an extraordinary fancy to me. His greatest delight was then, and for several years afterwards, to sit in my sleeve, from which, when we were by ourselves, he would come out and hop over the paper when I was writing, and seize my pen in his beak, looking up at me at the same time in a merry way out of the corner of his eye. I brought

him home to England with me, and there he selected as
his special perch a particular row of my books near the
door in my study, from which he would descend on the
head of any whose entrance into the room he disliked,
and beat them with his wings, scolding all the time at
the top of his voice, but doing them no injury. Several
times he flew through the window into the garden to
the top of a tall oak-tree, but on my going out and
calling him he would come down and pitch on my
head, and so allow me to carry him indoors again.
When he had gone to sleep for the night, if anyone
else came near him, he scolded with the greatest
indignation, but always received me with soft little
sounds of affection. After four years I had to leave
home for several months without him, when he pined
away and died, apparently of grief.

A curious story was connected with him while at
Hyères. One of the visitors, named Lady James, lost
a favourite canary, and was greatly distressed in consequence. Madame Joseph, a Frenchwoman, hearing
this, thought that she saw an opportunity of making
a little money, so she came and demanded of us the
sparrow as having belonged to herself and being such
a favourite with her that she could not part with him.
Not being able to disprove her story, we gave him
up to her, and she immediately carried him to Sir
Kingston James for a present to his wife; but Pierrot,
as he was named, would have nothing to say to Lady
James, and only flew at her and pecked her furiously.
Sir Kingston then determined to return him to
Madame Joseph. Meantime I had learnt that Pierrot
had never belonged to Madame Joseph, but to a Mr.
Sweeny, who had purposely set him free, because he
pecked his servant. We were quite welcome to him,
he said. I therefore told Sir Kingston James that I
declined to allow the bird to go back to Madame
Joseph, and resumed possession of him. In the idle-

ness of a foreign hotel Pierrot's history became the
subject of a drama, called 'The Comedy of the Birds.'

During our stay at Hyères we had a visit from
Archbishop Plunket, who was inquiring into the progress of Church reform in Italy.   Italy had her chance
of setting up a National Church apart from the Papacy,
and she lost it in 1866, just as France had a similar
chance and lost it in 1801.   What has been the result
in both countries ?   Speaking generally, it has been
that the *men* in both countries have given up belief in
Christianity, regarding it only as a useful discipline
for women.   In Italy the generation that had made its
effort after self-reform in the sixties, remained silent in
sullenness or despair, while Döllinger in Germany
and Loyson in France were making their protest in
the seventies.

In 1881 a movement on a much smaller scale than
that in the sixties commenced in Italy.   Count Henry
di Campello, Canon of St. Peter's, Rome, threw
up his canonry, and declared himself no longer
able to take his part in maintaining the Papal
system.   In 1861 the Pope had conferred upon him a
canonry in the Church of Santa Maria Maggiore, and
in 1867 translated him to St. Peter's.   At first he
thought that reform might take its rise within the
Roman Church, and for this purpose he claimed the
ancient right of the clergy and people of Rome,
usurped by the College of Cardinals, to elect the Pope.
With this view he formed an Italian Catholic 'Association for the Revindication of Rights belonging to the
Christian People,' which was excommunicated as soon
as its existence became known to the Pope.   Finding
that nothing could be done from within, Campello
wrote to Cardinal Borromeo resigning his canonry;
'No other course,' he said, 'being open to him as a
Christian or Italian citizen.'   To make an entire
breach between himself and the Italian Curia, he read

his letter of renunciation at a public meeting. But in giving up Popery he guarded himself against being thought to have swerved from the true Catholic faith, by declaring : 'I accept whole and entire the faith of the Christian Catholic and Apostolic Church, which was formally expressed in the ancient creed of Nicæa.'

The case was laid before Archbishop Tait, who, after consultation with the other members of a committee of the Lambeth Conference, delegated the supervision of him to the Bishop of Long Island, who was the superintendent of the American congregations on the Continent. The Bishop, accepting the charge 'as a Bishop in the Church of God,' gave Campello a license to execute his functions as a dispenser of the Word of God and of His holy Sacraments. Acting on this license, Campello formed a congregation in Rome, where he was joined by Monsignor Savarese, a learned but unstable man, who after a time went back to the Roman communion. Before he fell away from his faith, he had prepared a liturgy in the Italian tongue, which was used in the congregations of the reformed communions.

Count Henry di Campello paid me two visits. The first was shortly after his rejection of the Papal authority, when he was naturally anxious to find sympathy in England. The second time, in 1886, he came in great distress, Savarese being about to return to the Roman communion through fear of not finding sufficient support as a reformer to maintain him suitably, and (it so happened) the Bishop of Long Island at the same moment resigning his office of superintending American congregations on the Continent and supervising Campello's work. To meet the latter difficulty, Bishop John Wordsworth, at the desire of Archbishop Benson, undertook the office given up by the Bishop of Long Island, so far as Campello was concerned. In regard to his other troubles, Archbishop Plunket instituted a society for granting financial support to the Italian reformers, called 'The Italian Church Reform Association,' and Campello requested me to undertake the revision of the liturgy prepared by Savarese, the more as Savarese claimed for himself the copies hitherto in use in the churches. Undertaking to give what help I could in this direction, I engaged the interest of Archbishop Plunket in the subject. Consequently, many days and nights were devoted by the Archbishop and myself to the revision of the liturgy and the framing of Offices for Matins and Vespers, for Baptism and the Occasional Services, out of manuscript material supplied by Campello. When the preliminary work had been thus done, the revised book was taken to Bishop John Wordsworth, as the Bishop in charge of the Italian Mission, and was reconsidered by us with him at meetings in the Lollards' Tower of Lambeth Palace. The Liturgy or Communion Service was then recommended to the Italian Synod, and, being approved by it, was brought into use in every Old Catholic congregation in Italy. The remaining parts of the Prayer-Book did not receive their final shape till 1903, when they were reconsidered and completed by Professor Mayor and Signor Cichitti. Bishop Herzog, the Swiss Bishop, presided over the first Italian Synod, and ordained deacons and priests when need required, after an examination which had satisfied Bishop Wordsworth of the candidate's competency.

A grave question arose as to the consecration of Campello as Bishop. On the one hand, he was the leader of those who took part in the movement, and there was no one who could be placed over his head; on the other, he had not all the qualities desirable in a Bishop. Especially, he had the hasty temper often found in Italians, and a want of quiet firmness and confidence when difficulties arose. The question was placed in the hands of Canon Thornton, who went to Italy to make inquiries on the spot. The Synod chose Campello as Bishop-elect, and he was recognised in this capacity by his English friends on their receiving Canon Thornton's report ; but he was never consecrated. In his old age his infirmities, both in body and mind, grew upon him, and in reply to one of his letters I advised him to resign his office. He did so ; but, pressed with financial difficulties, and so broken down by sickness as not to be master of himself, he followed the example of Savarese, and reconciled himself to the Roman Church. He died in 1903, and the reformed communion organized itself afresh under the presidency of Professor Cichitti, who had been ordained by Bishop Herzog, and was nominated by the Synod as Bishop-elect.

CHAPTER XIX

The West Indies—Codrington—J. A. Froude—The West Indian
Question—Bishop Rawle.

In 1886 I accepted an invitation of the Society for the
Propagation of the Gospel, conveyed to me through
Lord Stamford, to undertake the headship of Codrington College, Barbados, for a year. This college had
been established by the society under the will of
Christopher Codrington, and it serves as the theological
training college for all the West Indian Islands. Codrington had been educated at Christ Church, and
became a Fellow of All Souls in 1690. He was a
warm supporter of William III., and followed him to
Flanders in 1694. Returning from service in the field,
he was appointed by the King Captain-General of the
Caribbean Islands in succession to his father. Having
held this office for a few years, he retired to his estates
in Barbados. At his death he left to All Souls
College his books and £10,000 to erect the library in
which they might be placed. His two plantations in
Barbados he left to the Society for the Propagation
of the Gospel, with instructions to take care of the
negroes and to establish a college, similar to the
colleges of Oxford, consisting of Professors and scholars
who should study divinity and medicine, but leaving
the particulars of the institution to be determined at
the discretion of the society. The society at once
sent out a catechist to instruct the slaves, and after

some difficulties had been surmounted the present college was established.   Having two such Principals as Pinder and Rawle, the college became the alma mater of the West Indian clergy, and established the Pongas Mission on the West Coast of Africa.   Some years before my arrival the college had been connected with Durham University, and the examination papers used at Durham were sent to Barbados for use by the Codrington students, and returned to Durham for the judgment of the Durham examiners.   A successful student of Codrington College was therefore equal in position and reputation to a B.A. of Durham, and he was allowed to take his Bachelor's degree at that University in his absence.   There were about twenty students during the year that I presided over the college.   But Barbados was at that time suffering, as it has ever since suffered, from the depression of the price of cane-sugar, and Codrington's estates, which had been calculated to produce £2,000 a year, had now very much decreased in value.   A Principal, a tutor, a medical lecturer, and a missionary clergyman for the blacks, who had been till lately slaves, had to be provided, and most of the students required help for their college expenses.

Of the students in my charge, two were quite black, two were brown, and the rest were white, being the sons of English planters.   One of the black students was a son of Bishop Holly of Haiti, who, being himself an African, had married one of the Caribbean Indian women.   Of this old race there are not many remaining.   Most of the survivors are settled in the island of St. Vincent.   My student at Codrington College had inherited from his mother the straight nose, and refined lips, and straight hair, which distinguish the Caribs from the Africans.   There was no ill-will between the black, brown, and white students at the college, all of whom lived together on the most friendly terms and studied the same books in the same classes. I found no difference in the capacities of black and white at the age during which they were under instruction; but there was not so much staying power in the blacks, and they could not equal their white rivals in after-life. It was singular to see how little jealousy and antagonism existed between the two races throughout the islands. Both at Bridgetown in Barbados and at Port of Spain in Trinidad, I preached in the cathedral to a congregation of several thousands made up of blacks and whites intermixed one with another. And yet it had been only one generation ago, just before the emancipation of the slaves, that the authorities at Bridgetown had fined a clergyman for having so transgressed proprieties as to administer the Holy Communion to some black slaves with their masters. The fine was only one shilling, but Bishop Coleridge, who had just gone out to the West Indies as Bishop, wrote home to the Secretary of State in England, and had the fine formally remitted.

Connected with the college, there was a mission chapel for the labourers on the estates, at which I occasionally officiated. The emotional piety of the blacks was very great, and the churchwardens, themselves black men, had to be careful to prevent men morally unfit from attending the Holy Communion. The congregations of blacks were as well behaved and as attentive to the service as any congregations in England. Unhappily, however, their emotional religion was not always connected with high moral conduct; but what was to be expected of those who had only been free men and free women for one generation?

An occurrence which took place at the college exhibited some characteristics of the negro in their least satisfactory form.

The college, comprising the Principal's house, stands in beautiful grounds, planted with palm-trees and other shrubs and trees. One evening I was taking

20

a late stroll by moonlight, when I was surprised to see someone coming towards me. As soon as he saw me, I noticed that he passed behind one of the palm-trees, and then came forward to meet me. I asked him what he was doing, and he said that he was the brother of the college gardener, and was acting as watchman for his brother.

Some conversation passed between us, and I proceeded on my way. When I reached the palm-tree, I found that behind it was deposited a sack half full of potatoes. Calling the man back, I asked what it meant. He said that they were his brother's potatoes, grown in his own patch of ground, and that he was carrying them home for him. I desired that he would call on me the next morning to make a full explanation. The next morning he did not appear, and I told the gardener to send him to me. About the middle of the day he entered my room, saying, in an off-hand manner, ' I believe, Mr. Principal, you wish to speak to me.'

' Yes,' I said : ' I want to know about those potatoes.'

' Potatoes !' he said, with a blank face of amazement —'what potatoes ?'

' Those that you had last night.'

' I can't think what the Principal can be talking about,' he replied ; ' I don't know anything about potatoes,' nor would anything induce him to confess.

I told him that he was to come back in the course of two hours and make acknowledgment, or it would be the worse for him, and I sent his brother to give him the same instruction.

At the end of the two hours I heard a timid knock at the door, and in he came in a deprecating fashion, saying, ' I hope the Principal will overlook it this time.'

I made him take back the potatoes to the place they had come from, and, after giving him a severe warning, let the matter pass. The blacks have not yet enjoyed their freedom long enough to get rid of peccadilloes of this sort, but they are thoroughly trustworthy in greater matters.

During the Trinidad Races it is customary for owners to leave their houses, which stand round the course, unprotected, and nothing is ever lost from them; but the temptation to take a few potatoes, or perhaps a worthless old piece of wood, is very difficult for the negro to resist. There was never any risk to plate or valuables left unprotected. Our butler was equal in honesty and in attention to the very best of English butlers, and I shall not easily forget his despair when a spoon had disappeared while we were giving a large tea-party in the park, which, however, was found to be quite safe after the party had broken up. None could be more faithful and affectionate to their masters and mistresses than black servants, and they exhibit a courtesy unknown to Englishmen of the same rank. When they have plenty to eat they are tempted to be idle, because they never think of yesterday or to-morrow, but only of to-day. When, however, they really work, they can do as much as an English navvy, and with far better temper. I suppose that no subjects of the English Crown are so happy, loyal, and contented, as the blacks of the West Indian Islands, and that in spite of efforts on the part of Mr. Pope Hennessy, when Governor, to teach them the dangerous arts of political combination and agitation.

The case of the West Indian planter in 1886-1887 was very grievous, as it is at the present day. This was owing to the subsidies paid by Continental Governments to the growers of beetroot, in consequence of which they were able to put sugar into the market at a lower rate than that at which it could be produced. The result was ruin to the Barbados planters, who had given up the whole of the island to the cultivation of cane-sugar, which now would not pay for its transmission to Europe. Morning

after morning we used to hear of planters becoming bankrupt. A bitter feeling naturally arose in
their minds : they argued that England was rich and
powerful, that Barbados was an English colony
which was being ruined by no fault of its own, and
that England, therefore, was bound to help it in one
way or another, either by preventing the markets of
the world from being made unfairly favourable to
beet-growers, or else by subsidizing the cane-growers
to such an extent that they could compete with the
subsidized beet-growers. The sentiment throughout the colony was that, if it was worth the while of
the Continental Governments to pay a sum of money
to beet-growers in order to keep the people from
emigrating, it was worth England's while to pay to
cane-growers in like manner enough to save them
from ruin. Taking no higher view than £ s. d.,
it would pay England to make the small expenditure
that was necessary ; and besides this, was it nothing
to have and to retain this beautiful colony in the
tropics, once counted the fairest jewel in the English
Crown ? Was it nothing to have English officials
ruling, and English influence predominating, 4,000
miles from the seat of the Central Government ? Was
it nothing to have this vast outlet for our home
population, where in ordinary times men who are
willing to work can earn a competency and rise to
wealth ? Nay, further, was it wise to let our West
Indian industry be ruined with the likelihood of the
foreign subsidies being hereafter withdrawn, in which
case the price of beet-sugar would rise to the present
price of cane-sugar ? The tone of the West Indian
mind was that of sons and relatives hurt by neglect
where they looked for sympathy. Such a state of
mind is dangerous to disregard :

> ' For to be wrath with those we love
> Doth work like madness in the brain.'

Yet nothing was done by England to prevent so flourishing a limb of the body politic from withering and dropping off for the lack of a little blood which the heart could supply without feeling the loss, until Mr. Chamberlain became Secretary for the Colonies, and then at length, in 1902-1903, steps were taken by him and the Chancellor of the Exchequer to put an end to the foreign subsidies, and meantime to help the West Indies by an annual grant until those subsidies should be withdrawn.

The visit of Mr. J. Anthony Froude to the West Indies for the purpose of investigating their estate, and making it known in England, took place during the year that I was in Barbados. Mr. Froude was to have paid a visit to me at Codrington College, where his brother once held office, but he was prevented from doing so through lack of time. I went to Bridgetown to meet him, and spent a day with him at the house of the Governor, Sir Charles Lees. Froude had been at Oxford just before my time there, and had left many memories of himself at the University. He came up ear-marked as one of Newman's followers, being the younger brother of Hurrell Froude, Newman's great friend and admirer. Newman employed him to write one of the series of *Lives of the Saints*, which he was editing, and a characteristic of these publications was to accept any idle legends, specially if they were miraculous, for the genuine history of the saint in question. When Newman joined the Church of Rome, the reaction took place in Froude's mind, which must have come at some time or other. He would not follow Newman to Rome, nor did he care to stand shivering about the brink ; he saw that a natural result of Newman's teaching was to produce in the minds of those who did not accept it an angry hostility and disbelief, and he put himself mentally in that attitude. He wrote two tales, *The Shadows of the Clouds* and *The Nemesis of Faith*, from this point of view, but they represented rather his theoretical apprehension of what might be than his own real position. For himself he chose the position of an eighteenth-century Protestant, unemotional, unecclesiastical, and unspiritual, but not unbelieving.

His two tales were read a good deal by the Oxford undergraduates, and were supposed by tutors to be mischievous. On one occasion an undergraduate at Exeter College brought into the hall at the time of the college examination a copy of *The Nemesis of Faith*. It was a transgression of rules to bring in any book, and Dr. William Sewell, who was conducting the examination, seeing the book, desired that it might be delivered to him. Finding what the book was, he shook his head, and said: 'Shall I show you the best place for this book?' 'If you please, sir,' said the undergraduate with a smile; whereupon Sewell walked across the hall and put it on the fire. Extraordinary exaggerations of this occurrence were made, and it was reported in and out of Oxford that Sewell had made a bonfire of Froude's books in the quadrangle. Some years afterwards I spent a day at Froude's house in Devonshire, and found him using Bishop Blomfield's book of family prayer in most orthodox fashion.

At the time that he came on his visit to Barbados, Froude had made his reputation by his great historical work, in which he proved himself to possess an unusual power of handling the English language. He had just brought out his book called *Oceana*, and soon after his return to England there appeared his *English in the West Indies*, the gist of which is as follows:

1. If the West Indies are left to drift as at present, the result will be the disappearance of the white population, and the establishment of negro communities throughout the islands.

2. The consequences of such an abandonment on the part of the whites would be the creation of such monstrous republics as that of Haiti, which is 'Paris in the gutter,' where the negroes have gone back in secret to serpent-worship and cannibalism while professing to be Roman Catholics.

3. The reason why the whites are abandoning, and will continue to abandon, the colony is the extension of the suffrage, and the policy which places blacks and whites on an equality, which equality must become a black supremacy, owing to the superiority in numbers on the part of the blacks, and their constant increase.

4. The remedy is that England should recognise the difference between colonies and colonies; between Australia, New Zealand, Canada, etc., to which self-government is properly granted, because they are of the same instincts and character as ourselves; and India, the West Indies, etc., where an imperial race must rule those that are inferior, dispensing justice to all alike, whether members of the ruling or inferior race. By applying the principle of East Indian government to the West Indies, Mr. Froude believed that the apprehensions entertained by the whites of being ruled by black Parliaments would be removed, that confidence would be restored, that capital would return, and the tide of prosperity once more set in which had been so long ebbing.

Mr. Froude's remedies were political, but the West Indian difficulty was, and is, mainly commercial. It is the low price of sugar much more than the fear of political control by blacks which makes English people fly from the islands. They fly from them, and they cease to crowd into them as of old, because a livelihood is to be no longer made in them by the cadets of English families. Mr. Chamberlain's negotiations for the abolition of the sugar bounties, and the subsidy to the producers of cane-sugar in the West Indies, would do more for the colony than any assurance that the hollowness of doctrinaire theories of equality had been recognised at home. Yet Mr. Froude's advice may be well pondered over by British statesmen. It amounts to this : Have confidence in yourselves, and remember what in the din of the oratory of Parliamentary demagogues you are liable to forget, and are forgetting : that you have an imperial task before you, and it must be performed imperially, or it cannot be performed at all.

During the Christmas vacation I went to the Island of Trinidad, passing St. Vincent and Grenada on the way.

The Soufrière, which has since devastated St. Vincent, was at this time calm and apparently peaceful. Trinidad is a much more beautiful island than Barbados, as it has not, like the latter island, been devoted to the production of the sugar-cane ; the hills are clothed with verdure, and the cocoa-trees grow freely in it, as it is not exposed to the trade-winds. We stayed with Bishop Rawle, one of the very noble band of colonial Bishops sent out by the home Church in the last generation, to be reckoned with Selwyn, Gray, Field, Patteson, and inferior to none of them in nobleness of life and devotion to his Master's work. Third Wrangler at Cambridge, and fourth in the first class of the Classical Tripos in the year 1805, and Assistant-Tutor at Trinity College, he undertook in 1847 the office of Principal of Codrington College, Barbados, where he spent seventeen years of his life, and to which he returned in his old age to die. To Mr. Rawle's energy, and the wise support given him by Mr. Ernest Hawkins and Mr. W. T. Bullock, Secretaries of the S.P.G., is due the preservation, as a theological college, of Codrington College, which the Barbadian authorities were desirous of turning into a sort of High School, whence some boys might proceed to English Universities. On his arrival Mr. Rawle found only eight students, which number he soon raised to twenty, and in connection with the college he established a mission - house, where coloured students might be trained for work in Africa. He would not leave the principalship for the bishopric of Antigua, which was offered to him, but in 1864 his health compelled his resignation, and he returned to England. On recovering, he was elected the first Bishop of Trinidad, a position of great toil and difficulty, of which the chief recommendation was that it offered opportunities for God's service and for building up the West Indian Church. In addition to his episcopal work, the Bishop undertook the charge of a parish and of a leper asylum and hospital. At the time of my visit he had been in residence for more than twenty years, living in the chief town of the island, the Port of Spain, and towering by head and shoulders above everybody else in the island. Every Sunday his cathedral was filled at each service with a congregation of about 2,000 persons of every rank and colour. He had negroes, coolies, and Chinese under his charge, all of whom required different treatment, and most of the churches in the island having fallen into disrepair, he rebuilt them, being his own architect, and, though he was a poor man, finding the greater part of the funds necessary for their restoration.

At the end of 1887 he came to England to recruit his health, and there had the irreparable misfortune of losing his wife, who had been a sharer in all his hopes and efforts. Unable to continue his work, he resigned his bishopric, and finding that Codrington College was without a Principal, he was induced once more to accept the office. But his strength was now almost exhausted, and in the spring of 1889 he fell asleep, and was buried in the churchyard outside the Society's chapel, on the brow of the hill overlooking his old college.   Bishop Rawle was a true English Churchman, such as the English Church forms in some of its clergy.   There was nothing extravagant about him; no love of asceticism for its own sake; an absolute and entire freedom from cant and pretence.   He was a man who simply did his duty to the utmost of his power in the positions in which God had placed him, giving himself up to God's service without reservation, without a shadow of self-consciousness, or imagination that he was ever doing anything great or good.

At the end of the academical year I returned to England, and an occurrence, slight as it was, during the voyage made me feel how widely extended is the belief that the West Indies are a derelict, and a fair spoil for any who have more energy and enterprise than their present owners.   I was conversing with a fellow-passenger, whom I regarded as an Englishman, as his accent was perfect and his knowledge of English affairs full.   A passing word of disparagement, referring to the straightforwardness of Russian diplomacy, brought a flash into his eye and a quick question: 'How not straightforward?'   I explained that I meant that Russia sometimes concealed her further purposes.   'Oh,' said he, 'we intend to have India, if you mean that; and,' he continued viciously, 'as you don't seem to know what to do with these islands here, we will have them, too.'   I do not mean, by recounting this conversation, to imply that there is any apprehension from the side of Russia, but the answer bears corroborative witness to the fact that, in the judgment of the world, Great Britain is letting one of her fairest colonies slide, and showing a deficiency of the spirit which makes and which preserves empires.

CHAPTER XX

WHEN I left England in 1886, I have said that an
arrangement had been made that Bishop John Wordsworth of Salisbury should give episcopal supervision
to the Italian Reformers; that Lord Plunket, Archbishop of Dublin, should raise money for their support
by means of the Italian Church Reform Association;
and that I should help in the revision of the existing
Italian liturgy, which had been drawn up by Monsignor
Savarese, and in the formation of an Italian Prayer-
Book out of manuscript supplied by Count Campello.
Archbishop Plunket's interest was also engaged for the
work of the revision, and to carry this out effectually,
as well as for other reasons, I paid a number of visits
to the Archbishop at Old Connaught House, near
Bray. And this brought me into very close relations
with him.

I had first met Lord Plunket at the Conference at
Bonn in 1875, before he had yet become a Bishop. His
large heart was much moved at the prospect of embracing as brethren the earnest men who had been
stirred into action by the claims put forward at the
Vatican Council, and from this time forward his interest
in the Old Catholic Reform Movement was keen and
constant. As soon as he had returned from Bonn to
Ireland, he forwarded to me £50, given by himself and

a few Irish friends, for the support of Old Catholic theological students at Bonn, and thenceforth he attended the Old Catholic Congresses as far as his engagements would allow. I accompanied him to the Congress held at Lucerne in 1892, at which he gave a sketch of the reformation in Ireland, claiming that the Irish Church, both by her lineage and by the character of her teaching, was no other than the Old Catholic Church of Ireland, and ending with an expression of the affection that he entertained for his brother Bishops—Reinkens, Herzog, and the Archbishop of Patras, the last of whom had come from Greece to attend the Congress.

His warmest interests were for Spain and Portugal, for, feeling that the application made from the Peninsula to the Lambeth Conference of 1878 for the sympathies of the Anglican Church and episcopal help ought not to be overlooked, he paid frequent visits to the Peninsula, and convinced himself that the Spanish and Portuguese reformers were worthy to receive the spiritual assistance that they had asked for.

At the end of 1892, accompanied by the Bishop of Clogher and myself, he went to Madrid for the purpose of consecrating a church, first paying a visit to Valladolid, Salamanca, and Villaescusa, where he held Confirmations. On his arrival at Madrid, he held a Synod of the Spanish Reformed Church, attended by nine Spanish presbyters, the Bishop of Clogher, M. Loyson, Count Henry di Campello, Signor Janni, two English presbyters, and two English laymen. When the time for the consecration of the church arrived, permission to proceed was refused by the authorities, and the congregation that had met for the consecration were kept standing in the street. The Archbishop, the Bishop of Clogher, and myself were residing in the clergy-house adjoining the church, and, as one entrance led to the clergy-house and to the church, we were told that if we went out from it we could not be readmitted. Nothing could surpass the 'superb temper' shown by the Archbishop in these trying circumstances. Judging that God's time had not yet come for his intended action, he waited patiently, and going out of his house (for it was his own house) to ordain a presbyter, on the policeman's refusal to readmit him, he went quietly with his companions to an hotel. A change of ministry occurring two or three days subsequently, it was understood that no further obstacle would be put in the Archbishop's way, provided that a foliated cross inlaid in an outside wall was removed, on the ground that the cross symbolized or suggested that the building was or contained a church. In matter of fact, when the Archbishop, the Bishop of Clogher, and the Bishop of Down subsequently presented themselves, no objection was made on the part of the State authorities to the consecration of the church or of a Bishop, though the Papal Nuncio, some devout ladies of Madrid, and some Ultramontane newspapers, tried in vain to raise a disturbance on the subject.

The journey to Spain with Lord Plunket was full of interest. The first place that we stopped at was Valladolid, where we were met by Señor Cabrera and by Señor Martinez, the latter of whom was the clergyman of the reformed congregation of the city. This congregation was the growth of twenty-five years ; for till Prim's Revolution in 1868 no Spaniard dared call himself a Protestant or breathe the name of reform. After a Confirmation service held by the Archbishop, we walked to the Campo Grande, the site of the burnings by the Inquisition. Here Philip II. is said to have sat in state, and allowed his soldiers to help the friars in setting alight to the faggots piled round the victims of an *auto-da-fé*. Two *autos-da-fé* were held here, one in the presence of the Regent, Juana, the other under the eye of Philip himself. The first of these *autos-da-fé* was held on Trinity Sunday, May 21, 1559. It was conducted, as usual, by the Dominican friars, who led to the place of trial sixteen penitents who were to suffer penalties, and fourteen adjudged impenitent, who were to be burnt. The sermon was preached by Melchior Cano, Bishop of the Canaries, and as soon as the sentences were given, those who were condemned to death were carried on the backs of asses to the Campo Grande to be burnt. On October 8, 1559, a similar scene was enacted, and on a grander scale, Philip II. himself being present, when thirteen men and women were committed to the flames. The sole fault of the sufferers was their holding Protestant opinions, and their occasionally meeting secretly together for the consolation of common prayer. In 1559 there were 1,000 Protestants in Valladolid; in 1560 there was not one. All of them had been burnt, or strangled, or exiled, or imprisoned, or driven into conformity. This outward conformity lasted till 1868. In 1892 I took part in the service in which Archbishop Plunket confirmed fourteen members of a congregation of some 300 souls. Some advance, therefore, had been made towards liberty of conscience in Spain.

From Valladolid we went to Salamanca, especially interesting to me as the ancient University town of Spain. After visiting the buildings of the University, I made inquiry as to the conditions under which Englishmen could receive a Salamanca degree, Mr. Frederick George Lee, like Titus Oates, having claimed to have had the degree of a Doctor of Civil Law granted him by the University. I had known Mr. Lee as an undergraduate at Oxford. There he was unable to pass the first examination, called Responsions or Little-go, the reason of which was not far to seek; for, instead of studying the books required by the examiners, he occupied himself in going about and, as he said, 'talking in behalf of the Catholic party.' Not content with talking, he kept a triptych in his rooms, which from time to time he opened in the presence of congenial companions, and performed some services before it, dressed as a Roman priest. After many failures to pass his Little-go, the University, in compassion, allowed him to become a Scholar of Civil Law without further examination, but he was unable to progress further in his University career. Having, however, gained the English Prize Poem, he was ordained, after which he was designated Doctor of Civil Law of the University of Salamanca. On inquiry, I was informed that by a law of 1845 anyone who received a degree from the Salamanca University had to be (1) a Spaniard, (2) a Roman Catholic, (3) a student resident for a certain length of time, (4) one who had passed the appointed examinations; and that the University insisted so strongly on these conditions that it had felt itself precluded from giving an honorary degree to the Prime Minister, Espartero, because he had not fulfilled them. The Rector stated that the name of Mr. Lee was unknown to him.

From Salamanca we drove to a large village named Villaescusa, where the Archbishop was expected for a Confirmation. As we drew near to the village several groups of men and women, about a hundred in all, came to welcome the Archbishop, and he got out of the carriage and walked with them. After a service in the church at Villaescusa, I shook hands and had some conversation with Señor Hernandez, whose story is as follows: Going some years previously to a neighbouring town, he had bought a copy of the New Testament, and was so struck by it that he read it to his sister. Others asked to hear it read also, and in this manner a little congregation of inquirers used to meet at his house. The priest of the parish grew angry, and gave public notice that on the next occasion when the image of St. Mary, called St. Mary of the Elm, was carried round the village, as was usual every year, she would show her indignation. When the day came, and the people gathered for the procession, it appeared that St. Mary had lost her arms. 'This,' cried the sacristan who had charge of the image, 'is the doing of the Protestants,' and one of those present said that as he passed Hernandez's house he heard a girl using the word 'arms.' The people rushed tumultuously to the house, and demanded of the girl what were the arms which she had spoken of. 'Baby's arms,' she replied in great amazement. This was regarded only as an excuse, and Hernandez, who was her uncle, was seized, carried off to the neighbouring town, and imprisoned in a cell lighted only from the top, for having stolen the arms of the Virgin of the Elm. Here he was kept for about a fortnight without trial. But meantime the Guardias Civiles had been summoned to Villaescusa to investigate the charge, and they found that the arms had been unscrewed, and were lying hidden under some hay in a stable to which the sacristan had access. The discovery of this fraud created a great revulsion of feeling in Villaescusa against the worshippers of the Virgin of the Elm. Hernandez was delivered from his prison, and his few readers of the Scripture swelled into a large body, for whom a church was built, which was attended on the day that I was there by 400 persons, of whom forty were confirmed.

Before leaving Villaescusa I had an instance of Spanish courtesy and good manners. The rest of the party were out of the house, when fifteen schoolgirls came to pay us a visit. As I was the only one at home, they introduced themselves to me, sat round the brazier, and talked with the greatest ease of manner, and at the same time with the utmost respect. They told me which of them had been confirmed and which of them were going to be confirmed, described what they had learnt at school, told me their names one by one, asked what my name was and the names of my children, and made some intelligent inquiries about the state of religion in England. The Archbishop and the Bishop on their return were surprised at finding me the centre of an animated group of children, whom I then presented to them.

Having returned to Salamanca, we travelled by night to Madrid, and took up our quarters at Señor Cabrera's clergy-house. Here, as I have already said, we were kept shut up, while the congregation, which had come for the consecration of the church, was prevented entering by two policemen sent by the Mayor of Madrid. Bishop Stack made an effort to go out in order to explain the circumstances to the disappointed congregation in the street. The policeman told him that if he went out he could not return to the house. 'That is stupid,' said Mr. Jameson, one of those who were standing in the street. 'You will take back that word,' said the policeman, striding to him; but Mr. Jameson had been for a long time a resident in Spain, and he knew Spanish ways. Drawing himself up, he refused to do as he was told, and the policeman withdrew to the door without further altercation. The Bishop returned and joined me at the window, where we could watch the scene in the street below; some of its features were so odd that we presently began to laugh. The Archbishop, looked up with surprise at our unexpected light-heartedness, and we asked him to come and join us. Our spirits gradually rose, and the Archbishop, having beckoned a friend to his prison window, asked him to arrange for an ordination, that he had intended to hold in the church, to be held in a room lent by some Presbyterians

21

for the purpose.   The ordination took place at 3.30, and Señor Regaliza, who had been ministering as a deacon at Villaescusa, was ordained priest.   Hands were laid upon his head by presbyters, who represented many Churches.   The English Church was represented by Dr. Noyes and myself, the French by M. Hyacinthe Loyson, the Italian by Count Henry di Campello, the Spanish by Señor Cabrera, while the Archbishop and the Bishop represented the Irish Church.   After the ordination a Confirmation was held.   We then went to the hotel, to which we had previously sent our luggage, and here M. Loyson was visited by Señor Castelar, the leader of the advanced Liberal party in Spain, to express his regrets and apologies for what had taken place.   The same night (for trains generally run by night in Spain) we went on to Lisbon, and stayed at the house of Canon Pope, and the following night proceeded to Oporto.

Here I was the guest of Mr. Andrew Cassell, a man who had been ordained deacon by the Archbishop of Dublin in his private chapel in Dublin, about which act of the Archbishop some scandal had arisen, as though he had performed an act of schism.   I had expected to see a young deacon, but I found an elderly man of good position, with a delightful household, consisting of himself and eight children, the eldest of whom was fifteen.   Three of these were confirmed the following day, together with twenty other candidates.   In his school there were 150 children, and in his brother's school (the Rev. James Cassell) there were 190.   Mr. James Cassell (an Englishman born in Portugal) was ordained priest by the Archbishop on the petition of the Portuguese or Lusitanian Synod, a meeting of which was held, attended by nine representatives.   The next day we returned to Lisbon.

CHAPTER XXI

THE Reform Movement in Portugal, though closely connected with the Spanish movement, did not commence in the same manner with it. The first preacher of reform in Portugal was Dr. Gomez, a Spanish ecclesiastic who, being expelled from the neighbouring kingdom on account of his Liberal ideas, took refuge in Portugal about the year 1842. In 1849 the S.P.C.K. published the Liturgy of the Anglican Church in Portuguese. In 1860 Mrs. Helen Roughton, an English lady, opened a school and held a class for Biblical study. In 1867 the Rev. Angel Herreros de Mora, another persecuted Spaniard, fled to Lisbon, and there instituted a congregation for reformed worship. In 1870, after the expulsion of Queen Isabel from Spain, and the introduction of Protestantism into that country, the Portuguese Government recognised the legal existence of the Evangelical Church of Portugal. In 1875 the Rev. Godfrey P. Pope, British Chaplain at Lisbon, invited the Rev. L. S. Tugwell into Portugal that he might see the reality of the effort after reform ; and after consultation between all interested, four reformed congregations were established, three in Lisbon and one at Rio de Mouro, under Senhores de Mora, Pereira, Miranda, and Da Costa, who were joined by two more priests. De Mora's death soon followed, and he was succeeded by Senhor Mello, who, like the rest, had received his orders from the Roman Catholic Church.

In 1878 the Portuguese joined with the Spanish Reformers in memorializing the Lambeth Conference, and praying for a Bishop for the Peninsula, to be nominated either by the Archbishop of Canterbury and the Bishop of London, or by the Archbishop of Armagh.

At the time of my visit in 1892 only one of the four original clergy was still living; this was Da Costa, of Rio de Mouro. On the day after my return to Lisbon I went to Rio de Mouro with the Archbishop and the Bishop. Da Costa had been originally a Roman priest at Rio de Mouro. He now kept a school, and had a large congregation in the same place. In 1882 he had been excommunicated, and the form of his excommunication, and that of his wife, is very characteristic.

'The crime of these unhappy persons,' declared the Archbishop of Mitylene, 'is horrible. It is the awful sin of public heresy, manifested externally, with all the anti-Catholic demonstrations which the furious fanaticism of error can inspire against the truth; the public teaching of Protestantism carried on by the heretical school founded in Rio de Mouro, at the expense of the dreadful Protestant Propaganda; the circulation of Bibles and pamphlets, where attacks are made on Catholic dogma, upon the worship of the sacred images, not to mention the pious homage which we pay to the Mother of God and Our Lady, the lofty patroness of the Portuguese; the denial of the various Sacraments, and the scandalous imitation of the most venerable rites of our holy faith. . . . Fly from them, Christians! You must avoid them as persons struck with pestilence. Hold no intercourse of any kind with them! At present there presses upon them the justice of God, who punishes them with the thunder-bolts of the anathema. Afterwards light will come and enlighten these blind persons, so that they may see that which at present they do not see—Protestantism decomposing, being reduced to the filth of error, and all its members in whom a sincere desire to know the truth exists reconciling themselves to the Church of Rome, and sheltering under the shadow of that portentous moral force which governs the world.

'Given in Sao Vicente under our seal and the stamp and arms of His Eminence [the Cardinal Patriarch of Lisbon] on the 23rd of November, 1882.'

Ten years after this fulmination I was happy to find Senhor Da Costa and 'his female accomplice'—that is, his wife—in good health and high spirits, carrying on a prosperous work at Rio de Mouro.

On the day following our visit to Senhor Da Costa, Senhor Torres was ordained priest in St. Peter's, Lisbon, of which Senhor Candido de Souza, who, if his health be equal to it, will probably be the first Portuguese reformed Bishop, is the clergyman. In the six schoolrooms and churches visited by the Archbishop in Portugal during this week, there were 1,500 adults and 500 children present.

On our return to Madrid, after an absence of ten days, we found that Sagasta had become Prime Minister, and that no further obstacles were to be put in the way of the consecration of the church. So strong, however, was the influence of the Court ladies (ten Duchesses, eight Marchionesses, and seven Countesses) and of the Nuncio and of the clerical papers, and so short was the time at the Archbishop's disposal, that it was thought better to defer the consecration to a later date, when both Señor Cabrera and the church might be consecrated together. The fury of the Ultramontane press was indeed astonishing, and only equalled by the calmness of the people and the indifference of the Government. The following is a specimen : ' Is it just or equitable, reasonable or politic, to disregard the way in which 18,000,000 [*sic*] of Catholics choose that we should be religious, we who have a right to be governed in a Catholic way by the State which we serve with our blood and money, in order to favour the filthy, immoral, and obscurantist demand of that group, of microscopic dimensions, headed by a few monks living with their concubines and trebly apostate ? The religious opinions and worship of Protestants are manifestly contrary to and subversive of Christian morals, for they teach and preach, in opposition to them, doctrines horrid in theory and profoundly immoral in practice, offensive to God, degrading to man, and ruinous to society ' (*El Siglo Futuro*).

On September 23, 1894, Bishop Cabrera was consecrated by the Archbishop of Dublin, the Bishop of Clogher, and the Bishop of Down. This was described by the Bishop of Madrid in a pastoral letter as a pretended consecration held in the presence of ' pastors, proselytes, and masons,' by ' three English individuals who bear the name of Bishops, although it is a thing certain that English Protestantism has been without a true episcopate from its cradle, not simply because its consecrations have been conferred by heretics and schismatics, but on account of its defect of succession and the essential faults of its ordination formula.' There were laymen in England who were as angry as the Bishop of Madrid at the consecration of Bishop Cabrera, and Viscount Halifax and others tried to get up a pro-Roman agitation in England on the subject. In consequence of the attacks made upon the Archbishop, I drew up the following address, which was largely signed, in 1895 :

'MY LORD ARCHBISHOP,

'We, the undersigned clergy and laity of the Church of England, approach your Grace, with reverence for your high office, to express to you our thanks for the action that your Grace has taken in fostering the Reform Movement in Spain, and giving your weighty support in the time of their need to the members of the Reformed Spanish Church.

'We desire to express to your Grace not only our thankfulness, but our admiration both of what you have done and the manner in which you have done it.

'1. You have come to the help of the Lord's people struggling to free themselves from the corruptions of a corrupt Church. You have stretched out the hand of sympathy and encouragement to some of God's servants in the time of their deepest distress. You have given them for many years past those consolations of religion and that spiritual support which a Bishop could alone give, and, when the full time was come, you and your two colleagues, to whom we also offer our thanks, transmitted to a man selected by themselves from among the presbyters of their Church, and found by your Lordships apt and meet for his learning and godly conversation, the gift of the Episcopate, which he may exercise to the honour of God and the edifying of His Church. And while this act of your Lordship's will, we humbly trust, bring forth good fruit in Spain, it vindicates at the same time the position of the Bishops of the Anglican communion as Bishops of the Church of God, interested in the affairs of the Church Catholic, and bound by every principle of right and duty to make response to an appeal calling upon them to come to the assistance of their brother Christians suffering for their fidelity to the Gospel, and refusing to accept the novel inventions of man for Evangelical truth.

'2. We venture, too, to congratulate your Grace on

the manner in which you have carried out this great
Christian work.   We regard with admiration the
courage, the patience, the prudence, the perseverance,
you have exhibited.   We have seen with a feeling
akin to indignation the insinuations and charges,
mostly arising from ignorance, which have been poured
upon you, and we have rejoiced at the meekness and
gracious courtesy with which you have instructed
those that oppose themselves.   We are equally impressed with the deference you have paid to the
judgment of your brother Bishops in Ireland, and of
the Bishops assembled in the Lambeth Conference.
We do not doubt that the question hereafter will be
rather why the gift of the Episcopate was not sooner
made to these brethren than why it was made so soon.
We pray—and in this we feel assured that we are
joining our prayers to yours—that the brotherly act
that your Grace and your two colleagues have performed may be abundantly blessed by God, that the
Church whose organization has thus been completed
may serve as a light in a dark land, and that its
members may be the highly favoured instruments of
restoring to their countrymen that pure faith which
their ancestors held, and for which martyrs died in
the fourth and in the sixteenth century.'

After his return from Spain, Lord Plunket continued
his work for Spain, for Italy, but above all for Ireland.
In 1896 he invited me to hold a quiet day for the
clergy of his diocese, at which the Holy Communion
was administered in the morning at St. Paul's Church,
Bray, and I delivered five addresses in the course of
the day.   At the end of the year 1896, Archbishop
Benson and Mrs. Benson paid a visit to Old Connaught,
and the two Archbishops had long and earnest discussion as to the proceedings of the Lambeth Conference
to be held the following year.   At that Conference,

however, neither of the Archbishops was present, Archbishop Benson having died suddenly in Hawarden Church, and Archbishop Plunket being carried off by an attack of influenza.

It is easier to say what Lord Plunket did than to describe what he was. Perhaps the most notable characteristic in him was his simplicity in the highest and noblest sense of that word. He was utterly unspoilt and unaffected by his position in the State and in the Church. He was not fenced about with either secular or spiritual pride. He did not know what condescension meant. He dearly loved, and was dearly loved by, his intimate friends and associates in his work, and he recognised all who loved the Lord Jesus Christ as his brethren and equals before God. The next thing to notice in him was his temper—his 'superb temper,' as Bishop Thorold designated it. Immersed as he necessarily was in controversy, he never spoke harshly of an opponent, never tried to misrepresent his arguments, never failed to acknowledge the right of others to their opinions, as he to his. When he was assailed even anonymously, and when acts and motives which he had not done and did not entertain were attributed to him, he did not shut himself up in a haughty silence, or express a justifiable indignation, but graciously and meekly instructed those who opposed themselves, without a hint that their charges were an offence to charity or a proof of their incompetence. He was grieved at misunderstandings, but seldom moved and never angered.

Behind these engaging qualities there was a firmness and courage not always united with them. When he had made up his mind that a course was in accordance with God's will, the Archbishop was not to be diverted from it, and he was brave enough to face obloquy without shrinking, leaving the result with God. Added to his courage in choosing ends and abiding by them was an astonishing perseverance in taking the means to attain those ends. He knew that the day of little things leads on to greater things, and he never shrank from the wearisomeness involved in doing the little things if they were conducive to the greater. He was prudent and patient as well as firm. If he judged that a thing had to be done, he did it, but he avoided all methods of doing it which might give unnecessary offence. Cabrera was consecrated, but no pomp and pride surrounded his consecration. He was consecrated, but the Archbishop waited some twenty years till all the obstacles that could be removed were smoothed away. Not many persons would have allowed themselves to be shut out of their own house in Madrid without complaint; but he was patient under the injury (which, indeed, he was too much occupied with other thoughts to dwell upon), and too prudent to irritate the Spaniards on a personal question when he wished to conciliate them. In a funeral sermon, full of pathos and of eloquence, Archbishop Alexander speaks of him thus: 'A noble Archbishop, a humble Christian, a man full of sympathy for sickness, sorrow, and suffering, who stooped to wash every foot that was stained with earth's dust, and to heal every foot that was stabbed with earth's thorns.'

CHAPTER XXII

Durham University—Congress of 1895—Retrospect of half a century
—Blickling Hall—Constance, Marchioness of Lothian.

In 1893 and 1894 I went to Durham University to
examine candidates for a License in Theology. I was
the more interested in this as it was to Durham
University that the papers of the students of Codrington College had been sent. My brother examiners
were, on the first occasion Dean Spence of Gloucester,
on the second Dr. Gibson, Vicar of Leeds, afterwards
Bishop of Gloucester. At Durham I was able to
renew my acquaintance with Canon A. S. Farrar and
Dean Lake, who had been my colleagues as examiners
in the Final Classical Schools at Oxford, and with
Dr. Plummer and Dr. Robertson, both of them, like
myself and Dr. Gibson, members of Trinity College,
Oxford. Dr. Robertson, now Bishop of Exeter,
was my godson. When the examination was over,
I went to Cosin's Library with Mr. Fowler the
librarian, and borrowed from it the Prayer-Books
containing the MSS. of Bishop Cosin. On a comparison of the handwriting, it became perfectly clear
that the notes published in the Anglo-Catholic edition
of Cosin's works, under the name of the 'First Series
of Notes,' were not in Cosin's handwriting. His
authorship of them is also otherwise disproved to
demonstration. They were probably written by Mr.
Heywood, a nephew of Bishop Overall.

In the year 1895 the Church Congress was held for the second time at Norwich, and a new departure was made by the committee in inviting Bishop Herzog to take part in the discussion. This implied an acknowledgment of intercommunion existing between the Church of England and the Old Catholics, as only those that are in communion with the Church of England can address the Congress. On Bishop Herzog's arrival I took him, to rest after his journey, to the house of Miss Temple Frere, and in the evening to Earlham Hall, where Canon and Mrs. Ripley received him for two nights. He read a valuable paper on 'National Churches' at the Congress, after which he went to luncheon with Bishop and Mrs. Sheepshanks, and the next day he returned to the Continent.

At the same Congress I read a paper on the hindrances to communion with the Oriental Church, which I represented to be not so much the doctrine of the Procession, or even of the Holy Eucharist, or of Icons, as the question of the acceptance of the Second Council of Nicea and the Eastern tenet of the Infallibility of the Church—that is, of the Orthodox Communion, consisting of the local Churches of Constantinople, Russia, Greece, Roumania, Bulgaria, Servia, Herzegovina, and Montenegro. At the same time I pointed out how much more we have in common with the Oriental than with the Roman Church in respect both to doctrine and to sympathies.

In 1898 I resigned the office of Secretary of the Anglo-Continental Society, which I had held since the institution of the society in 1853. The work for which it was established, if it were not done, seemed at least less pressing. The Old Catholic Churches of Germany and Switzerland did not now need the sympathies which they grasped at in their first years, and there were special societies formed for fostering and giving spiritual aid to the reformers in Italy and in Spain and Portugal. Archbishop Maclagan, who had been president since the death of Bishop Harold Browne, resigned at the same time. With a new president and a new secretary, the character of the society began to change, and in 1904 it altered its name to the Anglican and Foreign Church Society. In the year 1899 I brought to a close the publication of the *Foreign Church Chronicle*, which I had edited for more than twenty years, to advocate the views of the society.

Relieved of these preoccupations just as the century closed, I was led to institute in my own mind a comparison of the state of the Church in England with what it was half a century ago, in order to see where the Church now most needed the sympathies and efforts of her sons. Amidst much that was cheering, two losses offered themselves at once for notice : (1) The loss of the Universities as Church institutions ; (2) the loss of the labourers from our parish churches. Of the former I have already spoken. Theological colleges, necessary as they are, are no adequate substitute for our ancient Universities in the formation of the character of our clergy. With regard to the latter, I remember that there were in my father's church two galleries, one assigned to men, the other to women, in each case of the labouring class. There was nothing that is now considered attractive in the manner in which the service was conducted : no ceremonial effects ; no music, except such as was forthcoming from a fiddle, a violoncello, and a trombone, and an untrained body of village singers, who sat in the 'singing-gallery' at the west end of the church. Yet the men's gallery and the women's gallery were full twice a day, and a considerable number of the labouring class presented themselves at the (infrequent) celebration of the Holy Communion. Now where are the labourers at morning and evening services (to which they are to be attracted by music)? and still more, where are they at the Holy Communions, which have been multiplied and multiplied? It may be said, not without truth, that politics will go far to explain these things. No doubt it was the action of a political party desirous of weakening the Church, which it generally found in opposition to itself, and also desirous of strengthening other religionists who generally support it, which to a great extent (not wholly) led to the unchurching of the Universities; and it is the misrepresentation of the parson and the squire by agitators who constitute themselves leaders of the labourers which makes the latter shun our churches. But this is not sufficient to account for the indifference of the labouring classes to religious worship, now prevailing so much more widely than formerly. Is the disregard of the obligation of Sunday observance by all classes the cause or the effect of the phenomenon?

Take another case for comparison. Half a century ago there were, no doubt, as there always have been, men who disbelieved; but agnosticism was not then proclaimed as a principle justifying the ignoring of God, nor was faith in Holy Scripture, and therefore in our Lord, undermined by a criticism which is now affecting all classes of society.

Again, fifty years ago none of the clergy were disloyal to their Church, except those that had come under the spell of Dr. Newman, and they felt the position so impossible that, one by one, they left the Church. How do we stand in this respect now? There is a large and organized body of clergy who think that there is nothing wrong in disloyalty to the Church as she has been reformed, and whose object it is to restore her to the estate in which she was before the Reformation, and to reintroduce the ceremonies and practices and doctrines of the mediæval Church which have been repudiated by her.

The struggle with rationalism is impending; the struggle with mediævalism (the prevalence of which would disable us in our battle with rationalism) is upon us at the present moment. Under the circumstances it seemed right to co-operate with the Church of England League, established for the maintenance of the hitherto accepted doctrines of the Church of England; and I wrote three books in defence of the Church of England as she is and has been: *Scriptural and Catholic Truth and Worship* (1901), *Old Anglicanism and Modern Ritualism* (1901), *Sunday Observance* (1902); I also joined Dr. Wace, Dean of Canterbury, in issuing our Appeal to the early centuries (1904). In this appeal it was my part to show that mediæval and still more modern ceremonies, practices and doctrines are not to be forced upon us on the plea that they are 'Catholic,' the fact that they are not Catholic being proved by their being shown not to have been the common use of the Church in the first five or six centuries.

Blickling, in which I have lived for the last thirty-five years, is a village with a history. King Harold once resided in it, when he was Earl of the East Angles, and the foundations of his house still remain beneath the soil. Then the manor passed, by the Conqueror's grant, to the Bishops of Norwich. A new house on the present site was built in the fourteenth century, and in it lived, among others, Sir Thomas de Erpingham, the 'good old knight' of Agincourt; Sir John Fastolfe, the 'base knight,' the 'cowardly knight' of Patay; and the Boleyn family, one of which was Queen Anne, the mother of Elizabeth. That house was pulled down at the end of Elizabeth's reign, and a new house was built by Sir Henry Hobart, the then Lord Chief Justice of England. A descendant of

Sir Henry was created Earl of Buckinghamshire, and from him the present owner is descended by the female line. The house, or Hall, built by the architect by whom Hatfield was also built, besides its architectural beauty and picturesque surroundings, has an excellent library and a few good paintings, and it attracts visitors every summer in great numbers.

On December 9, 1898, a visit to Blickling Hall was made by the King (then Prince of Wales) and the Empress Frederick of Germany. Lady Lothian being absent, I had, at her request, together with Mr. Bertram Talbot, cousin of Lady Lothian, and Mr. Wright, agent of the estate, the office of receiving them. They first walked round the gardens, which was as much as the Prince could do, as he had not yet recovered from an accident, and his sister was afraid it might overtire him. In the house they visited the library, where I had previously arranged the most interesting books for inspection. In the room known as George II.'s, because George II. had slept there and the furniture has remained unchanged since that time, there is a portrait of Sir Henry Hobart, the founder of the present house, and Lord Chief Justice in the time of Elizabeth. He wears round his neck a chain with the letters SS on it. This chain has been supposed to be a sign of his office, such as is now worn by the Lord Chief Justice, and the SS to represent *Sanctus Spiritus.* The Empress demurred to this explanation, saying that the chain represented a token which Henry IV. gave to his partisans while he was in exile, before he had succeeded to the throne, and that the SS meant *Souvenir et Souverain.* Before leaving the library, the Prince and the Empress added their names to a list of visitors, inscribed in the first page of a large MS. Bible, which begins with Arthur, Duke of Wellington, and had ended with Alexandra,

Princess of Wales, who had visited Blickling ten years previously.

After luncheon, at which there was no formality, the Prince, it was said, liking to be treated in Norfolk more as a Norfolk Squire than as the Heir Apparent, the visitors went to the church, where the Prince was greatly struck by the beauty of Watts' monument to Lord Lothian, and the Empress was much interested in the historical brasses of the church, especially those of the Boleyn family, of which there are four in the chancel.

The school-children of the parish had taken great delight in the coming of the Prince, and had welcomed him with flags and singing. Not long afterwards the attempt to assassinate him took place at Brussels. The children were very indignant, and asked leave to write and express their feelings to the Prince. We told them that they might each write a letter in his or her own words. The following is a type of the letters produced: 'My dear Prince,—We are very angry with that naughty boy who has been shooting at you, and we are very glad that he did not hurt you, and we hope you will enjoy your holiday all the same, and that you will come back here to see us again soon.' I selected the six best of these letters and sent them to the Private Secretary of the Prince, saying that I thought it possible that the Prince might like to see the expression of the sympathy of his young admirers, on the principle of Shakespeare's Theseus in the *Midsummer Night's Dream*—

> ' For never anything can be amiss
> When simpleness and duty tender it.'

In a few days a letter was received returning the Prince's thanks for the children's letters, which was couched, not in merely formal terms, but was full of kindly feeling, such as might be expected from the son of Queen Victoria.

22

In 1901 the Hall witnessed a touching scene. Constance, Marchioness of Lothian, who had been its occupant since her husband's death in 1870, died, to the sorrow of the parish and neighbourhood. Thirty-one years ago I had gone to Scotland to bury her husband in that part of Jedburgh Abbey which is reserved for the family of the Kerrs. My son, the Rev. F. J. Meyrick, now Vicar of St. Peter Mancroft, Norwich, fulfilled the same office for his widow. I held a short service at the entrance of the Hall, consisting of some sentences from Holy Scripture and a few prayers and two hymns, at the time that the body was brought to be placed upon the hearse ; and as soon as that had been done, Mr. Lewis, curate of Blickling, and myself, in surplices, led the way as far as the confines of the parish, followed by the choir, the hearse, the mourners, and almost all the parishioners, the choir from time to time singing hymns, and the church-bell slowly tolling a farewell On the day of the funeral a service was held in Blickling church, attended by the villagers and the neighbours, at which Mr. Köblich, Minor Canon of Norwich, sang 'Oh, Rest in the Lord.'

Lady Lothian, the second daughter of Lord Shrewsbury and Talbot, was a highly cultured lady who would have shone in any society. But as soon as she became the owner of Blickling she made it the chief object of her life, laying aside the pursuit of other things, to give as much happiness as she could to the villagers, all of whom were dependents on the Blickling estate. 'There is little one can know, but there is much to do,' she has said to me, 'to make this our little corner of the world better and happier.' If anyone was sick, she supplied him or her from the Hall with all that the case needed, and she frequently sat by the sick-bed, giving comfort by her presence and consolation by the passages of Scripture which she read. The parish school was supported by the estate, and Lady Lothian took pains to provide it with the best possible schoolmistress; and she paid constant visits to the school, where the children, who were much attached to her, looked forward with delight to her coming. The education given was in accordance with the principles of the Church of England, and was under the religious direction of the Rector of the parish. Lady Lothian's place in church on Sunday was always filled, generally twice in the day. She had restored the church, with Mr. Street as architect, in memory of her husband, and had erected the beautiful monument to him, sculptured by G. F. Watts, opposite to which she sat. A monument to herself has since been erected by her sisters.

During Lady Lothian's residence at Blickling she had many interesting guests to visit her. Among others, I met at her house Carlyle and Browning. Carlyle was very much bent, and looked a rugged old man, not too particular about personal neatness. It was easy to trace in his conversation his peasant origin. He had a massive forehead, bushy eyebrows, and keen eyes, and he showed himself very well read on any subject that came under discussion. In his 'philosophy' he exhibited a curious combination of Scotch Puritan and German Rationalist influences, and he presented his views to London society very courageously, with a diction that was entirely his own. What he taught was the value of work, and the use of strong men to control the rest of mankind, whom he regarded as 'mostly fools.' His *French Revolution* is rather an epic and a drama than a history.

Browning's appearance and conversation were very different. After luncheon I went for a walk with him and the late Lord Carnarvon, whom I had known in Oxford. It was a pleasure to take part in the easy,

22—2

yet intellectual, talk that passed. Browning was of middle height, and he wore no beard at the time I saw him. The most striking feature about him was the brightness of his eyes.

Some years earlier I had met Hallam, the father of Arthur Hallam and the author of *The Constitutional History of England.* He was a quiet, reserved man, of a kindly disposition, with little power of every-day conversation ; but what he said was well worth hearing.

The later years of my life have been spent as a country clergyman at Blickling. The life of the clergyman in the country who is trusted by his parishioners is full of the deepest interest to himself, and not without benefit, it may be hoped, to them and to the Church ; but it does not, as such, supply matter for record. The tragedies and comedies of village life, which he soothes or witnesses, are sacred, and not to be exposed to the public eye, even when the actors in them have passed away.   The pastor's village friends

> ' Along the cool sequestered vale of life
> Have kept the noiseless tenor of their way.'

And after a long incumbency he has laid many of them to rest in the hallowed ground overshadowed by the church, which has been the symbol of their spiritual life.

> ' No further seek their merits to disclose,
>   Or draw their frailties from their dread abode :
> There they alike in trembling hope repose
>   The bosom of their Father and their God.'

APPENDIX

OFFICES HELD

1843-1847. Scholar of Trinity College, Oxford.   (Age sixteen to twenty.)
1847-1860. Fellow of Trinity College.
1847. B.A.
1848. Secretary of the Oxford Architectural Society.
1849. President of the Oxford Union Society.
1850. M.A.
1851-1859. Tutor of Trinity College.
1854. Master of the Schools (Responsions).
1855-1856. Select Preacher before the University.
1856. Public Examiner in Classics (Pass and Class).
1856-1857. Preacher at the Chapel Royal, Whitehall.
1856-1857. Examiner at Winchester College.
1857. Proctor.
1858. Examiner at Rugby School.
1859. Examiner for the Johnson Theological Scholarship.
1859-1869. H.M. Inspector of Schools.
1865-1866. Select Preacher before the University of Oxford.
1868-1885. Examining Chaplain to Bishop Wordsworth of Lincoln.
1868-1905. Rector of Blickling and Erpingham.
1869-1905. Non-Residentiary Canon of Lincoln Cathedral.
1875-1876. Select Preacher before the University of Oxford.
1886-1887. Principal of Codrington College, Barbados.
1893-1894. Examiner in Theology at Durham University.
1897. Member of the Cretan Relief Committee at Athens.
1853-1898. Secretary of the Anglo-Continental Society.

PUBLICATIONS.

As Author.

1850. What is the Working of the Church of Spain ? (Pamphlet.)

1851. The Practical Working of the Church of Spain.

1853. Evidence on the University and Collegiate Systems.

1854. Two Sermons preached before the University on November 5 and May 29.

Clerical Tenure of Fellowships. (Letter to Sir W. Heathcote, Bart., M.P. for University of Oxford.)

1855. Liguori's Theory of Truthfulness. (Pamphlet.)

Liguori's Theory of Theft. (Pamphlet.)

Liguori's Morality discussed in Nineteen Letters with Dr. (Cardinal) Manning. (Pamphlet.)

Papal Supremacy tested by Antiquity. (Pamphlet.)

1856. Liguori's Glories of Mary. (Pamphlet.)

Examination of Rev. R. I. Wilberforce's Inquiry into Church Principles. (Pamphlet.)

Moral and Devotional Theology of the Church of Rome.

God's Revelation and Man's Moral Sense. (Sermon published by the Vice-Chancellor in a volume entitled ' Christian Faith and the Atonement.')

1858. The Outcast and the Poor of London.

1859. University and Whitehall Sermons.

1860. Articles in first volume of Smith's ' Dictionary of the Bible '—*e.g.*, ' James.'

1863. Articles in second and third volumes of ditto — *e.g.*, ' Mary,' ' Prophet,' ' Church,' ' Antichrist,' ' Confirmation.'

1864. But isn't Kingsley right after all ? (Pamphlet.)

On Dr. Newman's Rejection of Liguori's Doctrine of Equivocation. (Pamphlet.)

Sulle Chiese Suburbicarie. Una Lettera ad un Uomo di Stato. (Pamphlet.)

1865. Jehovah or Baal? A Sermon before the University.

1866. Patriotism. A Sermon to Volunteers in Norwich Cathedral.

The Bible, the Church, Conscience—which is Supreme ? A Sermon before the University.

1867. Our Schools of the Prophets.   Ditto.
     Intercommunion.   Ditto.
1868. Vita della Santa Maria con tutte le Legende le più
     notabile.
     La Chiesa.
1872. Undergraduate Life at Oxford in 1844 to 1847 (prefixed
     to ' Memoirs of W. B. Marriott ').
1874. Sermons at Lincoln Cathedral and St. Paul's Cathedral
     on the Bonn Conferences.
1875. Articles in ' Dictionary of Ecclesiastical Antiquities '—
     e.g., ' Marriage.'
1876. Commentary on Joel and Obadiah in the ' Speaker's
     Commentary.'
     Episcopal Succession in the English Church. (German.)
1877. The Schism of East and West and the Seventh Council.
     Sermon before the University of Oxford.   (Also in
     French.)
1880. Commentary on the Epistle to the Ephesians in the
     ' Speaker's Commentary.'
1882. Commentary on Leviticus in the ' Pulpit Commentary.'
1883. Is Dogma a Necessity ?
1892. History of the Church of Spain.
1894. Lessons on Joshua and Judges.
1899. The Doctrine of the Holy Communion restated.
     Fourth edition.   (The same in Italian.)
1900. Article on ' Confession ' in ' Church and Faith.'
     Article on ' The History of the Holy Communion ' in
     ' The Church Past and Present.'
1901. Scriptural and Catholic Truth and Worship.
     Old Anglicanism and Modern Ritualism.
1902. Sunday Observance.
     Ritual and Ritualism.   (Pamphlet.)
1904. Articles in ' A Protestant Dictionary.'
     ' Prayers on the Ten Commandments.'
     ' Appeal from the New to the True Catholics ' (jointly
     with Dean Wace).   (Pamphlet.)
1905. Commentaries on the Epistles of St. John, the Pastoral
     Epistles, the Colossians and Philemon, in Rev. J. R.
     Dummelow's forthcoming Commentary.

1905. Letter to the Dean of Canterbury.
1850-1905. Articles, Reviews, and Letters in the *Colonial Church Chronicle*, the *Christian Remembrancer*, the *Observateur Catholique*, the *Union Chrétienne*, the *Literary Churchman*, the *Quarterly Review*, the *Emancipatore Cattolico*, the *Guardian*, the *Church Quarterly Review*, the *Churchman*, the *New York Church Journal*, the *Revue Internationale de Théologie*, the *Norfolk Chronicle*, the *Eastern Daily Press*, the *Church of England League Gazette*, the *Church Family Newspaper*, the *Foreign Church Chronicle*.

As Editor.

1853. Bishop Cosin : Religion, Discipline and Rites of the English Church. (Latin.)
1854. J. Meyrick : Papal Supremacy. (French, Italian, German, Modern Greek.)
1855. Extracts from Ussher, Bramhall, Taylor, Ferne, Cosin, Pearson, Bull, Hooker, Jackson, on the Holy Catholic Church. (Italian.)
1858. Bishop Cosin : History of Papal Transubstantiation. (Latin.)
1861. Bishop Beveridge : Ecclesiastical Rites. (Latin.)
1865. Bishop Andrewes : Private Devotions, Part I. (Latin.)
1867. Ditto. (Greek.)
1870. Bishop Andrewes : Private Devotions, Part II. (Latin.)
1872. Bishop Andrewes : The Roman Primacy. (Latin.)
Bishop Andrewes : The old Catholic Faith. (Latin.)
1873. Bishop Andrewes : Private Devotions, Part III. (Latin.)
1874. Bishop Hall : Noah's Dove. (Latin.)
1875. Isaac Casaubon : Letter to Cardinal Perron. (Latin.)
1876. Charlemagne : The Second Council of Nicæa. (Latin.)
1874. Correspondence with Old Catholic and Orientals, including letters to Dr. v. Döllinger, etc.
1875. Ditto.
1876. Ditto.
1877. Ditto.

1888. Extracts from Dr. Crackanthorp's 'Defence of the English Church.' (Latin.)

1889. Ditto.

1867-1899. Bishop Harold Browne: 'Exposition of the Articles,' in seven parts. (Spanish.)

1877-1899. The *Foreign Church Chronicle*.

1905. 'Private Morning Prayers,' from Bishop Andrewes' 'Devotions.'

Bishop Jewel: 'The Faith of English Churchmen.'

Bishop Jewel: 'On the English Reformation.'

INDEX

BILLING AND SONS, LTD., PRINTERS, GUILDFORD

ImTheStory.com

Personalized Classic Books in many genre's

Unique gift for kids, partners, friends, colleagues

Customize:

- Character Names
- Upload your own front/back cover images (optional)
- Inscribe a personal message/dedication on the
  inside page (optional)

Customize many titles Including
- Alice in Wonderland
- Romeo and Juliet
- The Wizard of Oz
- A Christmas Carol
- Dracula
- Dr. Jekyll & Mr. Hyde
- And more...

Lightning Source UK Ltd.
Milton Keynes UK
UKOW06f0608130717
305253UK00009B/575/P

9 781290 224710